CHINA HIGH

CHINA HIGH ZZ

MY FAST TIMES IN THE 010

A BEIJING MEMOIR

ST. MARTIN'S PRESS ❧ NEW YORK

CHINA HIGH. Copyright © 2009 by ZZ. All rights reserved. Printed in the United States of America. For information, address St. Martin's Press, 175 Fifth Avenue, New York, N.Y. 10010.

www.stmartins.com

Book design by Greg Collins

Library of Congress Cataloging-in-Publication Data

ZZ, 1975–
   China high / ZZ. — 1st ed.
       p. cm.
    ISBN-13: 978-0-312-53108-9
    ISBN-10: 0-312-53108-7
  1. ZZ, 1975–   2. Chinese Americans—Biography.   3. China—Social life and customs—2002– I. Title.

  CT275.Z88A3 2009
  951.05092—dc22
  [B]

                                                                2008035870

First Edition: April 2009

10 9 8 7 6 5 4 3 2 1

To

life's higher moments

and

Jenjen,

without whom this work

would not have been possible

Special thanks to

Nicole,

for her kind tutelage and unwavering support

throughout this endeavor;

Bonnie,

for believing in a project of passion by a rookie writer;

and

Alex, Belina, Catalin, Chris, Coco, Helen, Henry,

Hwa, Joanna, Jocelyn, Joe, Kemin, Kevin, John,

Phil, Shannon, Steven, Yang, Zan, Zhen, and Zu,

for being my beloved Beijing crew.

OCTOBER 13

I

"Sha—bi!"

I should have totally spit onto that Mercedes S600 instead of just calling the driver a "stupid cunt." Does he not look to his left before making a right turn on red? Pay attention, Mao damn it! Had I not fixed the horn on my motorcycle just an hour ago he would easily have run me right over.

Seriously, is it not enough to put up with all those in this town who never shower, spit everywhere, and squat on the sidewalks with their littering, peddling, and gambling (collectively, the "Spit 'n' Squatters") without having this Armani Wong hog up the road as if he were Mad Max? Considering that he paid twice the regular price for his show-off wheels (thanks to China's 100 percent import duty on cars), why didn't he spend a little more and buy some class, too?

I know China doesn't have a uniform traffic law yet, but courtesy ought to be a part of human nature, right? Whatever happened to all that wonderful Chinese culture stuff that *National Geographic* always tells us about? Pardon my French, but even though *shabi* is the nastiest word in the Chinese language, it just doesn't quite capture all the stupid-cunt-ness of China's modern-day Mercedes-driving sons of bitches!

Ah, knock it off. What am I doing? It's autumn in Beijing, for Mao's sake, the best—if not the only good—season around. Blue sky, white clouds, a beautiful breeze—things that one might take for granted elsewhere but are an absolute treasure trove right around here. If I don't look too closely, I wouldn't even notice that the entire city is under construction and the pollution that once made London the foggy capital has now made Beijing the smoggy capital. No need—in fact, it'd be an absolute crime—to tarnish a rarity like this with a loogie on the windshield. What am I, a Spit 'n' Squatter?

Besides, after three years in China, I really ought to be accustomed to the One A Days by now: in any given twenty-four-hour period, something about this country is guaranteed to piss me off. But, hey, what doesn't kill you only makes you stronger, right? Worst comes to worst, the clock still strikes 4:20 P.M. here in China; and I am back on sin street to help make the most out of it.

2

Once the boondocks for peasants too poor to live closer to the Forbidden City, Sanlitun is now Beijing's default pasture for sex, drugs, and rock 'n' roll. Here one can find countless bars, restaurants, lounges, cafés, massage parlors, boutiques, flea markets, kebab stands, cigarette peddlers, even sex shops with real latex vibrators.

And, of course, yours truly.

When I first touched down on this strip in 2001, the scene was a little different. For the relatively affluent the place to be was 88, a converted warehouse whose name rhymed with "get rich, get rich." From ambassadors to Internet boomers, the auspiciously named nightclub always had the most beautiful people. Whether on a Friday or a Monday, it was always packed, with some patrons who never bothered to leave the place throughout the entire weekend. Like repressed virgins, once the government decided it was okay for its people to party, everyone who could afford techno and ecstasy came out with a vengeance.

Then on those nights when I did not feel like paying 40 *kuai* (or a whopping US $5 at the then prevailing exchange rate of roughly eight to one) for a Tsingtao beer, the alternative strip in Sanlitun was Southie. Every night some local band would be playing "Hotel California" at a grease spot like Dirty Nellie's, where 20 *kuai* (US $2.50) would buy you two and a half vodka tonics. Sure, the Stoly might have been bootlegged in the Northeast and there have been stories of alcohol peddled on the street being tainted enough to blind lab rats, but I was even younger and more robust then; and no one had anything left to complain about after two rounds of the hibachi-grilled lamb kebabs that sold for 5 *kuai* a dozen.

But nothing lasts forever. In late 2003, Club 88 was torn down for a new residential development. A few months later, all of Southie was bulldozed to make room for a shopping mall.

Now, of course, new places are opening up in the neighborhood every day, including some rather lavish clubs such as Angel, Baby-face, Cargo, and Deep. But somehow it just doesn't feel the same. For one thing, the crowd has changed. Many of those whom I used to party with have either left town or left the party scene; some have even gotten married (imagine the horror). Granted, fresh blood keeps pumping in every day from around the globe, and let's not forget the *shabi* Armani Wong who just flattened me (almost) into pavement pancake. Then pile on the tourists, the pimps, the dust from all the construction happening up and down the block. . . . Mao save Sanlitun.

3

With its rusty doors, wobbly tables, and leaky glass panels that even Eskimos would condemn in the winter, Café 44 is not exactly high on creature comforts. Nine times out of ten, half of the menu items are unavailable; and the same Café Del Mar album will play over and over again until the resident bootleg salesman replenishes his stock at the end of every two to three weeks. As there is no drainage on site (hence no bathroom), the underaged kitchen crew must lug a bucket of liquid gunk across the room every two hours or so for dumping into the sidewalk sewers. And whenever they drip or spill it onto the creaking linoleum floor, which they always do, an angry mop that also belongs in the sewer will remind you that here in China there should definitely be no five-second rule if you happen to drop your food on the ground.

Yet unlike its bigger and flashier neighbors with on-site toilets, 44 holds a special place in my heart—it was here on a breezy night three years ago that I met my first ever Beijing babe.

In Chinese her name meant "Sunshine Sunshine." Fresh off the boat (FOB) from Washington, D.C., I thought that was the cutest thing I had ever heard. At twenty-two years of age she had just re-turned from university abroad with a bunch of similarly well-off Chinese kids who all drove BMWs. And like her worry-free peers, she never graduated, spoke almost zero English despite having lived in Melbourne for two years, and still lived at home with her parents.

But looking into her big brown eyes, I wasn't bothered by any of that in the slightest. Whether it was the way she snuggled into me when I took her on the back of my motorcycle or how she pouted her lips as the morning-after sun shined on her sleeping visage, she was the delicate flower that bathed in the rays of my masculinity.

Then after two weeks of easygoing fun, she told me that she loved me. And I completely freaked out. No man should move to a new city of fifteen million inhabitants (more than half of whom are female, by the way) and get tied down by a girlfriend in less than a month! For crying out loud, she didn't even know how to talk dirty yet, in Chinese or English.

So in a conversation that I now wish to have worded differently, I told her that I would never love her.

Yet for three more months Sunshine Sunshine hung around,

spending the night several times a week, often without my invitation. We never really talked, as she usually responded to my various attempts at an adult discussion with two blinks of her big brown eyes and "Um . . . never really thought about it." In retrospect, she was probably trying to make me grow more attached to her by simply being around me more. Unfortunately, physicality without communication is never the way to win someone's heart.

Then one day she told me she was pregnant.

Without having to think about it for more than two seconds, I knew that I was not ready for a child. To put it nicely, I was not fit mentally and financially. To put it bluntly, I just did not want the responsibility.

Had this happened outside China, I would probably have told the girl that I'd respect whatever choice she made while praying silently that she would indeed choose abortion over birth. Here in China, on the other hand, I did not have to pray at all.

Under China's one-child policy, the default rules of which limit any married couple of the Han ethnicity (which constitutes 95 percent of the population) to bearing only one child, abortions for unplanned pregnancies are more than just a "fundamental right" (as so held in *Roe v. Wade* in 1973), they are an encouraged practice. Rather than restricting abortions for pregnancies beyond the first trimester, the law prohibits an abortion only when the procedure is reasonably certain to cause death or injury to the woman. Even when a minor becomes pregnant, she does not need the consent of her parent or guardian to obtain an abortion. After all, face dictates that no Chinese girl should ever give birth to a child without having been married first, at least not yet.

So when Sunshine Sunshine told me she was getting an abortion right away, I didn't object. It was her body, her decision, my get-out-of-jail-free card. On the occasion that we managed to talk about it briefly, she said something along the lines of "Don't worry about it. Some of my friends have done it twice already."

But even so, I still went to the hospital on the day of the operation to make sure that she was all right. In the hours that I had breakfast and lunch by the steamed pork-bun stand opposite the gate (for I had no documentation to show relationship and thus could not enter the hospital), I saw many girls who looked about Sunshine's age going in and out of the hospital, alone.

From that day onward, I started showering Sunshine with more attention than I had ever given before. As relieved as I was by her decision, I nonetheless felt like a jerk. Even though she had never brought up the issue of protection during intercourse, I should have insisted on wearing a condom every time. After all, sex education was never a part of her school curriculum, and I was older and therefore should have been wiser.

But of course, no matter how many gifts, poems, or Valentine's Day roses I gave her, we could only grow apart. By the middle of my first winter in Beijing, she told me that she was not going to come around my place anymore.

In the months that followed, I kept swinging by Café 44 out of some subconscious urge to find Sunshine and patch things up as friends. Then before I knew it, I actually started to like this creaky little greenhouse. The glass panels let in plenty of light. The clientele has its share of young, friendly English speakers. And if nothing else, it is distinct from all the rest in Sanlitun by virtue of its name. Instead of abusing the auspicious 8 like everyone else, "44" sounds almost identical to "death death" in Chinese. Indeed, the number 4 is so unlucky in China that most building elevators go straight from 3 to 5, and hospitals never, ever have a fourth floor.

But if we just step outside the Chinese box for a bit, I can argue that 44 is actually a lucky number. In music, the fourth note in a scale is fa, which sounds exactly like the Chinese word for "get rich," thus making 44 no less auspicious than 88, and all one has to do to appreciate it is to watch a bootlegged copy of *The Sound of Music*.

Besides, had it not been for 44, I would never have met Baby Baby, Cutie Cutie, or many other girls with looks straight out of Final Fantasy and double-double names that I once thought were special; nor would I ever have found out from my fellow regulars that Sunshine Sunshine's baby *might* actually have belonged to a much older film producer with whom she was also cavorting at the same time as she was seeing me. Of course, no one would ever know for sure whether the baby was really his or mine, but somehow, it gave me a bit of relief. And then to help ease my guilt a little more, I just got word from her ex–best friend the other day that she had completely lied about her age and was only eighteen years old when I first met her!

No wonder we never had anything to talk about.

4

Through the glass I see Lao Chu, the owner of Café 44.

A "born in the soil, raised in the soil" Beijing-*ren*, Lao Chu grew up in a *hutong*, one of the many narrow alleyways that once crisscrossed to form the Beijing map. Though his name means "Old

Chu," he isn't really that old—mid-forties, healthy gait, a full head of salt 'n' pepper razed into a short, bristly buzz. As usual, he is playing *dou di zhu,* meaning "fight the land baron," a local card game with a revolutionary name and rules that have nothing to do with poker. And judging from the force with which he just slammed his cards onto the coffee table, this Mandarin-collared, kung-fu-shoe-dragging high school dropout just might make enough today from gambling to replace his rusting Chinese-made Jeep Cherokee with yet another Mercedes.

"How you doing?" I wave to Lao Chu.

But given how busy he was, my greeting was seen only by the young girl sitting to his right. Introduced to me only once (and by herself) as Wan Ren Mi, or "Desire of Ten Thousand Men," she is a winking machine who has become a Café 44 fixture. Now don't get me wrong, I was by no means trying to be flirty with her—given how many girls there are in this town who have long hair and flawless skin and weigh less than ninety pounds, I would never even have known that this one existed had it not been for Lao Chu, who came to me on a random day not long ago and said, "Hey, somebody really likes that thing."

"What thing?" I almost looked down between my legs by instinct.

"This." He picked it up. "Someone really likes this phone of yours."

"Yeah?" I studied my Nokia 2100 proudly—plain noncolored display, stubbly buttons with rubbery casing, the newest and cheapest economy model there was, simply ideal for this petty-theft-infested town at a bargain price of 750 *kuai.* "I just bought it today."

"Well guess what?" Lao Chu flicked an eyebrow.

"What?" I thought he needed me to translate his ever-changing drinks menu from Chinese to English again, for free.

"Did you see that doll sitting by the door when you came in?" He pointed to Desire with a chuckle. "She said that if you give her this phone, she'll spend the night with you."

"Really?" I tried to remember why I wasn't where I should have been when this offer was made. "Why?"

Okay, no need to answer that. This is China, after all, where a lot of random inexplicable things just seem to happen.

I checked out Desire from head to toe, and gave her a rating of around 6.8. It was a passable score, especially for a one-night stand. But the thing is, even if the offer wasn't some sort of a weird prank, my phone was nonetheless brand new. Granted, it wasn't exactly a James Bond gadget, but I'd still have to spend at least another hour shopping for a replacement if I actually agreed to the barter. No sex is worth that much trouble. Not around here anyway.

But to be polite, I still turned back to Lao Chu with a smile and said, "Maybe next time."

Then a few weeks later, it became apparent that Desire had become Lao Chu's *ernai* (pronounced "are-nai"), literally meaning "second wife." Polygamy, you ask? No, that would be illegal in today's China, even for a Muslim. Instead, *ernai* is the Chinese equivalent of a mistress. The deal is simple—he pays her bills, she pays him sex and time. Of course, Lao Chu never came out and said, "Hey, y'all, check out my *ernai*." But when a girl her age spoonfeeds ice cream to a guy his age—who is, by the way, married with a kid in high school—it is pretty obvious.

So does that make Desire a hooker? Well, not to Lao Chu or most other men in China. Conceptually, an *ernai* services only her keeper, which is arguably—and I emphasize "arguably"—no different from a housewife who cooks and cleans and lives on a husband's income; except that Desire definitely doesn't cook, and the only cleaning she does is of Lao Chu's wallet.

Now to anyone who goes to church on Sundays, Lao Chu might have to burn in hell for his Desire. But can you really blame him? Like most locals his age, he probably married the first girl he ever slept with. Worse yet, he might never even have seen his wife until they were married at the behest of his parents. The China of Lao Chu's youth was like that. People were too occupied with war and poverty to worry about sex and romance; and marriages were usually done out of more practical considerations.

Nowadays, on the other hand, priorities have shifted. With money in the pocket, a lot of Chinese can now afford what they wish they'd had when they were young, including sex. Out of ten married Chinese businessmen, at least five would have an *ernai;* and the best of these women can earn up to 50,000 *kuai* a month, with a Land Rover to drive, a platinum American Express card for shopping, vacations around the world, and another 2 million *kuai* (US $250,000) by the end of a two-year "contract period." By comparison, fresh graduates from China's top universities make 18,000 *kuai* a year, the equivalent of US $2,200, with no insurance, no paid vacation, not even a rusty bicycle to speak of.

Don't you just love development?

5

"Perrier, please." I sit down at my usual sidewalk table.

"Huh?" The young waiter scratches his head.

"Perrier. You Know, water, bubbles, Per-ri-er?" I'm trying to be as French as I can with my hands.

How the hell does one say Perrier in Chinese anyway?

The kid has no clue.

See, this is what I mean by "One A Day"—it's been less than ten minutes and I've already had two. Nothing against Lao Chu person-ally, but if he wants to make money selling Perrier, which costs twice as much as any Chinese carbonated spring water for no good reason, he should at least teach his staff to know its damn name!

"Okay." I take a deep breath. "It's in a green glass bottle with a yellow label. It has bubbles. Goes 'pss' when you open it. Get it?"

"You mean one of these?"

"No! It is not a Tsingtao beer!"

If this were any other day, I'd be teaching this boy a lesson by now—a lesson so loud that everyone in 44 would hear it. It would be harsh, even insulting, delivered in a way to make him feel really, re-ally stupid. It's ruthless, even draconian; but this is China, where the people have been told what to do for generations and genera-tions. And as far as I know, yelling seems to be the only way of get-ting through to these people.

It's just that, right now, I don't want to spend the energy.

Earlier this afternoon, I had to fire someone—as in *zai jian* (good-bye), hit the road, Chang, don't you ever come back no more. He was not much different from the waiter standing before me now.

Shaggy hair, a bag of bones, skin bronzed permanently by the elements even though he was barely eighteen years old (or so according to his identification). A villager from Henan Province, he was one of eight couriers in my employ.

By way of background, I run a small company called Foodiez. Since its birth two and a half years ago, it has been Beijing's only gourmet food network that delivers hot, freshly made foods from over thirty restaurants right to the customer's door. From American to Italian to Tibetan, Foodiez offers every culinary style meaningfully represented in this town and delivers only the best, or at least the best available.

The idea came to me on a night in December 2001 after an unexpected snowstorm had completely crippled Beijing's roadways. Being a noncook who had to eat out every meal but had no way of going out due to the snowed-in traffic, I turned to the city guides for a delivery service that could bring me something good. To my chagrin, all I found were Subway and McDonald's, which delivered only within two kilometers of each outlet and were not delivering at all on that particular evening.

At first, I was peeved—how can this place expect to be a real metropolis without even a decent delivery service? Take a look at every other industrialized city around the world—food delivery is a way of life. People like it. People demand it. People depend on it. Yet the capital of the most populous country in the world, which has fifteen million people and over one hundred thousand restaurants, has no such thing?

So why don't I do it?

The business model was deliciously simple: round up a network of restaurants, generate orders for them through a hotline, pick up the ordered foods from the vendor's location, and deliver them to the customer while they are still hot and fresh. From the vendor's end, I'd take a commission on every order; from the customer's end, I'd collect a small delivery charge depending on the distance. Given just how many potential customers I had out of Beijing's fifteen million, it was going to be my first-class ticket to early retirement.

Funny how reality never follows the model.

First, it took me three weeks and many desperate pleas to finally convince the local business registry not to reject my license application on grounds that a business like Foodiez had never existed. Then, nine out of ten vendors I tried to recruit insisted on using cheap, grease-leaking packaging instead of the sanitary ones I had recommended, and refused to provide any receipts for the revenue that I would have generated for them (thus socking me with their share of the onerous income tax). Because no one in China was selling food-to-go thermoses even though they were all made in China, I had to spend ten times the amount to import some simple plastic boxes that had to be replaced within a matter of months. And finally, how do you train Chinese telephone operators to distinguish between curly fries and chili fries—in English, no less—when they have never had either?

But thanks to youthful fire in the belly, I still managed to round up thirty restaurants after three months of hustling, with something for every palate, plus a decent pastry shop that made Beijing's closest-to-real cheesecakes, and even a wine supplier.

To launch the network, I needed money for marketing. Given that I had only US $25,000 to my name and that China has no such thing as small-business loans, I welcomed aboard a Chinese lady who promised to invest another US $25,000. Following the method that had been used by similar services in New York and Hong Kong, I printed and distributed a beautiful catalog. The twenty thousand copies took up 30 percent of the start-up capital; but based on my pro forma, even at a "conservative" growth rate of 20 percent month on month, I could afford to make this catalog a Beijing fixture.

Sometimes I surprise even myself with my optimism.

From the get-go, over 90 percent of my customers turned out to be foreigners, especially overpaid expatriates working for giant multinationals who would never speak Chinese if they didn't have to. To these folks, it was all too easy to embrace my bring-the-outside-world-to-China idea, even if I had just taken out a tiny ad in *That's Beijing* and never bothered with the catalog. Unfortunately, their number was far too small to meet my volume-driven targets.

As for the locals, they just didn't get it. One day a woman said to me over the phone, "As much as I like your catalog, why should I pay you twenty *kuai* to deliver the food to my place when I can just take a taxi for fifteen *kuai* and pick up the food myself?" Until then, I had never realized just how much I had to educate this town on a simple concept called the value of time, which meant that my *actual* market potential was much smaller than what I had been counting on all along.

But even so, I still had more customer complaints than I had time to handle. Call me crazy, but how does someone actually gather the nerve to bitch about his food being ten minutes late during peak traffic hours after having already eaten the food without paying for it? Yet it has been done, more than once, by the same guy. And given how spread out Beijing is, even Domino's most fast and furious would take forever to get to the suburban villas where some of my customers like to hide, so give my employee a break if his rusting, one-speed "Flying Pigeon" bicycle gets a flat tire along the way instead of bitching about the fries being a little soggy.

But of course, the customer is always right.

After six months, my "angel" investor split, leaving me with a big fat duck egg in the company account. Her justification? The business wasn't profitable enough, so she took her money back, shifting all the risk to me.

At the time, I could have dropped Foodiez like a sack of hot potatoes. Sure, I could sign all the contracts up the yin-yang, but actually keep any of my vendors from walking out whenever they wanted? Get real. From accountants who couldn't prepare cash flow statements to receptionists too lazy to say "Thank you for calling Foodiez, how may I help you?" I had to train every employee from scratch even though half of them would jump ship immediately after completing their training.

And the worst of all—my delivery boys. When I first saw them, half looked like they had just rolled off a coal truck—dirt underneath their fingernails, sweat stains across their faces, dandruff even in their eyebrows. And the smell, Mao have mercy! Yet they never showered, for weeks on end. I don't know how many times I have yelled at them about cleaning themselves up. First to wash themselves; then to wash their clothes; and most recently to either cut that greasy lopsided hair or have it shaved off by me with a cleaver!

We always hear that starting up a business in China is cheap, but after you factor in the frequency with which you have to yell, it's hard to calculate the real cost of being a China entrepreneur.

But still, Foodiez was my baby. If I didn't save it, I'd just have to write my name backward and smear it with dog poop.

So first up, I fired the manager, who spoke decent English and had some restaurant experience but still had no idea when it came to something as new as Foodiez. Then I moved the office into my one-bedroom apartment, reducing my bed to a desk and sharing the one and only bathroom with my fifteen employees. Altogether, I saved 10,000 *kuai* a month.

But even so, simply copying a business model from the outside world without modification was just never going to work. Before the Chinese public realized just how busy its own life would soon become, a more cost-effective means of marketing must be found. And due to fundamental language differences, relying on telephone operators who'd quit as soon as their English skills become good enough for better-paying jobs would always put the quality of our customer service at risk.

So I moved Foodiez to the Internet. And why not? Everyone in Beijing has broadband; even migrant workers with less than a primary education know how to look for jobs online. By leveraging a user-friendly Web site that would have cost me US $20,000 in America but only US $800 here, I was able to minimize reliance on telephone operators and easily update restaurant information in real time. To incentivize our existing customers to use the Web site, I offered rebates on every order placed over the Internet. Then, let word of mouth do the rest.

At first, the move was resisted by everyone in the company, for ordering food by Internet was unheard of. But I had to take the gamble. Everything in China is changing, and with the market here being so different, something that has never been tried elsewhere just might work.

And thankfully, it did. As of January, Foodiez broke even for the first time on a monthly basis. After fifteen months of living in a room the size of a minivan, I finally managed to move into a duplex where I can live upstairs with relative privacy while the office works downstairs.

But the problems don't stop there. Last month I netted barely 2,000 *kuai*, or US $250, because my customers prefer to eat out during the warm weather rather than ordering in. In local talk, a

"250" is an idiot who would take 250 when he could easily get 500; and I would have made at least US $25,000 last month had I just stuck to my old office job.

Now looking back, starting my own business was like being in love. In the beginning, I hardly ever needed rest. Issue after issue, crisis after crisis, I loved being in charge and making all the decisions myself; and there has never been a better sense of accomplishment than building something from the ground up with my own hands. But time tends to mess with love. All the minuscule details of day-to-day management have cut into the passion I once felt. For a new idea—no matter how good it is—to really catch on in a place like this, one really has to be sure about one's commitment. And having to fire one of my boys today certainly did not help in that category.

According to the e-mail complaint I received last night, the kid shortchanged a customer 20 *kuai*. It was an unseasonably stormy night, and he probably thought he deserved a tip after battling the elements for an hour. But there is no such thing as tipping in Beijing; and even those foreigners who would always tip back home are quick to ditch the habit once here. When I confronted the kid, he of course denied it, which left me with no choice but to let him go. It always sucks to fire someone, and this one made it extra special by stealing the delivery moped that the company had just upgraded for him.

So now, what am I going to do about getting that Perrier?

"Forget it." I put up my hands in surrender. "Just get me a Coca-Cola, okay? Do you know what that is?"

"Yes. *Mei wen ti*." The waiter nods nervously while repeating the ubiquitous Chinese phrase for "No problem."

"Now don't you tell me '*Mei wen ti*' and then give me a bottle of cough syrup." I don't mean to be an ass, but this is starting to really get on my nerves. "And make sure that I get plenty of ice this time!"

6

Five minutes behind schedule, I can finally get on with my therapy.

In Chinese, this stuff is called *da ma*, or the "big numb." Translated into English, it becomes weed, pot, grass, cannabis, ganja, Mary Jane, or just plain old marijuana. What is lost in translation, however, is that given the dry climate in northern China that makes local cultivation of the cannabis plant rather difficult, the big numb found in Sanlitun is usually smuggled in from Africa or the Middle East and thus in the form of a solid resin called hashish. Made from the glandular hairs of the female cannabis plant, it has higher concentrations of THC than plain sun-dried marijuana, thus truly delivering on the promise of the big numb.

To get this stuff, I call Prince, who, unlike the singer of "Purple Rain," is paunchy, bald, very black, and pimped out like he just stepped out of a rap video. Like all the other dealers in Sanlitun, he claims to be Nigerian, which only adds to the speculation that much of Sanlitun's hashish supply comes in through diplomatic pouches of the Nigerian embassy.

Whenever we meet, Prince greets me with a lazy yet paranoid chuckle followed by a wet-palmed slap of hands. His voice is resonant yet raspy; his face, always smiling. To be safe, we take a walk 'n' exchange away from the main drag and swap the consideration in a slick slap-slide-squeeze-'n'-fist. Up until a few months ago, we always rendezvoused outside the KFC opposite City Hotel, which was the base for all African connections in Sanlitun. But as the new supermarket next door has drawn in too many people, our meetings have gradually relocated to Sanlitun's outer rim.

In terms of service, Prince is one crap dealer. Punctuality is not in his blood, and inconsistency is the only thing consistent. Half of the time, he doesn't even show up himself and instead sends in one of his FOB countrymen; but as a way of protecting his turf, he always adds the over-the-phone caveat "Please, don't give him your number, please!"

For 200 *kuai,* or the equivalent of US $25, he sells a chunk of hashish about the size of a quarter and a half inch thick. While the quantity is hard to beat—something that size will support three smokes a day for at least three weeks—the quality can practically roller-coaster. Always wrapped in layers of nontransparent cellophane (whether to seal in the freshness or hide the staleness), the stuff can be tested only by squeezing it—if rock solid, no good, if soft and gooey, possibly better, but only possibly.

Before each drop, I first estimate how many times I will have to yell at Prince for being late or just not knowing where the rendezvous point is, including something as easy to find as the *hutong* next to Café 44. And each time, he says, "Ohmygod, please, please, five more minutes," at least five times. The whole operation is like a druggie Foodiez network, just a lot less efficient.

Yet, I keep calling Prince. Somewhere deep down, I must enjoy screaming at a drug dealer without having to fear being shot by him. In the same way that Foodiez's own most demanding customers do, I bitch and moan to help improve another much-needed line of service here in the capital city—it's funny how one's perspective changes depending on the shoes one wears. And lately, the quality has been excellent—soft like Play-Doh, sticky like glue, more pungent than ever, and delivering an unprecedented high. It's good to see my efforts finally paying off.

To rock this baby, I like to roll. Even though various smoking paraphernalia can now be found on sidewalk rugs laid out by Tibetan migrants or their imposters, a good joint is still the best way to enjoy hashish; and I don't mean a half-baked job like most stoners put together. While I am far from being enlightened, there is one thing I am sure of: A good reward always requires a good effort, and a good high is often the best reward.

To start, I break a pill-sized chunk of hashish into smaller sesame-sized bits and mix in a sixth of a cigarette's tobacco to help the mixture burn evenly. To roll it up, I prefer the small-cut OCBs imported from France, but only after I remove about a third of the paper so that the end product will not contain too much tree bark. Then, most important, I always add a filter folded from a business card, which not only stops the hashish bits from flying into my mouth but also adds immeasurable class and grace. Unlike those who either burn their fingers or resort to "roach clips" toward the end of a joint, I'd never be caught dead holding my pleasure stick in such an unsightly fashion. After all, a joint is to be enjoyed by all the senses; and image is part of everything.

If you think the foregoing is easy, perfecting it takes much dedication and focus. The hash bits must be sufficiently small and evenly spread throughout the tobacco, or they will clump up to clog the drag. The filter must be long enough to grip comfortably between the fingers, have sufficient spirals in the middle for filtering power, be collapsed in the right places to have square edges to facilitate rolling, and be folded precisely to display the business-card holder's name through the translucent paper (with myself being the honoree in this case). And most important, the rolling action requires a fine balance of force and finesse such that enough air will be left in the mix to sustain a fine cigarlike burn without sacrificing the pull that comes only with a tight package.

Measuring measures a little less than 3 inches long and about 3/16 of an inch in diameter, it's called the Zigarette (or Ziggy for short), an elegant pleasure stick designed for one. Hands down, it is the best-looking, best-smoking joint I have ever come across, and I have come across a lot. Sure, some potheads might call it too skinny or even criticize me for a design unsuitable for sharing, but I'm not just any pothead. Would James Bond ever share his vodka martini? I think not. Just as the Japanese have tea ceremonies that no one else can duplicate, I've got a highway that's in a class of its own. Besides, I am no cheapskate—if you want one, just ask.

7

"Hey." The waiter returns with a glass of Coca-Cola with more head than I've ever seen on a soda. "Aren't you that guy?"

"Which guy?"

"That guy on CCTV?"

As in China Central Television—the government's propaganda network that once had the entire country as its captive audience?

"Yes, it *is* you!" His curiosity turns into excitement. "You were on that driving show back in May!"

Aw shucks. It's amazing how good the Chinese memory is—it's been five long months, and people still remember the crap show that aired during China's weeklong May 1 Labor Day holiday, the show that was supposedly watched over and over again by some two hundred million people.

Truth be told, I didn't ask for the gig. In fact, I don't even watch television. But then, there is *guan xi*, as in China's most famous (infamous) word for "connections."

One day in March, I got a call from Makeshift, a friend who dabbles in China's entertainment circles as a graphic designer, pianist, magician, comedian, and TV-show host, among many other things. "Do you want to be on TV?" he asked.

"Hmm . . ." I was actually quite surprised, as I had never studied theater or journalism, but heck: "Why not?"

After all, I'm not bad looking, and I'm definitely no dumb doorknob either. A lot of girls like me, and some guys, too; and it's got to be for more than just my eight-packs. Come to think of it, a professor back in college even suggested that I study theater after seeing my skit for her English literature class; I just never gave it much thought.

"I know a producer who is making a show for the May first holiday," Makeshift said. "I think you'll be perfect for it."

"Cool." It's always nice to hear that you are "perfect" for something. "Which network is it?"

"CCTV."

"Come again?" I instinctively flinched at the sound of the acronym, which should really stand for Completely Crap Television.

"Don't you worry," my brother from a different mother assured me. "I wouldn't have called you for something on CCTV-9. It's CCTV-2, the business channel."

Oh yeah? "So what's the show about?"

"Racing cars."

"Beg your pardon?"

"You know, strapped-in pedal-to-the-metal racing cars."

"But you just said it's a business channel. What's it doing racing cars?"

"Who cares? They all have to make money somehow. What do you say?"

A week later, I was summoned to the kickoff meeting, where I was told that six contestants would be split into three teams and compete in seven races, with three on a certified F3000 racetrack, three on an off-road racecourse, and a final showdown between the two top-scoring teams through a desert outside of Beijing. To hype up the show, the network had been recruiting contestants nationwide for months—Internet, television, radio, newspapers, you name it. But out of the six contestants sitting at the table that afternoon, everyone had some sort of *guan xi* with the producer, who then gave each of us a two-page document to sign.

So I asked her, "Is this like a *summary* of the contract?"

"No, this *is* the contract."

"But this doesn't even say what show we are doing."

"Don't you worry about that." She giggled. "We never even had any contracts until this time. All the previous shows just went straight into filming."

"But it doesn't say how much we get paid either."

"Oh now." The mole on her left upper lip bloomed with amusement. "Don't you forget that we are CCTV. Everything will be taken care of."

The motorcade to the filming grounds was impressive. As official sponsors, Nissan and Peugeot had donated more than twenty brand-new vehicles, each with supersized "CCTV" logos emblazoned across the doors and hood. Cruising alongside the entourage on my beautifully polished motorcycle, I felt pretty darn close to a superstar.

By the same time the next day, I felt much closer to a graveyard shovel.

"Why do I have to wear this even when I eat?" I tugged on the ill-fitting bloodred denim-and-Velcro overalls that would have made Michael Schumacher hurl his lunch. "It's more than ninety-three degrees in the shade!"

"We just have to." The producer shrugged while sucking on her Popsicle. "The network likes to see uniformity. That's what uniforms are for."

"But why does it have to be red and gold? I look like a damn Chinese cigarette box in this thing!"

"But those colors really pop on the screen. Need I remind you that they are the colors of the Chinese flag?"

"Then how about these white knockoff Puma sneakers? I don't recall the color white being in the Chinese flag. And 'Puma' is not spelled *P-v-n-a*."

"But they are cheap, twenty *kuai* a pair. We don't have five hundred thousand dollars to spend on each episode like MTV does."

"Well then what about the 'races'?" I quoted with my fingers. "What kind of 'race' did you guys have in mind?"

Earlier that day, I'd had to roll my team's car down a bunny hill and try to start it by fiddling with the clutch instead of using the ignition, which was a neat trick if I were to ever steal a car, but hardly a race. Then on the next day, we were scheduled to "compete" in parallel parking.

"Well." She squinted. "We have to be close to the people, you see? Our audience has never raced. Many of them have never even driven a car. The poorest ones haven't even been inside of a car. A real race would be too much for them. They wouldn't understand it. And then there is the insurance issue."

"What insurance?"

"That's the issue. There isn't any."

"Then what about my partner's hair? Why did he have to lose his dreadlocks?"

"Oh, that's just too weird."

"But he has a ponytail to begin with!"

"Yeah, ponytails are okay. We [the Chinese] have worn ponytails for thousands of years, but not whatever he is wearing."

"So are there any other rules I should know about?"

"Well, now that you asked." She opened the floodgates. "You use too many hand gestures when you talk—stop that. You criticize the race officials on camera—the network doesn't like that. And please laugh instead of making faces when the host tells a joke. I know it's not funny, but remember, it's a show."

"But I thought it was supposed to be a re-al-i-ty show!"

"Look, darling." Her pupils were visibly dilated by this point. "China needs happy television, okay? There are nine hundred million peasants in this country; half of them are in primary school now, and the other half never graduated. Whatever we put on TV, they will follow it. To keep them quiet and happy, we need happy scenes, happy songs, happy people—that's why the show is called *Happy Heroes*. Get it? So be happy and stop complaining! The last thing the government wants is for everyone to mimic the *real* you and start questioning this and that. Don't forget, this is China. There are cultural differences, okay?"

How could I argue with an excuse as civilized as that?

As Confucius said (and if he didn't, he should have), the less you have, the more face you crave. Having attained the relative pinnacle of culture a long, long time ago when the outside world was still undiscovered boonies, China loves to use "cultural difference" as a defense against questions of why the China of today is the way it is, even though not everything about China is cultured and not every difference between China and the outside is a cultural one. To rebut it, you'd almost have to challenge what Chinese culture means, which, given the nationalism that is growing in sync with the exploding economy, just might invite a collective ass-whupping.

So for what seemed a lot longer than the next ten days, I sucked it up and did my part. As expected, my team made it to the final race. As expected, my team lost. It's all a conspiracy. And as icing on the rice cake, I was given 1,000 *kuai* in a lovely little red envelope for my time and effort, or the equivalent of about US $12 a day.

According to the producer, the show scored unprecedented ratings during the ensuing May 1 holiday. For three weeks, I didn't leave my apartment without wearing dark shades.

So yeah, "What about it?" I signal the young waiter at Café 44 to keep his voice down.

"I loved that show!" he gushes. "All those neat tricks. All those cars. Especially that driving lesson you had to give."

Right, which almost killed my teammate when the peasant whom we had to teach how to drive a manual shift but who had never driven any motorized vehicle in his life floored the accelerator, launched the Nissan Pathfinder straight up a forty-five-degree anthill, and got stuck at the top with my teammate still screaming in the passenger seat.

"You remember all that?"

"Oh yeah." He fails to discern my sarcasm. "I watched every episode. Reruns, too. Say, do you still race?"

"Still? It was only a show, kid."

"But . . ." He looks confused for a second, and then says, "I wish I could be a Happy Hero someday too. Like you. So cool."

Aw shucks.

8

"Excuse me." A young man with a European accent leans in from the next table. "Is that what I think it is?"

He is eyeing my Zigarette.

"Well what do you think it is?" I smile back.

A look of surprise flashes across his eyes. "Is it legal to smoke it in public?"

"Well, that really depends."

For him and all others uninitiated, let me make one thing very clear: drugs are not legal in China, period. Unlike California and some European countries, there is no such thing as "drugs for medicinal use" or "legal to consume but not legal to sell." Instead of "Just say no" or "This is your brain on drugs," the government takes an emphatically harsh stance against all narcotics—with executions and life sentences being the punishments of choice for anyone caught dealing drugs and something that might as well be from the Dark Ages, as I was recently told, for anyone caught using drugs.

Since 2001, summer in Beijing has been synonymous with the Great Wall Rave. Ingeniously, some party organizers figured out a great modern-day use for China's foremost national treasure: parties. The last time I went, some big-ticket DJ from England (I believe Paul Oakenfold) took over one fortification on the Great Wall while the alcohol stand took over another. From an early Friday afternoon onward, close to a thousand revelers packed into the cobblestone walkway and littered the entire place with beer bottles and cigarette butts. As the venue was more than two hours away from city limits, the music was as loud as the equipment could handle, and the thousand-year-old structure saw a war that it was never intended for.

But on the morning after the last assault (which happened in July of this year), cops roadblocked the hungover revelers on their way back to the city, needled and pricked everyone who was not a foreigner, and arrested anyone who tested positive for something. As an instance of extreme happiness begetting tragedy, a friend named Tiger was caged for smoking some big numb.

"So what happened?" I couldn't hold back my curiosity upon seeing him again months later.

"Compulsory rehab." Tiger had a different look in his eyes.

"Where?"

"Some mental institution up in the mountains."

"You mean you were treated like a lunatic?!"

"I wish I was actually crazy."

"What did they do?"

"Well, for the first hour, they stripped me naked and dunked me into a pool of ice water; then a bunch of heroin addicts took turns beating me up."

"And the rest?"

"Let's not go there."

"Right, sorry. So how long did you stay?"

"Forty-five days."

"For smoking some damn hash?!"

"It would have been eight months if my girlfriend hadn't found some *guan xi* and paid the money."

Then he turned down my consolation Zigarette with both hands. Twice.

So the question becomes: Why is China so harsh on drugs?

Well, the whole story dates back to the early 1800s, when the British fell in love with Chinese tea. To import it by the boatload, the Brits had to pay the Chinese large quantities of silver, which was the only currency that China would accept. As teatime became a pastime and thus a serious drain on the silver reserve, the Brits had to sell something to the Chinese in order to balance out the trade deficit. And sure enough, the brilliant minds at the East India Company came up with just that special something: opium.

Quickly, the black, oily resin that looks rather similar to hashish but is ten times more potent took off like nothing China had ever lit up. By the 1830s, the Brits had turned their trade deficit with China into a huge trade surplus, all at the expense of addiction, drug wars, and broken homes among the Chinese populace.

So in 1839, after violent protests by angry citizens in various parts of the country, China's imperial court banned the importation of opium. Following a series of communiqués in which China called itself the "Kingdom of Heaven" and Britain the "Boondocks of Devils," some Chinese official with a supersized hard-on seized a reported 2.3 million pounds of opium and burned the whole lot over twenty-three days.

Pissed off that the Chinese had had a huge shindig with Britain's stash without inviting the Brits, Her Majesty's Royal Navy fired its cannons upon the birthplace of gunpowder, igniting the Opium War of 1840. The one-sided onslaught ended with China's paying 21 million *liang* of silver in reparations (with each *liang* measuring about thirty-eight grams or 1.2 ounces), the ceding of foreign-controlled areas in five different port cities including Shanghai, and the severing of the entire island of Hong Kong plus neighboring areas as a British colony.

But that was just the beginning. China's defeat in the Opium War signaled to the world that the once mighty Middle Kingdom was now economically weak and had an army of addicts. In 1900, the unified armies of America, Austria, Britain, France, Germany, Italy,

Japan, and Russia again invaded China and drove the then-incumbent emperor from the Forbidden City, looted the imperial gardens, and further expanded their concession areas. Then to add further insult to injury, the army of "little Japanese ghosts" (as some of the older generation still call the Japanese to this day) did so much to China during World War II that we still hear about the Nanjing Massacre more often than just from time to time.

So out of shame for falling off the wagon too hard once upon a time, China has held a grudge against drugs for over 160 years. And it makes perfect political sense—to secure public support for its rule, the government must keep reminding the country of its shameful past and how the Communist Party was the savior.

But in an autocracy of one-party rule, the government rarely has to explain why it does anything. Even though banners and billboards keep telling everyone to resist the temptation, they never show what the temptation actually looks like. So even though drugs still exist in China, since they are as endemic to human existence as is the desire for entertainment, 99 percent of this country can't tell an eight ball from a cue ball.

So even though I've lit up in Beijing's many bars, restaurants, clubs, shopping malls, subways, hotel lobbies, and government buildings, and even in the Forbidden City, the closest complaint I have ever gotten was when some patrons at a bar mistook the smoke for extra-potent incense. Fact of the matter is, as long as the cops do not consciously look for drugs (I have smoked within a stone's throw of completely ignorant cops many times before), no one is ever going to find out.

And even if they do, nothing is going to happen, for my immunity is none other than the words coming out of my mouth—in English.

9

Of course, there is nothing in the books that says English speakers are above Chinese law. We just are.

Ever since China opened its doors to the outside world in 1980, much of its double-digit annual growth has been the direct result of foreign investment. To help maintain the momentum, it is the unwritten policy of the Chinese government to give extra face to foreigners who live, work, or study in China, which means that as long as a foreigner refrains from raping, killing, and pillaging, the government is not going to worry about his various bad deeds. And of all the indications of foreignness, the ability to speak English without a Chinese accent is certainly the easiest one to spot.

But what does this mean exactly?

Well, take my Yamaha, for example. It's an XJR400 from 1994, cobalt blue, completely stock except for an upgraded Yoshimura exhaust. Churning out a max of fifty-seven horses at the back wheel with a weight of about 450 pounds, including a full tank of gas, it is not exactly a ballistic missile but is nonetheless perfect for zipping through city traffic. Compared to even the best Chinese-made motorcycle, it has better brakes, better ergonomics, better emissions, and way better looks, which is quite embarrassing for China, as it is already ten years old. Since purchasing it earlier this year, I have already taken it on dozens of road trips, and I would feel positively naked without it.

But it has one tiny problem: no license plate.

Back in 1985, Beijing's city planners decided that it was in the best interest of the public to restrict its use of motorcycles. Simultaneously, the city stopped issuing new license plates and imposed geographic limitations on where licensed bikes could travel within the city.

Under this ban, a person can only take over someone else's existing license plate rather than getting a new one. This means that I must buy a used motorcycle that I don't really want and transfer the plate to the bike that I do want. Currently, a used bike with a real plate would cost me at least 13,000 *kuai,* or the equivalent of US $1,600, even if the bike itself is completely shot.

Assuming that I make this investment, I must then take the plate to the Registry of Motor Vehicles, file an application to transfer the plate, pay a bunch of processing fees, and submit simultaneously therewith the title to the bike that I want to ride, which brings me to the second problem.

Despite being the world's largest motorcycle producer, China does not make bikes with engines bigger than 250 cc's. Why? Because most of the buyers use motorcycles for transportation rather than pleasure, and neither need nor can afford a bike like my Yamaha. But for an enthusiast like me, the technology and design of a Chinese bike are just not up to par.

So if I want to ride a fully licensed Yamaha XJR400 on the streets of Beijing, I must first purchase a brand-new one—as China does not allow the importation of anything used—from a dealership in Japan at a price equivalent to 40,000 *kuai* (US $5,000); then pay a shipping company approximately 20,000 *kuai* (US $2,500) to ship it to China within a reasonable time; then pay another 40,000 *kuai* (US $5,000) in import duties to the Chinese customs (thanks to 100 percent tariffs); then 13,000 *kuai* (US $1,600) for the old license plate; and finally 2,000 *kuai* (US $250) in filing fees to complete the entire process. That brings the total to 115,000 *kuai,* or US $14,350, for a toy originally priced at US $5,000.

So if you were a single male with good sense, good riding experience, a desire for wind in your hair, but not a lot of money to waste, what would you do?

Here in Beijing, there are about a dozen garages that moonlight as special "distributors" for bikes smuggled in from Hong Kong or Japan. Walk into one of these dingy holes-in-the-wall, and you'll find nothing but a bunch of beat-up replacement parts and maybe some helmets made in Korea. On the surface, it's just another Chinese garage that uses nothing to fix crap. But as soon as you flip open one of the many bike magazines scattered around the room, the boss will come over and say, "Whatever you want, my friend, you get."

So you point to the picture of that razor-sharp rocket ship rounding the Isle of Man; put down some Mao bills to show good faith; and wait for some really nice folks down south to "locate" it in Hong Kong, "acquire" it when it's convenient, disassemble it so it won't be so conspicuous, and ship the parts in a crate to Beijing for your "dealer" to put together. For show, you can pay a few hundred *kuai* extra for a set of out-of-town plates that must be screwed on upside down to be not so conspicuously fake. Then, after paying roughly 50 percent to 75 percent of market price for the same machine had you purchased it on the outside, get ready to blast past China's many spanking new Benzes and BMWs while finger-waving to the Chanel babe riding shotgun.

But then, what happens if the cops catch you? Well, if your bike is anything faster than a Suzuki GN125, they will never even bother to chase. But just in case you make the mistake I did last week by sticking your neck out ahead of all the cars at a red light, what do you do? According to law, the cop can arrest you on the spot, confiscate the bike in perpetuity, and throw you in jail for an indeterminate period. According to me, simply bombard the overzealous trooper with a few minutes of English gibberish that you yourself might not even understand and wave *zai jian* (good-bye) as you casually pull away into the dusty sunset.

But hey, don't hate the outlaw; hate the system that makes him one. It was Mao himself who said that the essential underpinning of the proletarian revolution—and thus of this country at large—is *"zao fan you li,"* to "rebel with reason." Yes, motorcycles are dangerous; but so is every motorized vehicle. Instead of using emissions or adolescent high jinks to justify the moto-ban, just tell it like it is: the bigwigs in city hall prefer to see BMWs and Benzes on "their" streets rather than motorcycles. As a matter of principle, I hold in contempt all laws that are the result of brain farts; and it certainly helps to be armed with some English vocabulary in fighting such idiocy.

10

"So, you see"—I hand the day's first Ziggy to the inquisitive young European—"smoking this is not exactly legal. But that's kind of the point, isn't it?"

He has a nice smile, much like those young guns in old westerns who are always called "the Kid."

"So where are you from?" I ask.

"Germany." He lights up the joint with glee. "Just got in a few months ago."

"Doing what? Work? School? Bit of both?"

"An internship here through my university, and I'm studying Chinese on my own."

"Excellent. How is Beijing treating you so far?"

"I love it!" He grins from the heart. "I really want to stay here once I finish school."

"Oh, really?"

"Definitely. It's so different here. I come from a town with one hundred seventy thousand people, and it's considered a big city in southern Germany. Even Berlin has only three million. Whereas here you have fifteen."

"But Germany is beautiful, no? And there is the Autobahn."

"Yeah, but that's about it." He shrugs. "Otherwise, it's boring."

"Okay." I can't really debate him on that. "So what do you want to do?"

"To be honest"—he coughs a little—"I don't really know yet. My university is not so famous, the internship is pretty shit, but I know Chinese, so that's my advantage relative to everyone else in my class."

"Yeah?" But does he know it well?

Let's face it, Chinese is not an easy language to learn. After more than 4,500 years of evolution, it boasts more than eighty thousand pictogram-based characters. And instead of using long, run-on sentences in typical American fashion, the Chinese rely heavily on the use of maxims that are distilled from history. To engage in a fluid conversation with a local, one better know enough maxims to keep up, or one will just be told to go back to school and "good good study, day day up."

"Well for now"—the Kid blinks one eye playfully—"my Chinese is *ma ma hu hu.*"

Touché. Anyone who knows "horse horse tiger tiger" to mean *"comme ci, comme ça"* after just a few months should do just fine. Very good pronunciation, too.

"And where are you from?" he asks.

"China."

"No really." He chuckles. "Where are you from originally?"

"China."

"As in *China* China?"

"You got it."

"Then please, accept my apologies." He is unmistakably German in a nervously cute way. "I didn't mean to offend you."

"Oh, no worries, mate." Thanks to nature and nurture, even I have trouble figuring out my own nationality sometimes.

II

On a Christmas Eve almost twenty-nine years ago, I was born in the Chinese coastal city of Shanghai. Like my parents, who are both Chinese, I have black hair, brown eyes, and beige skin.

Growing up in Shanghai, I had a small reputation. Because I ditched the little red scarf that every Chinese kid must wear around his neck and tore down much larger banners of "Long Live Communism" hung in the school hallway, I never got grades as good in "morality" as I did in everything else. As early as seven years old, I already had my own little rat pack in the schoolyard. Before my eleventh birthday, I had already kissed the prettiest girl in school, a feat that was unheard of in the China I grew up in.

Then in March 1989, a surprise.

For three years leading up to that point, my father had been studying in America as an exchange scholar sent on behalf of the Chinese government. All along, the plan was for my mother to join him first and leave me to the care of my maternal grandparents. Yet, randomly enough, some unnecessarily generous visa officer at the American consulate offered—I repeat, *offered*—my mother the option of bringing me along as well, even though a wife and her kid going to America for the purpose of visiting the husband was probably "Reason #1 to Deny Visa for Intention to Immigrate." Being thirteen years old and only weeks away from my long-anticipated ascension to the household throne, I of course was not a happy camper. But then, I did not exactly have a choice in moving to the Land of the Free.

"No wonder you speak English like an American," says the Kid.

"Well it's not like I moved to New York City, my friend. There was no Chinatown where I went. If I didn't speak English, I didn't eat."

First day at my American public school, behold the cultural differences. Never had I seen pants worn backward and baseball caps worn sideways, not to mention big, flashy jewelry on boys. Some of my fellow thirteen-year-olds were already six feet one and one eighty pounds, while I was barely five feet six with half the weight. And the girls, Mao have mercy—none of the girls I knew in Shanghai had measurements like these, nor the odd habit of snapping gum as if making popcorn inside their mouths. And to top it all off, where did all these different races come from?

Being the resident FOB, I was welcomed warmly by Bruce Lee

impersonations and questions like "Do you put rice on your pizza?" Whether white, black, brown, red, or even yellow, they all made fun of me just the same, for I was green. In the first week, I got punched by one white boy, one black boy, and one mean-looking Latina whose cheeks outflapped her boobs. Fortunately, nothing was landed on the face, or it would've popped one of the many pimples I was starting to develop thanks to adolescence and America's hormone-based diet.

But after I found some friends who taught me the value of some key American maxims, aka four-letter words, things got better. By the time I entered ninth grade, I had a new mission: to regain the schoolyard prince status I once enjoyed in Shanghai. And it seemed that the only way to do so was to be "cool," which was apparently something that could only be felt but not spoken. So I looked at the "cool" kids around me for some clue, but the answer kept eluding me. The jocks were dumb. The Goths were scary. The artists stank of cigarettes. And the preppy ones were just, well, too rich. I tried talking to the popular girls on campus, most of whom were blond and did not give me the time of day. As for the few who did, the conversation usually ended with something like, "Ohmygod, you can count twelve to the second power in your head? What are you, like, a nerd or something?"

So for the first four years of my American experience, I lived as a nerd. Besides going to school for classes that required zero effort and hanging out with my equally "uncool" friends, there was not much to do besides daydream. At times I would curse my parents for bringing me to America; even to this day, I have yet to remember one good thing about high school. But as a silver lining, all the shenanigans that I was effectively excluded from by virtue of my nerdiness gave me time to read every textbook twice, which in turn allowed me to attend university without having to ask for a penny from my parents.

Then, just like that, life in America became pretty darn nice. Sex, drugs, and rock 'n' roll, all were done before the school bell tolled.

Of course, being Chinese, it took me a while to warm up to drugs. After all, every Chinese should remember the Opium War. But then, none of my friends looked like the emaciated addicts that I had once seen in China's history books. If anything, some of them were overdoing it on the munchies and should really lose some weight. So with a pounding heart, I emptied out the three-foot bong in one breath and coughed many times. Then just as I was about to complain that the whole exercise didn't work, a wave of tingling warmth buzzed from the tip of my toes all the way to the top of my head. It stayed there for hours, for as long as I laughed and laughed and laughed.

In the years that followed, I fell in love with America more and more. Clean air. Open roads. Space Museum. Rock 'n' roll. The way people held doors for each other. The smiles given by complete strangers as you entered their stores. Even milk and cereal, fries and ketchup, especially when served in supersized American portions. And all these things were made even greater by America's great big numb.

12

"So are you an American citizen now?" asks the Kid.

"Nope."

"How come?"

"Dunno. Could have filed my naturalization papers years ago. Just never did."

"Then do you consider yourself more Chinese or more American?"

"Hey, man, what is this? An interview?"

Because if it is, I would much rather get interviewed by MTV Girl, a local celebrity whose beautiful face once adorned the cover of *Time* magazine as the future of Chinese television. At some point in the past, I would have done anything to be with her; unfortunately, I was only twenty-six years old and did not drive a BMW. All the soap opera notwithstanding, however, I still have a soft spot for her, which is why when she texted me for dinner last night, I gladly accepted.

It took me two trips up and down Ghost Street to find our meeting place, which had red doors, red lanterns, and red-clothed bellboys in red silk caps, much like all the other establishments on the same street. As I pulled open the door that said "Push" in English but could actually only be pulled, a combination of stir-fried peppercorns and Chinese cigarettes woke up my sinuses.

Past the glass tanks stuffed with fishes and eels and reptiles, I saw an awesome wooden statue of Guan Gong, or Lord Guan, a badass from circa A.D. 220 who stood six feet five inches tall and wielded a giant spear-sword that would have given Hercules' weapon a run for its money. Having chopped off a lot of heads in his time, he died to become a demigod for all of China, with restaurateurs being among his most devout worshippers.

"This is my friend." MTV Girl introduced me to the four men and two other girls who were already seated at the table. "He grew up in America. So don't mind if he misses on a few things."

"So you are a *hai gui*." Mr. Wong brought up the term for "re-turnee," meaning any Chinese citizen who has lived extensively over-seas and then returned to China. "How is your Chinese?"

"It's okay."

"Are you a southerner perhaps?" Mr. Chen followed.

"Yes, born in Shanghai."

"Oh really? I don't usually get along with Shanghai-*ren*." Mr. Wu smiled genuinely. "They are always so . . . how should I say, cunning?"

"But you can understand everything we say, right?" Mr. Li didn't give me time for a comeback. "Like *'shabi'* for example?"

Thirsty from all the walking I had just done, I motioned for a cold drink while everyone else stuck to either hot water, hot milk, or hot almond juice. But since no waitress was assigned to any particu-lar table and tipping has yet to become China's incentive for effi-ciency, I was told to "wait just a moment" by at least six ladies who had sounded so pleased to see me upon my arrival. And when my "Coca-Cola on ice" was finally brought over, I had to ask for more than just a half-melted cube and question whether the flat, luke-warm liquid was actually Coke at all.

Rather irritated, I wanted to order something I was sure to like instead of relying on Mr. Li, who was apparently the bill payer and ordering for the table. So I broke every Chinese restaurant's rule of "one menu only no matter how many people are eating" and asked for a menu all to myself. But with the waitress standing uncomfortably close to me with her paper and pencil in hand, it did not seem appropriate to take the time to digest the menu and make sense of all forty pages of elaborate names that sounded too civilized to be eaten.

So I asked for the second thing under "Chef's Specialties." It was some kind of fish, nonendangered.

"Sorry, sir, we don't serve that anymore for today," the waitress apologized.

"Okay, then how about number five on the same list? I like beef, too."

"Sorry, sir," she apologized again. "We don't serve that anymore."

"You mean it's sold out too?"

"No, it's just no longer served."

"And how long have you guys *not* served this item?"

"Oh, at least a few months, sir." She was sure that I should have known.

"Then exactly what is available?"

She responded with the most expensive thing on the menu.

"And what's in this 'Thousand-Hand Buddha on Green Lotus'?" I didn't want to brave any mountain treasure or ocean delight that some environmentalists would have killed to save, especially not after SARS and now the bird flu.

"Sorry, sir, I've never had it."

So in the end, I decided to order a kung pao chicken—diced, boneless chicken cubes stir-fried with red chili peppers and freshly roasted peanuts. Spicy, slightly sweet, plenty of protein, and not too fattening; what could be better? And one of the two other pretty girls at the table almost seemed to agree when she said, "Wow, I haven't had kung pao anything with anybody on Ghost Street since I was two."

After a sip of the tea that the ladies at the table had to wait for until the men were served first, it was finally time to dig in.

"You are left-handed." Mr. Chen noticed something as I was try-ing to pick up the squishy, spongy sea cucumber that the girl in red had just put onto my serving plate.

"Then you must be really smart." The other girl in white re-minded me of China's strange respect for the left-handed species.

"And strong, too," the girl in red added. "Look at his muscles. Must be all that beef they eat in America."

"Do you play any sports?" Mr. Li quieted the girls with a squint.

"Yeah, used to be a swimmer, in high school."

"But you probably weren't very fast." Mr. Wu must have really liked me.

"And you don't hold your chopsticks correctly," Mr. Chen added. "Your hand is too high at the top. I bet you can't pick up the hard stuff too well."

Obviously not—for how else could a sea cucumber miraculously defy gravity and wiggle its way *upward* out of the grips of my chop-sticks?

Halfway through the meal, drinking kicked into high gear. But instead of beer, wine, or even just bootleg whiskey, it had to be *bai jiu* (pronounced "bye-geo"), which smells stronger than turpentine and goes down harsher than chlorine. If I were stuck in an icy cave in the middle of Siberia with nothing to live on, this stuff might be just what I needed to keep my soul from giving out. Otherwise, it's just too damn Soviet. According to legend, Guan Gong often cele-brated his kill with a shot of *bai jiu;* but I think the sequence was wrong—it was the drink that drove him to kill.

Just as I was about to muddle my way through with a sip of my Coke, Mr. Chen raised his glass and said, "Welcome back to the motherland, my little American friend."

"But I cannot drink." I spun for an excuse.

Truth of the matter is, I have the "Asian Flush," which is an enzyme deficiency that causes my face to turn lobster red after even just half a beer. It's never deadly, but it's still embarrassing enough for me to save myself for good-tasting alcohol.

"Nonsense." Mr. Chen poured a double just for me. "If you are really Chinese, you must drink Chinese liquor. Now, bottoms up."

I looked to MTV Girl for help.

Her wink suggested that Mr. Chen was someone crucial to her future career.

So I looked to the great Guan Gong, who held his three-foot-long beard in his left hand and his giant phallic weapon in his right. He didn't look like he gave a damn.

In the end, I took the shot. After turning down various offers of Chinese cigarettes throughout the evening, holding my chopsticks in the wrong way, and not eating much of anything besides the kung pao chicken, I had to give face somehow. And it was every bit as disgusting as I knew it to be. But after two or three more (or perhaps four or five), I didn't worry about whether I was "really" Chinese anymore.

Until each burp this morning brought back the aftertaste of being an outsider in my own country.

"But hey," I get back to the Kid. "These days, it doesn't really matter if I am Chinese or American. The world is converging. One day, all national borders will be irrelevant."

"So then where is home?"

"Home?" I laugh. "For me, it is *si hai wei jia*."

"What's that?"

"It's an old maxim, means 'To live among the four seas.' "

"As in the four China seas?"

"Well, it really means the whole world now."

And I'm not exaggerating. Between English and Chinese, I can talk to at least half of the people in this world, and the rest are all busy learning either English or Chinese or both. So I can literally live anywhere in the world—Asia, America, even Africa if I want to. It just happens that I'm in China now.

"Well, I guess that's pretty much what I'm doing." The Kid jots down the phrase in his handy notepad. "Rather romantic, *n'est-ce pas?*"

13

"So, do you go back to America often?" the Kid continues.

"No, not really."

"Not even to see family?"

"Oh no." At least not to see *my* family.

Thanks to the One Child Policy, my household never had more than three people. And ever since my mother passed away a few years ago from cancer, my so-called family has become just my father and me.

If I were to choose ten words to describe my father, "master" would come first, "boss" would come second, and "friend" would come nowhere near the list. Like generations of Chinese fathers before him, he was always rather quick to resort to corporal punishment. From being slapped in public to being beaten by two baseball-sized "family discipline sticks" until both weapons snapped in the process, I grew up with plenty of what might be considered child abuse in the West. And even after I had grown taller than my old man, I still carried a constant fear of testing his anger. After all, I was born a rabbit in the Chinese zodiac, and we rabbits don't like turmoil within the nest. More than poverty, worse than abstinence, it was the risk of being yelled at for everything I did that made me feel increasingly alien in my Chinese-style household.

So these days I stick to my friends, the family I never had, which is in every way much better. Having no relatives around means no bickering, no boring reunions, no headaches of mandatory courtesy that come with blood relations even though you cannot stand them otherwise.

Besides, when it comes to making friends in this town, it is like going to college all over again. Fresh bloods come in every day, and they all flock to Sanlitun for registration. Some of them are really quite smart and nice, like the Kid for example; and you'll shoot the breeze and exchange phone numbers and, before long, run out of name slots on your mobile phone.

Of course, just like in college, not all the friends you make in the first week become the ones you keep. Indeed, most become what the Chinese call "Dogs 'n' Foxes"—better-than-average acquaintances whom you'd party with. Come 5 P.M. on any given day, I'll text all the animals out there to find out what their plans are for the evening and see if I want to join the prowl. The friendship is superficial, for it usually started out with a business card and wouldn't stand up for two consecutive months without a drinking session. But it's all a part of growing up. When I was eight, I had only ten friends. That was my circle; and everyone was tight. Then my circle grew bigger and bigger, while my close friends became fewer and fewer.

But how many close friends can one ever really have? Personally, it's taken me three years to put together an inner circle I cherish and trust; and at this point, none is closer than the loose-cannon American who is storming down the street.

14

When I first saw Lethal Weapon in the gym, he was wearing a wife beater and gunning heavy curls in front of a mirror, while rapping "Baby Got Back" by Sir Mixalot. I almost pulled a hernia trying not to laugh.

In the ensuing chitchat, he told me that he had been in Beijing for about a year. His mission: to find a sponsor for his self-created TV show. "I want China to see itself through my eyes," he said, "and to learn just how funny it can really be."

China, funny? Good luck. Having just done *Happy Heroes*, I gave the obligatory nod and dismissed the idea right away. Did he not know how many foreigners had come before him wanting to make China into a comedy and failed, or worse?

"But I know it's possible," he rebutted urgently. "Talk to the cabbies, man. They don't buy any of that CCTV bullshit. Ten years ago there was no McDonald's; now look at all the fat Chinese kids hooked on that shit. Don't tell me that things can't *wo cao ta ma de* change."

"*Wo cao ta ma de?*" I had never heard of anyone cursing with a phrase that meant "I schtook his mother's holiest of holies." It wasn't the nicest thing I had ever heard, but it wasn't a well-recognized expletive either.

So to give him some face, I agreed to check out his demo the first chance I got and maybe give him some comments.

Two weeks later, I popped in the DVD when there was nothing else to do.

In a series of sidewalk interviews, Lethal engaged random strangers for random conversation. The original topic was nondescript—he just approached the locals in their native language. Yet surprisingly, everyone responded; and some conversations even developed into sidewalk discourses on economics, politics, the future, even sex and marriage. By the end of every conversation, there were at least three rings of bystanders circling Lethal and his interviewee. At one point, a silver-haired Chinese grandmother even raised her fist in the air and declared at the top of her lungs, "Isn't life beautiful?"

Shortly after that, Lethal and I started to hang out. You can tell a lot about a person from his work; and I have never met anyone, foreign or Chinese, who has a talent quite like his.

Since then, we have become the best of friends. It is rare to meet a person with whom you'd love to have a Zigarette any time of the day. And I've come to think his idea is brilliant—now that China is easing up its dragon gates, a show that adds a foreigner's perspective to everyday issues that are confronting the Chinese would be a great way to push open that door a little faster.

But of course, change is never that easy. Until Lethal came along, mainland Chinese television never had a full-time foreign host for a prime-time Chinese-language show—at least not one where the foreigner did not end up looking like an absolute dork. For months, Lethal was given the runaround. See this person. See that person. Find someone who would call this other person and see if he can help you with meeting up with this other person's other person. For months, a plethora of *wo cao ta ma de.*

Then a few weeks ago, after a year and a half of cameos on Chinese soap operas that barely paid for his travesty of an apartment, Lethal finally landed a talk-show gig on a semi-privately owned network that—thanks to some foreign investment—has become the most successful satellite network in the Greater China market.

Looks like Mao's spirit finally got sick of hearing his mother's something being *cao*ed.

15

"This is my very good friend . . ." I welcome China's soon-to-be TV icon with a high five.

To which Lethal Weapon responds lethargically, "Call me *er bai wu.*" He preempts my introduction.

"As in . . . 250?" The Kid looks puzzled, apparently unaware of the number's local connotation.

"What's with the long face, *ge-men'er*?" I squint at my partner in crime.

In Beijing, *ge-men'er* is what guys call each other. As an outsider, you absolutely have to master this word, which stems from the character for "brother" and pronounces like "gummer." Basically, whenever one would use the word "dude" or "bro" in English, one would use *ge-men'er* in Chinese. If you can't say it, you have no friends.

"*Cao!*" The Sergeant Briggs of Sanlitun gets in character almost too quickly. "Phoenix is run by a bunch of *wo cao ta ma de shabis*."

Oh, I forgot to mention, instead of the social commentary that he wanted to do, the show that Lethal has been chosen for is a rosy mouthpiece to glorify China's state-run sports machine. So nothing private, nothing negative, and definitely nothing political. Even though his network is partly foreign-owned, it is still regulated by the Ministry of Propaganda and is still, therefore, subject to the same censorship.

Nonetheless, it will make Lethal a star.

"Okay, let me guess," which has become a daily exercise ever since he got this gig.

"They won't let you interview migrant workers who built the Olympic stadium."

". . ."

"Challenge the local football hooligans to a match?"

". . ."

"How about that Yao versus Mao comparison?"

". . ."

"Sex life of Chinese Olympians? Gay Chinese Olympians?"

Okay, I'm not trying to be facetious—these are indeed some of the angles that Lethal has tried in order to get at the issues he is really interested in while staying within the boundaries of his mandate. After all, how many interviews can one really do on China's best Ping-Pong players?

"Remember the marathon three days ago?" he asks.

Sure, if you can call that a marathon. The cops blocked off only one lane on the Second Ring Road, and the racers had to run around the city alongside midday traffic. Just imagine all those buses, trucks, fumes, and . . . oh, Mao, have mercy.

"Well, did you know it was supposed to commemorate Sino-Japanese friendship?"

"No kidding? But wasn't there a mass demonstration against Japan just last week?"

In case you haven't heard it by now, China and Japan aren't exactly the best of friends. Since antiquity, China has looked down upon Japan for "usurping" the Chinese language and claiming to be the progenitor of many things that are really Chinese, including tofu and Zen. Then pile on World War II and the Nanjing Massacre, and it is no wonder that Sino-Japanese relations have long been a brewing volcano.

Most recently, Japan yet again petitioned to become a permanent member of the UN Security Council, which, if successful, would neutralize much of China's influence on the world order. Within hours, China's propaganda machine stirred this town to a boil. From TV to radio to newspaper, any medium capable of attacking the Japanese kicked into overdrive. Even in my gym, which is marketed as the most fashionable in town, a huge banner hung across the wall, condemning the "little Japs" for World War II atrocities and demanding a formal apology from the Japanese government. When I asked the attendant what business it had in a place where some members were known to be Japanese, the response was, "We're just following orders."

Then a few days later, the demonstration happened. The entirety of Ping An Boulevard was cordoned off so that tens of thousands of college students could march from their campuses on the city's west side to the central business district on the east, torching a few Toyotas along the way. Not since Tiananmen 1989 had Beijing seen a demonstration of this caliber.

And, randomly enough, an annual marathon that was meant to commemorate Sino-Japanese friendship had been scheduled for just days after.

"So for this week's show," Lethal continues, "I interviewed some runners at the marathon on what they thought about Sino-Japanese relations."

"And?"

"Beautiful footage all around—people agreeing with the government, people disagreeing with the government, people with no friggin' idea and don't give a damn . . ."

"Wait, you are not trying to exonerate the Japanese, are you?"

"No, of course not. I'm not trying to say who is right and who is wrong. The point is that the people actually had a difference of opinion."

"So what's the problem?"

"Can't show it."

"None of it?"

"The boss said the whole issue is not to be touched." Lethal's left pectoral is starting to twitch.

"Well," I say with a shrug, "you kind of expected that, right? I mean, we're talking China versus Japan, the bad blood clots up the yin-yang."

"But *ge-men'er*, do you not know what year it is already?" He might as well tattoo *wo cao ta ma de* on his face. "World War II ended sixty years ago, the Nanjing Massacre even earlier than that. Why can't we talk about them intelligently? Why can't the people decide for themselves when to forgive? I mean, the Olympics is supposed to be about unity and humanity, right? Well, some people are ready to move on. Why can't we let them have a voice too? If this bad blood with the Japanese gets any worse, are we going to have ourselves another Munich?"

"Mm . . . Did you tell that to your boss?"

"Sure, though maybe not in so many words. Guess what he said?"

"Uh . . ." I hold down the coffee table in case of an earthquake. "Cultural differences?"

"*Wo cao ta ma de,* check out the big brain on you!" He takes a whale's swig of his Tsingtao. "No fucking shit China is different! I didn't live here for six years and pretend it's Phila-fucking-delphia. But which part of this bullshit is cultural? Is it the grudge? The lack of freedom of speech? Call me crazy, but I always thought culture is supposed to be something positive."

Yikes. Should I bother to mention the word "face" and explain why some "cultural differences" must be in quotes?

"It's just an excuse, bro."

"You think I don't know that?" He leans over the coffee table. "If it's censorship, just admit it. Don't try to sugarcoat bullshit with *wo cao ta ma de* 'cultural differences.' If I have to give face this way, then I might as well deface myself. Some of you think of yourselves as so damn cultured for inventing gunpowder; well, we invented something called freedom of speech."

"Whoa, hold on. Who is 'you' and who is 'we'?"

"Oh, don't even go there. You know exactly what I'm talking about. You and I are exactly the same."

Except that I am a returnee, he is a foreigner. Relative to the locals, we are all outsiders. Relative to him, I am an ally who doesn't always agree.

"Look, man, you know that I love China too," he continues. "But for fucking Christ's sake, don't feed me bullshit like I am a three-year-old."

"But you can't just expect everything to change overnight, right?"

"So you wait? Like everyone else? Six months, man. If things don't get better, I'm moving to Italy."

"And do what? Sell espresso?"

"I'll *wo cao ta ma de* teach Chinese if I have to!"

"Look, I've said it all along—go work for the CIA. Be a spy, work undercover. Beats taking shit from your network all the time. Heck, with all the technology China has these days, you can probably buy a cell phone that can do half the work for you. And you'd be perfect for it, with your Chinese being so *wo cao ta ma de* and all."

"Shut your mouth!" His right pectoral begins to twitch as well. "Confucius said—"

"Wait. What? Who? You mean, *our* Confucius or *your*—"

"CONFUCIUS SAID"—he almost crushes the wooden table into smithereens—"that a boy becomes a man at the age of thirty."

"And then something else at forty, then fifty, and sixty, and blah blah blah. Yeah, I had to recite that stuff when I was five. So what, you want China to change just because you are turning thirty?"

"No!" He grimaces. "I want to be more than just China's next exotic TV pet. Look at me, man—I am a goddamn Ivy League graduate for crying out loud!"

"Okay." I hand him the second Zigarette that I had originally made for myself. "You look like you can use one of these."

16

"Hey, is your friend okay?" the Kid asks with hushed concern.

"Oh, don't worry about him." I start rolling up another. "Celebrities, they are just moody like that."

The Kid laughs. "So how did you end up back in China anyway?"

"Chance."

"You mean you didn't plan on coming back?"

Well, of course not. Once you have moved to America from a developing country, you don't plan to go back. If you just learn some decent English and take it easy on the drugs, you eventually have a job, a car, a place to live, a bunch of party friends, a few sex partners, and too many credit card bills to worry about. China? That's on the other side of the world. If I really get a craving for some kung pao chicken, I just call for delivery from Chang's Golden Pagoda down the street.

But then in fall 2000, a headhunter called me and said, "How would you like to make twice the salary you do now, have your accommodations paid for, plus a cost-of-living adjustment of four thousand dollars a month, and a year-end bonus?"

At the time, I was working in Washington, D.C., in my first full-time job. My salary of $80,000 a year plus bonus was okay for a newly graduated twenty-four-year-old with no trust fund; but after taxes, loan repayments, and all the booze that I was buying at that age, there wasn't much left. By February, my girlfriend of six years had broken up with me because I wasn't ready for marriage. By May, my mother had passed away from cancer. My apartment was an oddly shaped studio on the ground floor of what I suspected to be the servants' quarters of an old plantation house. And I rode a bicycle to and from work.

"So what's the gig?" I asked the headhunter.

"Corporate finance associate. Top—and I do mean, top—Wall Street firm. One of the oldest and most respected in the world."

"No kidding. And what do I have to do to get it?"

"Easy. Move to Hong Kong."

As in the land of Jackie Chan and dim sum?

"But seriously, what do I have to do to get it?"

"You've already done all there is to it." He laughed. "You speak Mandarin."

17

After flying business-class for the first time ever on a United Airlines 747, I landed in Hong Kong's brand-new international airport. The Airport Express that connected the airport to Hong Kong Island was the fastest and cleanest subway I had ever taken. An episode of *Wallace & Gromit* played on the in-seat video screen, and the conductor announced the stops in English first, Cantonese second, and Mandarin last.

"Welcome to Hong Kong," the cabbie said upon hearing my first try at the local dialect.

"So you speak English?" I wowed.

"But of course." He laughed. "This is Hong Kong. Everyone speaks English."

As we made our way up the mountain to Mid-Levels, I marveled at the magnificent Hong Kong skyline. Like some long-awaited déjà vu, what I had once imagined America to be was finally before my eyes— only newer and in a "special administrative region" of China. Taking in a panoramic view of Victoria Harbor with its rows of yachts from the giant living-room window of my giant three-bedroom apartment, I said to myself, "Who knew China could be so nice?"

Like all the suits in Hong Kong, I worked in Central. Compared to everyone else in the office, I was always the first to leave, even though I was already averaging nine to nine every weekday, plus at least one more day on the weekends. On several occasions I had to burn double-all-nighters, including an episode where the time entry system said, "ERROR: You entered 56 hours for Tuesday. The maximum per day is 24."

But even in my most haggard state, I still took meticulous care of my wardrobe. On many occasions in the elevator, I had my tie turned over and my trousers pinched by complete and uninvited strangers who were keen to know whether my taste for brand was above, below, or on par with their own.

Fortunately, shopping is never a problem in Hong Kong. From tailor-made clothing at a fraction of American prices to Christmas sales of up to 80 percent off, I had never shopped so much in my life. Maybe it was the sea of neon signs that blinked in my face 24/7, or maybe it was just because I had never bought an Armani before, but after barely six months, I owned over a dozen designer suits, handmade shoes of every color and style, and even winter clothes that I could never wear in Hong Kong's sweltering climate. At times,

I asked myself, "What are you doing? You are a guy, for crying out loud!" But then I saw all the other guys shopping like this as well.

To help further assimilate into Hong Kong culture, I made a conscious effort to party constantly. After a century of British influence, Hong Kong does the nightlife right. Unlike Café 44, any decent venue in Hong Kong has a professional, English-speaking staff and a bathroom with sitting toilets. Of course, having gone to school in America, I had my taste of bumping nightlife in Boston already. But being a poor student on scholarship and tied down with a girlfriend, I never went too crazy even if I was tempted to. But now I was a twenty-four-year-old unattached male making almost US $250,000 a year in a city where at least fifty new clubs come and go every month—"partying" took on a whole new meaning and at ten times the Beijing prices.

A typical night out—even if it was Tuesday—would warm up with an exhibitionist workout at the California Fitness in Central, followed by street-side curry in the nearby "rat alley" to help lay the foundation for the dozens of drinks that would mark my path up and down the small hills of Lam Kui Fang; and on the off chance that I hadn't hooked up with a complete stranger by 2 A.M. (whether a random beer girl or some banker traveling through), there was still enough energy left in me for hours of dancing to Gloria Gaynor covers played by Filipino bands at Insomnia. The drinks were more expensive than New York's, but the last call was also way past 4 A.M. White, middle-aged European fat cats with a penchant for cigars were the default clientele at La Dolce Vita, while all the foreign-born Chinese kids in Gucci and Prada always filled out Red Rock and California. A continuous line of taxis trickling down from the hilltop of Lam Kui Fang shuttled partygoers to Club ING, Dragon Eye, One Fifth, Pink Mao Mao, and other hot spots around town, only to return after 4 A.M. so that the exhausted revelers could get their second wind at Drop and greet the new workday with dim sum at 7:00.

On extremely robust occasions—every Friday and Saturday—the party would move onto a "junk" by late morning and head out to the small neighboring islands that offered fresh daily catches of rainbow-colored fishes and prehistoric-looking crustaceans. A motored replica of the old wooden Chinese ships that the British had used to transport opium into Hong Kong, the junk came complete with beer coolers, suntan lotions, and small private chambers in case any couples felt the need. And of course we did. Although the sea could be choppy at times and do a bad number on hungover heads and roughed-up stomachs, there was always ganja on board to make one forget about the deluge of the night before.

Amid all the revelry, I made a lot of "friends," many of them females. One night a dirty blonde in a slinky black dress whom I had just met on the cobblestone steps in Lyndhurst Terrace suggested after a few mojitos, "How about you go home with me tonight?"

"Tonight?" I wasn't too sure. It was a Wednesday, she wasn't blond enough, and the weekend that never ended had actually left me a little tired.

"What's the matter?" She had a thick Australian accent and a feistiness reminiscent of the Outback. "You don't want to fuck me?"

"All right . . ." I still don't know how I could have answered it any better. "But just this once."

She had a tiny apartment in the back of Causeway Bay. Had it not been for the rusty air conditioner in its living-room window, she would have had a clear shot of someone else's kitchen.

"What do you want to have?" She veered her head out of the kitchen.

"Doesn't matter, anything is fine." I just wanted to get out of there as soon as possible.

A few minutes later, she returned with a large wooden serving tray. And there it was: from right to left, a rolled-up Ziploc of ecstasy, two eight-balls of cocaine, a smaller Ziploc of what I assumed was heroin, a tin box with a marijuana leaf etched on the lid, two unwrapped syringes, and two yellow rubber elastics.

"What would you have? Coke? Heroin? You can pick the syringe you want." She found my dropped jaw amusing.

"No needles!" I was emphatic. "Please?"

"Okay, then have some coke. My roommate just got these from Thailand. Good stuff." The woman I shall forever remember as Needle Queen started unfastening an eight-ball.

I had my doubts. For years I had used only the big numb, which suited me just fine. Never once was I curious about the hard drugs, as I found the whole idea of taking chemicals rather repulsive. And of course, all the public-service messages on American TV helped as well.

But I was now living in Hong Kong. And after my first experience working so hard, first time spending so much, and first time having so much sex, what was the big deal with trying cocaine for the first time, too?

After two lines, my mouth jumped into turbo mode. Needle Queen, on the other hand, took a few hits of big numb and settled into an ultramellow stupor. For an eternity, I told stories and she listened (which, for better or worse, left no time for much else). And when my soliloquy finally reverted to a normal conversation by 8 A.M., it was time to take another line and get back to work.

Of course, I knew that all this sex, drugs, and rock 'n' roll was bad for my health. But I hadn't even hit the quarter life yet, and I could run the Standard Chartered Hong Kong Marathon if I just took enough coke in the morning (which I did try, even though I had to turn back halfway because of severe dehydration caused by, well, you can imagine). Besides, what would a twenty-something do with a $50,000 bonus? Buy a car? A house? Life insurance? Nah, let's just buy some coke and call up some girls instead.

Thankfully, the bonus was *only* $50,000.

For someone new to Asia, Hong Kong is the perfect place to start. But given my age at the time, I only saw a side of Hong Kong that would eventually lose its appeal. After barely a year, during which my various first times turned into many times, I knew it was time for a change.

18

"Is that why you came to Beijing?" the Kid asks.

"Well, not exactly. All I knew was that I wanted a place more exciting, not less. So America was out, as was—no offense—Europe. Japan and Singapore—too clean and organized, everything in small, pretty boxes. India, love the curry, but I'm no techie. Thailand, Malaysia, Korea, red hot in the eighties and nineties, not so much anymore."

"Did you think about Shanghai?"

"Oh, sure. I was born there, you know." My old home is five minutes away from the city's busiest commercial district and ten minutes away from the nicest Buddhist temple around. Stand on the Bund at night and behold the Pudong skyline, it's hard to believe that it was all just farmland twenty years ago. I have old friends in Shanghai, even old flings if I count puppy love. Given my line of work at the time, I would have been popular even without a personality. And everyone knows that Shanghai girls are, for better or worse, *the* hottest.

But, nah. Been there, done that. Shanghai would always be great to me, but that's also because I never lived there as an adult. Besides, I've got relatives there.

"So what made you decide on Beijing?"

"Well . . ." It's kind of embarrassing.

"Was it a girl?"

The Kid sure catches on quick. But actually, "It was a woman."

In August 2001, I was sent to a remote town in Jilin Province to visit a Chinese manufacturer of herbal Viagra. Though it was still a balmy twenty-five degrees Celsius in Hong Kong, the temperature was already way below freezing in the snowy Northeast.

I arrived with two colleagues. The other party to the deal sent its own team of representatives, one of whom caught my—and everyone else's—attention right away. At five feet seven plus heels, she danced across the icy pavement while the rest of us skidded around like penguins. When we shook hands, I was struck by her supple skin, perky lips, big brown eyes, and lightly freckled nose. Even without makeup and jewelry, she was still more radiant than fresh snow under the midday sun.

Right away, I knew she was older. But I didn't know how much older. Maybe two or three years, maybe five or six, maybe even up to ten. It was hard to tell. As far as I know, Chinese women just don't age.

Throughout the daylong group meeting, I found myself looking at her more often than I should. The word around the table was that she was once a member of the song and dance troupe for China's People's Liberation Army, who then went on to graduate school and rose quickly through the ranks of the state-owned investment bank she was working for. In secret, my two colleagues chitchatted in rather vulgar terms about how they had never seen a banker quite like her. One even declared, "If I ever get a wife, she'd better look like that!"

By the end of the day, it was time for us to have dinner with the company management. And in typical northeastern fashion for that time of the year, dinner consisted of dog meat hot pot and *bai jiu*. Needless to say, everyone who was not a local ended up drinking the 52-percent-alcohol elixir on rather empty stomachs. After an hour of continual toasting, she and I were the only visitors left standing.

Being in the middle of nowhere, the company put us up at the "best accommodations available," which consisted of a dormitory without proper heating or private bathrooms. While I waited for the "hot" water to heat back up after my two drunken colleagues had finished cleaning themselves of the vomit and dirt that had gotten into their hair, thanks to an embarrassing misstep-and-roll down a bunny hill while puking, someone knocked on my door.

"Hey, what's up?" I was surprised to find her still awake.

"Are you tired?" She flicked her eyebrows and kept her hands held behind her back.

"Depends, I guess."

"It's cold out here."

"The dog meat helps."

"Let's drink." She flashed a half bottle of the *bai jiu* that we hadn't quite finished during dinner.

"Again? Are you sure?"

"Why, are you scared? My husband can down a whole bottle by himself."

"I beg your pardon?" Scenes from *The Graduate* flashed before my eyes.

Even though I had sensed a little something from her glimpse earlier in the day, the situation at hand was nonetheless unexpected. I knew she was married. I knew what I *should* do. But there she was, standing so close to me that I could feel her warm breath in the frigid air. All along, I had assumed women from mainland China were quite conservative, like my mother. And she looked so pure—no makeup, no ostentatious clothing, no bling bling. Was she just leading me on?

I was too busy thinking to do anything when she wiggled past me and into my room.

Before that evening, I had never been with a woman from mainland China, much less one married to a government official and a Communist Party member. In retrospect, maybe she just wanted my company for a few hours. But before long, she had become Mrs. Robinson and I, the Dustin Hoffman character.

Two puffs into her "after" cigarette, she told me that it was her first time cheating on her husband. Then she started to cry, saying that her husband treated her very well, which I suppose meant that he gave her everything except romance. It was an awkward moment to say the least, but it was also interesting to play the marriage counselor immediately after committing adultery with the client.

Then, perhaps as a return favor, she said, "Maybe you ought to move to Beijing. I think you will like it. It's bigger than Hong Kong, not so clean and neat. For someone with your personality, it's perfect."

"And was she right?" asks the Kid.

"Well, she was certainly right about Beijing being not so clean and neat."

19

"Fruits." Lethal Weapon calls for my attention.

"Where?" I can certainly use one of Beijing's delicious autumn peaches for after my Ziggy.

"There." He dips his chin.

"You mean those girls?" I see a trio walking our way.

"Yes." He giggles. "Fruits."

"Isn't that a little demeaning?"

"Oh, and 'babe' or 'chick' or 'bird' is not? But don't you worry, little buddy. I didn't invent this word. People at the network taught me."

"Great, leave it all to China's talented TV people."

"Would you feel better if I told you the word for guys is 'ape'?"

"Perfect. What else did you learn?"

"Did you know that a pretty girl is called a 'ripe fruit'?"

"And an ugly one?"

"Rotten fruit."

"*Ge-men'er,* you are never going to get laid like this. Girls need to be respected."

"Oh yeah? When was the last time you got any?"

"That's besides the point." Although it *has* been seven months, going on eight.

"Well I've been dry for nine!" His eyes scream *wo cao ta ma de.* "It's already fall, *ge-men'er*. I've got to get some before this year is over. I mean, come on, we are good-looking guys."

Okay, see, that's where Lethal's problem is—what does he mean by "good-looking guys"? We are GREAT-looking guys. Strictly in terms of everything, the two of us should just have so much more game than any local guys do. For one thing, half of our local competition can really use a shower, preferably followed by deodorant. Then even the most basic fashion sense would help, like not wearing white socks with a black suit or clutching a man-purse under the armpit. And, most important, a great number of them still have to decide whether they are gay or just boys. Personally, I just don't understand why any straight man would hang Hello Kitty figurines on his rearview mirror. It pains me to say this, as I have nothing but Chinese blood flowing in my veins, but when it comes to a lot of local guys, they really do look like apes.

Of course, it's not all about appearance. Girls like guys who are interesting, witty, and charming, right? Well, I've got a long résumé and plenty of stories to score me high marks in each of those categories, too. And now that China has met *Sex and the City,* there are more local girls with jungle fever than one could shake a stick at. All around Sanlitun, some of the oldest, fattest, baldest, most grotesque foreigners are hooking up with some fine-looking Chinese babes. The fact is, even Einstein could get laid here without being a genius.

Yet, unbelievably, Lethal and I have seemingly become the Ambiguously Gay Duo of Sanlitun.

"What are we doing wrong?" Lethal sighs. "You know a lot of girls. Why don't you just pick one and be done with it?"

"Well why don't you? At least I don't have to take my own hands out to lunch the next day."

"So what are you gonna do? Hold out until you find the right one?"

"Dunno, haven't really thought about it. And you? Shouldn't you be banging like a rock star these days?"

"Theoretically." He rubs his forehead with the ball of his palm. "Did I tell you about the striptease I got last night?"

"The what?"

"Yeah, some fruit wanted to showcase some lingerie she had just bought."

"And?"

"Nothing. Fooled around a bit and threw her out."

"Rotten fruit?"

"No, pretty ripe actually, some college babe from the gym."

"Then what's the matter? Thought you said it's been nine months."

"Yeah . . . Just sick of giving test drives, you know."

"So you want a girlfriend?"

"Don't you?"

"Nah. It's good to be single."

"Yeah, single and dry."

"Well calling girls 'fruits' ain't gonna help either."

"But that's what they are." Lethal lets out a torrent of smoke. "I mean honestly, you've seen the girls I hang around with. Models, actresses, *wo cao ta ma de* TV personalities. They look great. But are they girlfriend material? Or do you just take a bite and throw them out?"

"Oh come on, *ge-men'er,* you can't generalize like that. Not all pretty girls are fruits, okay?"

"Oh yeah, like who?"

"Well . . ."

20

When I first met Mirage in 2002, I didn't think much was going to happen.

Wearing a dark blue button-down and straight uncolored hair, she looked almost square compared to the other glittery attendees at the dinner party. But I was drawn to her features right away: clean, strong, dignified—interestingly reminiscent of Sophia Loren. And unlike millions of Chinese girls bent on lightening their skin color with lotions and potions, she had a glowing tan that dimmed the pasty white.

So I introduced myself, expecting her to just nod and smile or perhaps give me a pet name as would most Chinese girls in similar situations; but she gave me her full name, first and last, and even wrote them out in midair so I could identify the characters. To push the envelope, I asked her how old she was, a question that no local girl I had ever met would answer without asking me to guess and guess again and then end by deciding not to tell me. Without hesitation, she told me she was twenty-four.

Naturally, I was intrigued. But before I could make a move, I was told that she was a rising star for China's biggest modeling agency, which meant that I might as well save myself the trouble and back off, for any decent-looking Chinese model is by default taken or kept, and she was way more than just decent-looking.

But as luck would have it, I managed to bump into her over and over again. It's true what they say: no more than two degrees separate any two Sanlitun regulars. Through all the chance meetings, I saw that Mirage was more than just a pretty face, or a leggy five feet nine with Lorenesque endowments. Never vulgar or ostentatious, she rarely wore makeup and was a fan of T-shirts and jeans. Unlike all the other Chinese models I had known, she could paint, write poetry, and even beat me at a game of chess. At the time, she was dating the son of a powerful army general, who would have sent in an entire platoon if I had dared to lay hands on his prize. But no matter how I watched myself, I am sure she still knew exactly how I felt about her.

Then on a moonlit summer night in 2003, Mirage and I met for a casual drink in what was then still Southie. Somehow, the topic moved on to her boyfriend, who apparently drove Beijing's first ever Hummer and had oversized insecurities to match. Under his reign, she was not allowed to have any male friends or stay out past midnight, and had to ask all men within five meters of her to be quiet whenever he called just so that the guy would not fall into a jealous rage upon overhearing a baritone voice. The punishment for disobedience included slapping, kicking, and sometimes even choking.

"So why put up with it?" I was calmly furious.

"To help save the money I earn as a model," she said. "So one day I can buy my mother a new house."

Her mother, by the way, lived alone on a remote military base on the edge of the great Taklimakan Desert.

Naturally, I started reminiscing about my own mother and the house that I had once wanted to buy her. When we both got a little teary-eyed in the end, she held my hand for a few seconds of quiet comfort. It was the closest I had felt to any female in years.

The next day, she disappeared. No phone call. No text message. Even her mobile number was no longer in service.

I didn't know what to make of it.

Then a good two months later, right before I was about to write her off altogether, she called to say, "I've been working in the South for a while. Want to come for a visit?"

Apparently, her modeling agency holds a beauty pageant for aspiring models every year on beautiful Hainan Island, a place as picturesque as Hawaii but at one-tenth the price. And for the first time in her career, she was going to be the event's assistant coordinator.

But seriously, flying all the way to Hainan for a girl I hadn't kissed or even seen in months? I am a man, for Mao's sake, and I get enough girls as is!

The flight was excruciating, with a three-hour delay in Guangzhou before I finally landed in Sanya at midnight.

Then, I saw her, statuesque in her white T-shirt and faded blue jeans. Her hair was much shorter with brown tinted highlights, her skin even more glowing than before. As usual, she wore no makeup. As usual, she stood out from the crowd.

"Have you eaten yet?" she asked, after a split-second pause.

I don't remember how I responded. It was the first time that a girl had picked me up from the airport in years. I wanted to kiss her on the cheek, or at least give her a hug. But I just mumbled.

By the time I checked into the Cactus Resort, it was already 1 A.M. Shortly after I unpacked, she led me to the beach.

As I took in deep breaths of the ocean breeze, she said, "I am free now."

"As in . . . What about . . . him?"

"It's over." She shrugged. "No more *yuan fen* between him and me."

"I beg your pardon?"

Okay, I knew how to write the word *"yuan fen"* in Chinese; but as is the case with many words we know how to write, I still have no idea what it really means. As far as I can tell, *yuan fen* is China's default explanation for everything hard to explain. Once you've gotten past all the usual reasons and excuses for why everything works out the way it does, there stands *yuan fen*.

"Well as far as I am concerned, it's just fate." She smiled. "I thought I was going to put up with him for life. But then you came around. . . . And now . . . Who knew that you and I would have such good *yuan fen*."

And it was only going to get better.

Before our first time, she asked, "Why do you like me?"

"Well . . ." I thought about it constructively for the very first time. "I am not too sure."

Because if I were to be strict with my standards, she wasn't the prettiest, the smartest, the most successful, or even the nicest, and she greeted people with "Have you eaten yet?" even when it was four o'clock in the afternoon. But I just liked her. It was something visceral, something outside of logic, something that hinted at the big L. And Hainan Island was just perfect for making a four-letter word beautiful.

The pageant took place on the eve of my departure; half of the island showed up to watch. Dashing around the set with her walkie-talkie and directing over two hundred guys and dolls, she was—for me—the event's main attraction. And when some guy sitting next to me pointed to her and asked, "Who is that fox over there?" I answered with a proud grin, "That's my girl." Hokey, sure, but it felt good.

By 2 A.M., we finally made it back to the hotel. To make the most of our remaining hours before my early-morning flight, we put aloe on each other's sunburned skin and kissed to some old tunes on her portable stereo.

Until her boss called.

"Do you have to go?" I didn't think it was reasonable for anyone to work at 3:30 A.M., especially not for some VIP session involving government officials at a karaoke bar.

"But it's my job, baby." She kissed me softly. "I have no choice."

At 7 A.M., she stumbled back into the room, reeking of alcohol and cigarettes. I could imagine what the karaoke had been like, or even worse, but I wasn't going to think about it like that.

In perhaps my best handwriting ever, I wrote her a letter as she fell asleep. It was the first one I had written for anyone in years, and in Chinese no less.

Soon after I had returned to Beijing, she called to say: "I miss you."

Already? Me, too! Her voice was so soft and lovely that I felt it was the perfect time to ask, "Where do you think we should go from here?"

To which she answered: "I'd feel the same way as you would."

Great! Awesome! Mission accomplished—she agreed to be my girlfriend! I heard it loud and clear.

From then on, I wrote poems for Mirage every day. All around town, I told people that I had found my girl. Even in my sleep, I smiled at the thought of her.

Then two weeks later, a most-anticipated phone call.

"I am back in town," she said, "and I want to spend tomorrow with you."

But what should we do? I kept tossing and turning that night. It had to be something different, something cool, something that would take our *yuan fen* to the next level. . . .

At 11 A.M., she arrived.

"Looking for someone, sweetheart?" I greeted her with my biggest smile.

"Yes." She looked fabulous in her new Versace outfit, her legs running a mile long in flowing black trousers and her bosom ripened

beneath the snug white top with a silk bow tied in front. "I'm looking for someone who thinks he is my boyfriend."

I beg your pardon? Oh, right, I get it; she's being cute.

Walking through the apartment that doubled as a buddy's office
for his software start-up, she counted the computers in the living
room and said, "This is . . . interesting."

"Actually"—I ushered her into the oddly shaped cubicle with a
single bed that was smaller than the one I had in college—"here is
my room."

"Nice . . ." She swept the bread crumbs off the Mickey Mouse
bedsheets left by the previous tenant. "This is, uh . . . different from
before."

Yup, that would be one way of putting it. When we first met, I
had a 2,000-square-foot spread with two balconies, courtesy of the
megasalaried job I'd had. But my new place wasn't so bad. Okay, so
the water heater didn't work and it was only 100 square feet of
space, but was 700 *kuai* a month with utilities, and there was still a
bed. Besides, I had already told her I wasn't employed anymore.

"So how have you been?" I could barely hold back my plung-
ing kiss.

"Good." She nodded. "Done with the pageant, made some money,
came back on Monday."

Yeah? But this was already Thursday. How come she didn't
call me right away? I definitely would have called her first if it had
been the other way around. Was there someone else she'd rather
see? Oh, silly rabbit. Maybe she had to spend time with her
cousin, who doubled as her roommate. I am not so into family, but
some people are.

"Well, I missed you. . . ." I reached for her hand. "A lot."

"And I you . . ." She let me caress her fingers. "But I was so busy
that . . . Oh, you haven't told my cousin about us, have you?"

"Uh, no. Why?"

She let out a quiet sigh.

"Want a beer?" A little midday alcohol might warm up the cold air.

"No, not in the mood."

"Then how about a smoke? I rolled it up already."

"No, too early for that." She frowned for a second. "Notice anything different?"

"You mean other than no beer and hash? There is only one way to find out."

"Oh, behave!" She laughed. "Not on this bed anyway. I'm talking about, you know, the aura. See anything different?"

Now that she mentioned it, she did seem a bit more . . .

"They want to put me in a TV show." She preempted my response by continuing, "The same network that sponsored the pageant. I've been meeting with them all week. A show about traveling to the Middle East by car with me as host."

"Then we should really celebrate! I was thinking that we'd go to the Red Gate Gallery for an art exhibit, then go for a walk along the Forbidden City and—"

"Why a gallery?" She crinkled her nose. "How about we go shopping instead?"

Or how about I hara-kiri myself with a rusted knife? And had she not noticed that I was sleeping on a Disney bunk?

"Okay!" I don't know where I got the conviction. "We can go shopping if you like."

And I even meant it. For once in my life, I would enjoy walking through a sea of people and breathing in recycled carbon dioxide.

Then Mirage's phone rang. And when she finished, she said, "Let's do shopping another time."

"Great!" Barely two weeks into our relationship, and she already understood the beauty of compromising; talk about some incredible *yuan fen*. "We can go see the foliage at Fragrant Hills. There is a little café there—"

"Sweetheart . . ." She added a frown to her smile. "The network people want to meet for lunch and talk business. Now."

"But . . ."

"I know, baby, and I am sorry." She gave me a consolation kiss. "But those guys are still of great use to me."

Later that night, the temperature plunged well below zero. Shivering under my Mickey sheets inside my unheated room, I waited for the phone call that she had promised me. Instead, all I got was a text message from an unknown source that told everyone to brace for the incoming cold front.

Three days later, I met her for lunch at the China World Hotel. It was the first time I had ever seen her in a skirt, which made it that much more difficult to say, "It's time to go our separate ways."

Of course, I didn't really want to break up. According to my master plan, Mirage would immediately shower me with hugs and kisses and beg for my forgiveness, thus allowing me to purse my lips for a few seconds and then generously let bygones be bygones.

My plan failed miserably. And I will never forget her calmness when she said, "Let's hope *yuan fen* would have us meet again when we least expect it."

A week later in Sanlitun, I bumped into Mirage's cousin, who told me that the woman who had said "I love you too" just a few days before had been sick for a few days and was leaving for Shanghai first thing in the morning.

"When is she coming back?" I am sure I sounded even more anxious than I looked.

"She is not," her cousin replied.

Like clockwork, I couldn't sleep again.

At 5:30 A.M., I tiptoed into the only restaurant on Ghost Street that hadn't locked its doors yet and sneaked a flask of chicken soup past the waiters and cooks who were snoring up a storm in the dining room. It was for Mirage's cold, a token of my goodwill.

Shielding my gift from the rain under the foyer of a convenience store across from her building, I called at least twenty times before her cousin finally got out of bed three hours later to let me in.

Three seconds later, I realized just how little I had actually known her.

The place was a dump. Chipping walls, greasy floors, a lone lightbulb without a lamp shade, candles stuck on the radiator. Except for clothes scattered everywhere and cosmetics in the bathroom sink, nothing indicated that this was a girl's home, much less the home of a once rather successful model.

Coming out of the kitchen, I spotted Mirage in the bedroom to my right. Wrapped from head to toe in a blanket on a metal-framed bed with not much of a mattress, she was curled up in a fetal position with her back toward me. Two well-traveled suitcases leaned against the wall, perhaps bound for Shanghai, as her cousin had told me.

I wanted to grab her and hold her and tell her how much I had missed her.

My feet didn't budge.

I realized that we were from different worlds. Leaving her abusive ex gave her freedom and independence; but it also gave her bills to pay and duties to fulfill. Even the best models in China don't make much, and at twenty-five, Mirage's best years were behind her. Unless she wanted to go back to the desert or allow herself to be another Desire of Ten Thousand Men, she needed to be practical, and loving me the way I wanted to be loved was a luxury that she could not afford. Call it fate. Call it luck. Call it bad timing. As much as I wanted her to be "the one," she could be only my Mirage.

Such was our *yuan fen*.

"Look, I suggest you stop thinking about her, okay?" Lethal says. "Another buddy of mine is dating her now."

"Oh, really?" How I hate this two-degrees business sometimes. "When did you see her last?"

"Just a few days ago. Went to her birthday party. Good-looking broad, I must say. She doesn't look a bit like she's twenty-nine."

Really? I thought she was one year younger than I am, not older.

"Is this the month of Virgo already?" I can still picture our conversation on astrology vividly.

"I think that was September. Last week should be Libra."

"So what's she doing these days, anyway?"

"Nothing."

"What happened to that TV show?"

"Nope. My buddy is a movie producer. She doesn't have to do jack."

Well then what about the house that she wanted to buy for her mom? Or has that come out of her new boyfriend's wallet too? Could it be that she liked me only because I had a good job once? How many guys did she call to visit her on Hainan Island before she called me? Was I the only one who said yes?

Good thing my Zigarette is almost ready.

21

"Shuai ge!" Someone just called me a "handsome chap."

Well if it isn't the trio Lethal just called "fruits."

"Mei nu!" I rise for the Sanlitun protocol.

And fortunately, I didn't have to lie this time—the three girls actually qualify as "good-looking."

"Mmw . . . ah" for the left cheek; as much bullshit for the right cheek.

China sure has changed. All those years when my mother was around, my father never kissed her even once in my presence. In today's Sanlitun, everyone is hugging and kissing even if they barely know each other; the habit is not just for the French anymore.

Out of the trio, I know HH the best. One of the most active social butterflies in town, she is well known for her signature curly hair and near-perfect English. Often mistaken for someone from Malaysia or Thailand, she can breeze in and out of Beijing's heavily guarded diplomatic compounds without any hassle from security. The last time I saw her, she was engaged to some American guy who was going to take her out of China. Judging from the way she is scanning Lethal right now, the wedding is either coming up very soon or not coming up at all.

Next up is DD, whom I met only a few days ago. Once a catwalk kitten, this thirty-something claims to be a celebrity makeup artist. Almost a twin for another model I once knew, but with bigger boobs, higher cheekbones, and long, braided hair with brownish highlights, she seems to be very popular with young foreigners under the age of twenty. On Monday, she was being served by some

French garçon named Jean-Luc; but today is Wednesday, which might be either German or Italian day.

"Hi!" The last girl's grin is bigger than the occasion requires. "Good to see you again."

And of course, there is, well, some girl whom I just kissed on both cheeks but whose name I can't remember.

I used to hate it when that happened.

But it happens almost too often these days. Meet a girl, talk for ten minutes, get her number, don't call her for a few days, forget about her in a few weeks, and delete her number in about a month. It's just the way it's done. Usually I'm pretty good with faces, but this one just draws a blank. . . . Oh well, as long as she knows mine.

"So what's going on?" I ask HH. "No work today?"

"What work?" She shrugs. "Left that place ages ago. Just waiting on America now."

"Your fiancé is working on it, is he?"

"He'd better."

"Are you guys in love?"

"Well . . . Yeah . . . You know."

"And you?" I glance over DD's breasts, which look very good today in her low-cut blouse. "What have you been up to?"

"Nothing really." She stretches out her arms in a lazy yawn, her cleavage spreading and tightening. "Waiting for you to call me, I suppose."

"Then where would you take me today? It's almost five o'clock."

"I don't know. . . ." DD pouts for a second. "How about we go dancing? Like Mix?"

Again? "I was just there on Saturday."

I know. It's embarrassing. Having been around since the days of 88, I really shouldn't be going to places like Mix anymore. But when you know a lot of Dogs 'n' Foxes who'd care to see you only when there is food 'n' alcohol involved, it's hard to be creative about nightlife.

To get to Mix, I had to walk through an entire parking lot of Beemers, Mercs, Hummers, Porsches, and hey, one nice new Ferrari. Half of them don't even have license plates yet; and most of their drivers don't have driver's licenses either (at least not officially).

At the door, a gang of black-uniformed bouncers wielding metal detectors greeted me. All ex-military, all six one and above, all wearing skinhead buzz cuts, and all really, really able to kick my ass. To any guy who comes in, they just gesture like robots. To the pretty ladies, especially the blondes, they can be very, very friendly. For now, not many of them will take bribes, as Chinese clubs have yet to turn away anyone at the door on account of his or her appearance or due to overcapacity and potential fire hazard. But all will happen in good time.

Inside, the decor was elaborately kitsch. Now that all of China is in a building frenzy, having the most modern installations is not a problem; having the most sophisticated taste is. In terms of software, these places still have a way to go before catching up to the hippest spots in New York or London, as well as the ones in Hong Kong or even Shanghai. The color scheme is usually a bit too red, the staff is usually a bit too slow, there are usually too many mirrors with too much unflattering lighting, and the music is usually too loud and not the most cutting-edge. But it's all right. Given the level of local taste, any converted warehouse with sofas, stereos, whiskey, strobe lights, and no windows or fire exits will make millions.

The crowd was about 60 percent locals and 40 percent outsiders, with the latter being mostly ABCs (American-born Chinese), BBCs

(British-born Chinese), CBCs (Canadian-born Chinese), and returnees like me. The difference between the two groups was almost too apparent—if someone looked rich or ultrafashionable, he or she was probably a local or a local's *ernai*.

As usual, the ones sitting down were busy playing a local dice game, where each participant shakes up five dice in an inverted shaker and then bets on how many of 1s to 6s are split among all the shakers in play, with 1s being wild. The basic rule is that if someone bets "two" of something (i.e., two 2s), the next in line must either call for an audit of all the dice or raise the bet to at least "three" of something (i.e., three 5s); and the bets will keep snowballing until someone blurs out "eighteen 6s" or something equally improbable, and an audit is called for everyone's true worth. If the "eighteen 6s" turns out be just another Chinese bubble, the person who led the hype must drink; otherwise, the punishment goes to the one who dared to question Chinese luck.

And speaking of drinks, nine out of ten tables would order at least one bottle of Chivas Regal to mix with bottles of green tea. Originally invented in Taiwan, this deceptively light but deadly concoction has become the local club drink of choice, relegating oldies like gin and tonic to the bar tabs of outsiders who have not yet assimilated. To help digest the alcohol, there was also a fruit plate on every table: a half-split banana standing upright in the middle, surrounded by triangular watermelon slices and big, round, dark grapes with two seeds inside each. But I don't think everyone appreciates the subliminal message, as no one ever seems to touch the bananas, and I have yet to come across any threesomes on the premises (except maybe at the gay clubs).

On the dance floor, a young crowd gyrated to European house mix, with DJ Noodle busy tooling the turntable. Dim lights. Heavy beats. Close dips. Some folks got the rhythm. Some folks really need some. It was certainly a blessing to have had black friends in America who taught me the moves—some white men just can't dance no matter where they are in the world, and most local Chinese girls dance even worse than they drive. But thanks to the dirty warehouse-grade horse-tranquilizer equivalent of ecstasy that half of them must have been on, more than half of them were whipping their heads from side to side in a deep trance, providing some form of comedy if not stimulation (as long as you didn't let their flying ponytails whip you in the eye).

In the thicket of human bodies I ran into one of my Dogs 'n' Foxes, this one being more dog than fox, even though he likes to think otherwise (especially with the ladies).

"What's going on?" I tried to scream over the ground-shaking beats of "*douche-douche*."

". . . " He was already quite drunk and slobbering.

"What? I can't hear you!"

". . . fuck . . . you . . ."

"And how was your week?"

". . . fucking . . . fuck . . ."

"So who did you come with?"

". . . fucking . . . fucker . . ."

"Any plan for the weekend?"

". . . fuck . . . fuck . . . fuck . . . fuck . . . fuck . . ."

"Alrighty then, good seeing you, man."

". . . fuck . . . off . . ."

In the background, through the loudspeakers, the sultry voice of an Englishwoman grunted to the Arabic beat, "Fuck me hard. Fuck me well. Wrapping my pussy all around . . ."

On my way to the bar, I checked out the talents who were heading in the other direction. Half of them wore very little on their bodies but had on shades that covered their entire faces. In Lethal's terminology, they would be tart fruits, bitter fruits, in-season fruits, past-season fruits, best picks, rare finds, plump 'n' juicy, sweet 'n' sour, and the occasional "ohmygod that was nasty" fruit.

At 2 A.M. the crowd was still coming in. There is a city ordinance that says only restaurants can stay open after 2 A.M. So every table is given free peanuts. Other than a code of "no flip-flops" at some of the snottier places (although a venue named Suzie Wong's hardly fits the profile of a high-class joint), there is no dress code and definitely no drinking age. As a male outsider, there is never a need to dress up. As long you are not grotesque, all the girls (hot or not), especially the ones who might be too young for you to be talking to back home, will check you out even if you wear just a torn white T-shirt.

Suddenly I spotted something fifteen feet to my right. Long black hair down to her buttocks. Eyes worthy of an Egyptian queen. She was an outsider, probably of mixed lineage but with a European flair. Next to her stood a chap talking into her ear. Was she listening? Or was she bored? Should I make the move? Or keep looking cool? The music was pumping; I had the bounce. She was still nursing her drink. What do I say to get her to dance? Walk up close and ask her directly? Look at her in the eyes and send over some electricity? Hmm, she started laughing. Bet that guy just made a fool out of himself. So what would be a good icebreaker for a girl who has probably heard it all? More important, do I really want to make the effort? And how much longer would I have to put up with this "*douche-douche*" if I did?

In all fairness, Mix is not a bad place. For any twenty-one-year-old male living in America, entertainment doesn't get much better than playing video games and drinking the cheapest beer in a frat house with ugly sorority groupies. Here, on the other hand, no one needs to play video games, because he is already living in one, with all the lights, noise, and technology that even Studio 54 couldn't afford for Gloria Gaynor in its heyday. And unlike one of those so-called legendary underground raves that can happen only once every so often these days in America, Club Mix happens every night, and there is absolutely nothing underground about it.

Unfortunately, I can't be twenty-one anymore, at least not on this particular Wednesday. Once upon a time, I too enjoyed stumbling out of Mix at 6 A.M. like a vampire before sunrise and scrambling past the retirees practicing their morning tai chi on the sidewalk. Now, it's getting more and more embarrassing.

"Wait . . ." HH checks an incoming message on her titanium Vertu mobile. "A friend of a friend just opened up a bar. Grand opening tonight. Want to check it out? This one is in Houhai."

"Oh sure, and risk my life trying to dodge all the speeding rickshaws before I even get to the front gate?"

Okay, I admit: in terms of pure (or, rather, *original*) aesthetics, there is hardly a place in this whole country that can beat Houhai. As the backyard to many members of the ex–royal family up until 1949, this man-made lake just north of the Forbidden City is still home to some of the most elaborate and best-preserved feudal architecture in all of China. Legend has it that the emperor ordered this lake to be dug as an extension of the Grand China Canal (which is twenty times longer than the Panama Canal) just so that he could board his royal vessel in a jiffy and tour his vast empire by water. And in memory of all the laborers that must have perished while digging this massive hole in the middle of an otherwise completely landlocked city, we can now all contemplate the ripples across the water whenever the wind blows.

And until recently, that was what I did. Starting in 2001, after a once-upon-a-time public toilet on the lakefront was converted into a hut called No Name, Houhai became the oasis where one could (believe it or not) escape the city's smell, noise, and congestion. The three or four establishments around the lake brought in a small, select clientele, and there was hardly any traffic in the area. After jogging around the lake on a not-so-polluted afternoon, I would watch the sun set over those Speedo-clad old men swimming in the industrial-green water and say to myself, "China can be romantic after all."

But then in 2003, SARS hit. To help contain the deadly virus, the government "advised" everyone to stay away from enclosed public spaces. And the people really listened. Overnight, the entire Sanlitun was emptied out. Even the Forbidden City, ordinarily the most heavily trafficked tourist trap in all of China, became a ghost town.

But the self-quarantine didn't last long enough. After a few weeks, the partying crowd brought its own virus into Houhai, by the tens of thousands. In a matter of weeks, dozens of rowdy bars landed on the old lakeshore drive. Neon Jack Daniel's and Budweiser signs replaced old street numbers. Cheap sofas in all shades of red crowded out the sidewalk. And cars just kept coming in with their horns blasting.

So nowadays, no Houhai for me after 4 P.M. Too many bars. Too many people. Too many tricycle rickshaws darting down the lakeshore drive at breakneck speeds.

"Well, there is also a fashion show tonight inside the Forbidden City," DD says. "Can get free invites if you guys want."

But, of course, fall is the season for high society. The last such show was at a temple adjacent to the Forbidden City where the emperors once worshipped their ancestors. I don't know how the organizers managed to book the place, as it must be Class A national heritage. But I guess for 400,000 *kuai* a night, even the emperors' ancestors can stay up a little bit longer.

Still, I doubt I'll be going to tonight's event. I'd rather get high than mingle with high society, and I definitely don't want to accidentally burn down any ancient wooden structure with a flick of my Zigarette.

"I say that we all go to Maggie's." Lethal makes the same bad suggestion that he always does when he is high.

Aka the "Mongolian Republic," Maggie's is "members only," which means it accepts only two types of patrons: Caucasians and anyone who flashes a credit card. Inside, a horde of Mongolian hookers with more makeup than clothes will vie for the next FOB victim. While most of them are uglier than a baboon's ass, they can still be quite exotic to a FOB foreigner who has never groped an Asian woman. Indeed, the owner made so much money from this place that he allegedly went on to finance either Banana or Kiss or Rock 'n' Roll, huge complexes that offer hookers in three-inch heels, gigolos in skintight Versaces, and a vibrating dance floor where nouveau-riche businessmen and their *ernais* can head-bang to neo-peasant techno after a few e-drops.

I never want to go to any of those places again.

"Why don't we just go chill at Transit?" I suggest one of my favorite escapes, where only the roses are red, the mirrors stay in the bathroom, and the music is never "*douche-douche.*" A small but immaculately converted warehouse with wood-beamed ceilings, frescoed walls, a trickling water fountain for good *feng shui*, and high arched windows designed by the owners themselves, it is where even the worst mood can find peace and conversation flows like wine for hours. Plus, the boys there make a killer Long Island ice tea—a splash of freshly squeezed orange juice really makes the difference.

"But did you know that it's right next to a garbage dump? Or was that a septic station?" HH and DD frown at each other. "What an awful smell!"

I give up.

22

"FRUIT!" Lethal almost chokes on his beer.

"Not again, bro."

"No, really, check her out."

All right, let's see. . . .

Big eyes. Wavy locks. Five feet seven. Golden tan. Beautiful shoulders. Curvy waist. Low-rise jeans way below the navel. Black toenail polish over pink sandals. And a tight yellow cutoff T that reads "Public School Girl."

Bling bling!

"Ah, whatever." It's just Ginger.

"You know her?" Lethal squints with envy.

"Oh, sure."

"But I've never seen you two hanging out."

"That's coz she was before your time, bro."

"Well how did you know her?"

I tap my lips with two fingers.

"You mean hash?" Lethal seems incredulous. "She smokes?"

Well, not exactly.

It was the night of last summer's Fetish Party, the annual costumed shindig where everyone tired of Mix, Vic's, and Babyface could party in his nastiest and sexiest.

Before going, I got a call from Huajiadi, the Englishman who coorganized the party. "Dude, you have to bring some stuff," he said.

"Naturally. You know me."

"No, I meant bring more. There is a girl who wants some."

"Yeah?" A girl who smokes, interesting. "But is she hot? I'm no errand boy, you know."

Honestly, I *hate* getting hash for other people. Just because I use it myself doesn't mean I will distribute it, or do anything more than pass on a telephone number. A lot of people come to Beijing for a few days' visit and the first thing out of their mouths is, "Hey, where can I get some drugs?" Who the hell do they think they are? Do you know how long it took before I managed to get Prince's number? A whole damn week, at least!

"Dude, she has a few friends in town; it's for them. She asked me first, but I'm busy here at the party. . . . Can you like sell them a spare chunk?"

"What, am I stocking up here? I have to see Prince again just to get one for her? And it's not even for her?"

"But *ge-men'er,* trust me. It's worth it."

"Why, is she hot?"

"*Ge-men'er,* is the sun hot?"

"Well have you seen the sun in Beijing lately?"

"Trust me, this is not British humor."

"But you are still white after all. We might have different tastes."

"Just hurry!" He hung up.

In keeping with tradition, the party was held at Vibes, a bar inside Factory 798, which up until 2002 was a state-owned factory that made something useless. By the time I arrived, the party had just kicked into high gear. Inside the elevated DJ booth, Sunshine Sunshine's latest beau was spinning drum 'n' bass. At the bar, five layers of people hollered for their Tsingtaos and mojitos. Up above, cross-dressers got down on the narrow black metal walkway, some of them looking positively fly in their feathers, stockings, and G-strings. On the dance floor, leather 'n' chains, masks 'n' whips, bunny outfits, angel wings, headmasters, dominatrixes; it was like Halloween, just sweatier.

Making my way through the thick crowd in my pink linen beach pants and nothing but a red suede tie, I looked for my damsel in hash-stress. Ordinarily, I don't like to be thought of as a sex object; but this was Fetish, and getting a few pinches from the boys and girls just came with the territory.

Then I saw someone under the metal staircase.

Dancing alone, she bounced her apple bottom with perfect rhythm. Wearing a black top, black jeans, and black boots, she didn't look like any of the other scantily dressed people at the party. But boy did she stand out. Maybe it's because I was chased down the hallway by a gang of black girls during my first week in America, but I've had a black fetish for years, and the Afro wig she had on was the first one that I had ever seen in China.

With a quick pivot and turn, she caught me staring before I could look away.

My abs tightened instinctively. I love girls with full lips, not to mention that naughty mark above her upper lip. Her nose was sharp and strong, but not overpowering. She looked Chinese, but not exactly. Unlike the chopstick-thin trio sitting to my left now, she was more womanly, her face with no sunken cheeks or bony edges.

Then, sunshine. And I couldn't help but smile back. Not since Mirage had I seen a visage that pleasant. For a second, I even thought I should have worn more clothes.

But I didn't walk up to her. It's just not my style.

"So where is this hot girl I need to save?" I asked Huajiadi, who was busy serving up absinthe shots under the DJ booth.

"There." He pointed to his left and gave me a wink.

"You mean the chick with the Afro?"

"You got it."

During the ensuing self-introduction, she told me she was a Taiwanese-born American studying traditional Chinese medicine in Beijing. Even though she had been in town for almost three years, we had never seen each other. And she didn't realize that I was the "dealer" sent to save her until I took out the chunk of hashish.

Throughout the evening, nothing happened. She seemed a bit aloof, and the place was loud. I met her friends and shared a few smokes, but that was all. Sure, I liked her; I was intrigued, in fact. But I also liked a lot of other girls. A fetish is just a fetish, and she wasn't really black.

Then on a Saturday a few weeks later, she woke me up at 10 A.M. with a phone call. Apparently, I had promised the night before while hanging out in a group that I would take her for a ride on my motorcycle. Honestly, I didn't think she was serious and my promise was more or less a "Yeah, sure, whatever." But a promise is still a promise, and I couldn't say no to such a pretty girl first thing in the morning.

When I picked her up, she offered me a yogurt drink for breakfast. Being a single guy without an office job, I never get around to eating breakfast. So this was nice.

"Beautiful day," she said, pointing to the rare blue sky and white clouds. "I want to get a tan today."

"How?" I was puzzled. "We are going riding, not sunbathing."

"Oh, it's okay. I just need a little color on my shoulders. I'll tan while we ride."

Yeah, sure, whatever. Girlie girl.

About two hundred miles and five hours later, during which we rode through a mining village where the soot turned her face black and had at least three close calls with trucks driving on the wrong side of the road, we finally made it back to the city. For refreshment, she took me to Baskin-Robbins, where I had Rum Raisin ice cream for the very first time.

On my way to drop her off, I said to myself, "So, this girl called me up first thing in the morning, brought me breakfast, put her life in my hands for the whole day, and just bought me ice cream. She *loves* me. Yeah, she is a bit girlie; but at least she didn't melt in the action like I thought she would."

So, I leaned forward. Her face was looking a bit dusty, her long locks not as bouncy; but it was all right. We had had a good day. Time to kiss, then kiss some more, maybe see each other for dinner, have drinks afterward, and retire to our respective quarters with the understanding that we would have sex by Wednesday.

I saw the twinkle in her eyes, those coquettish lashes demanding my attention with every blink. This was going to be good. Nice and soft. I have nice lips, and she certainly did too. When they met, sparks would fly. And she felt it as well, reaching up with her fingers to caress my cheek.

Which then pushed on it to give me the deflection.

How cute: she likes to play.

So I tried again.

And she gave me another deflection!

Wait a second, what the hell is going on?! Did this girl seriously think she could just drag me out of bed, cling on to me for five hours, go on a ride that I never really even intended, and then just buy me some second-rate ice cream and leave without a kiss? What am I, a sugar-craving taxi service? Did she have any idea how easy it was for me to get a bootie call? If she wanted me to wine her and dine her and tell her bullshit stories before we could even lock lips, then she might as well go back in time!

So I left, and deleted her number from my phone.

But again, two degrees—even if it's been months since I last saw her.

"Hey ya." Ginger gives me the finger-wave from two meters away. " 'Sup?"

"Beautiful day." She grins. "Did you go for a ride?"

What is that, some sort of sarcasm?

"So how is everything?" Not that I really care to know.

"Good. I've finished school."

"Oh, good for you. So what are you doing now?"

"Working for a game developer."

"As in PlayStation?" How juvenile.

"No, mobile phones."

"What happened to Chinese medicine?"

"Put that on pause. All the hottest games are being developed in China now. And you? What've you been doing?"

"Oh, you know." I raise my soon-to-be-lit Ziggy. "Just taking it easy."

"Same old, same old, eh?" She scans the trio to my left.

I know what she is thinking. But this is what happens when a son spends a lot of time with the mother while growing up—I just feel more comfortable hanging out with girls. It doesn't make me gay (necessarily) or even a player (necessarily), just more comfortable. The truth is, I'm never going to sleep with anyone in the trio; but it's always good face to be around pretty things that everybody thinks I do.

"Are you going out tonight?" Ginger continues.

"No plans yet."

"There's a fashion show inside the Forbidden City."

I heard.

"And it's Wednesday, ladies' night at Vic's."

Right. Hip-hop is for kids. "I'll text you if I go." But if I don't, "I have to babysit some friends from out of town."

"Okay." She finger-waves once more. "See ya."

Whatever.

"Ge-men'er." Lethal nudges me. "Why don't you ask her out?"

"What am I, in high school?"

"Why the hell not, man? She is hot. Do you even see what I see?"

"Ge-men'er, I'd rather just get high."

Because any way I look at it, it's just too much work for too little return. Everyone wants to be in love these days, whereas I outgrew crowded places long ago.

"Aw, *ge-men'er*." Lethal shakes his head. "I know where you are going with this. It's no good, I'm telling you."

"Cao." I don't generally curse in Chinese, but. "Look who is talking."

"Hey." Lethal wants to stick to my problems. "No matter what, I've got a year and a half on you. When I was your age, I was exactly the same way. I just don't want you to go down the same road I did."

"Oh yeah, the road to insanity, right? Thank you, Father."

"Oh, by the way." Ginger turns around all of a sudden, her long curls messing with the breeze. "My company needs some advice on intellectual property. Are you still doing the law thing?"

23

"Wait a second." The Kid looks confused as I send off Ginger with the usual have-your-machine-call-my-machine. "Are you a lawyer?"

"The last time I checked."

"But you don't look like a lawyer."

"Thanks."

"So do you work for a firm?"

"Used to."

"In Beijing?"

"That's what brought me here in the first place."

Back then, my mission couldn't have been sexier: help Chinese companies go IPO on Wall Street. As one of only two American lawyers in the office, I was assisted by a staff of ten, including Chinese attorneys who had to (by law) suspend their local licenses just so they could work under me. In terms of pay, the "hardship allowance" on top of my supersized expatriate package meant that I made even more in Beijing than I had in Hong Kong. And if my designer wardrobe alone weren't enough to earn me face, my office on the thirty-fifth floor of China World Tower One certainly did. Being a third-year associate at only twenty-five, I was on track to become the youngest partner ever in my firm.

But soon I got bored again. Sure, I could give thirty-second synopses of all the "sexy" deals I did and my meetings with the big shots; but it took months for those thirty seconds to happen (if they did at all), and most meetings were a complete waste of time. Then, as far as timing went, 2002 turned out to be a really slow year for foreign law firms in China. After the Internet bubble went poof, half of the deals stopped dead in their tracks. All of a sudden, hours of work e-mails turned into hours of surfing the Web.

Shortly thereafter, the whole Foodiez thing started.

For months, my colleagues warned that the firm was unhappy about my "profiteering on company time." Even the managing partner himself told me to "stop fooling around with being a delivery boy." But I let it go in one ear and out the other. Instead of pulling all-nighters for people who didn't even know my name, I wanted to be my own boss.

So, in July 2002, the firm decided to pull the plug on me. With one phone call, my life turned upside down. Good-bye fat paycheck, window office, personal assistant, and villa apartment. Instead of just wanting to be the boss, I had to become one pronto.

But of course, Foodiez didn't go so well in the beginning. To get by, I had to do something else. And the only thing that came to mind was to hang up my own shingle.

So what should I call the firm? Well, given how China has so many gray areas, it must have a degree of latitude, plus the ability to reach unprecedented altitude, and bottom-line, it'd better have some attitude.

How is Lawttitude?

"So what kind of clients do you have?" the Kid asks.

"Well, that would depend on what you mean by 'clients' and what you mean by 'have.'"

Because in two and a half years, I have been approached by many potential "clients" who think a lawyer in China should be bargain-able in the same way everything else at the Ya Show Shoe Cap Market is; but I didn't spend US $150,000 on my law school education just so that I could bill my services at $2.50 an hour. And, annoyingly enough, most of those who get into situations where they need the help of a lawyer still prefer their savior to be at least a few years older than twenty-eight—especially in China.

"But there is still work available, right?"

"Oh, sure." Between small commercial leases and piecemeal form contracts, I have so far amassed a whopping US $4,300 in my entire history as a "barefoot" international lawyer extraordinaire, or roughly a week's pay from my old law firm.

"Have you handled any interesting cases lately?"

"Well"—I don't mean to be too Clintonesque, but again—"that would depend on what you mean by 'lately.' "

And I'm not sure if "interesting" is quite the right word to describe it.

In March 2003, an unexpected phone call led me to the following lawsuit:

In mid 2002, a small Singaporean trading company abbreviated WIT contracted to purchase fifty thousand tons of low-ash metallurgical coal (aka "coke") from a company that I will abbreviate as GUNS, with delivery to be made within five days thereafter. But once WIT's cargo ship came to port, GUNS stalled. In a series of last-minute maneuvers (six to be exact), it pushed back the shipping date by more than sixty days, raised the price from US $74 per ton to US $92 per ton, demanded prepayment of the entire purchase price before anything was delivered (in contravention of industry norms), and turned out to have lacked the requisite licenses to be in the business of exporting minerals in the first place. In a nutshell, it promised the world without ever having the ability—or much else—to deliver.

"But why are you calling me?" I asked the gentleman identified as the Captain. "I do corporate work, not litigation. And you might want to call a Chinese-qualified lawyer instead of me."

"But we have, sir. Over twenty different firms. All the international firms are too expensive. None of the local firms can understand us. You are the only one who is reasonably priced and bilingual."

"Well, did you know that the party you want to sue is part of China $ & % × Industries?"—who just happened to be a giant state-owned enterprise that manufactured missiles and firearms for the People's Liberation Army.

"But please, sir," the Captain pleaded. "You are our only hope."

As a corporate lawyer, I had never handled any litigation before. Sure, I had studied the relevant subjects in law school, but this was for real; not to mention that I was in China now, where the only thing I knew for sure about the local laws was the moto-ban.

But hell, got to start somewhere.

Thankfully, it didn't take months to read through all the documentation that WIT sent me. Out of everything, the most favorable piece of information was a clause in the purchase and sale contract that read, "In the case of a dispute arising out of this contract, the parties shall resolve such dispute through arbitration in Hong Kong."

Based on this, all I had to do was file for arbitration in Hong Kong, get a judgment against GUNS or possibly even its parent and enforce the judgment in Beijing through powers of the local court, which by the New York Convention of 1958 is required to do so.

But first, we played nice.

The day after I couriered over the statement of claims, which took me forever to draft, someone from GUNS responded with an offer to meet in my office the next day.

Wicked! I high-fived myself.

Then, panic.

Being a soloist unaffiliated with any registered foreign firm, I have no license to practice law in China, which means that I have no office, either. Prior to WIT, it never mattered much as I dabbled mostly in small-time contract work; and it kind of played into the barefoot lawyer scheme of things. But now that my opponent was on his way, I had to put on something.

So I called up every employed individual on my Nokia and begged to use his office as a front. Here in China, face is everything. To knock the socks off of big shots who supplied the Chinese military, I needed something impressive. I am an American lawyer, after all, and in China's eyes, American lawyers should have big, fancy offices. Yes, it felt like a con, but desperate times called for desperate measures.

And it was certainly worth every last penny of that 200 *kuai* I paid in grease money (i.e., rounds of Starbucks' Iced Americano with shots of caramel): two China doll receptionists at the front desk, real bamboos lining the walkways, streams of water flowing underneath the glass floor, a grand piano in the reception area, a mahogany conference table that seated thirty, sleek orthopedic chairs straight out of a Sharper Image catalog, panoramic windows overlooking the downtown traffic, a ceiling-mounted projector, lights with twenty-some different settings, electronic gizmos that went up the yin-yang. . . .

Well then, how about support? Every real law firm has to have a team, with partners, counsels, senior associates, junior associates, summer associates, interns, paralegals, parahumans, and so on and so on. Here in China, where "unity equals strength," I'd better at least get some interns pronto!

Thankfully, China has one of the most extensive mobile telephone networks known to man. Within ten minutes of sending out my mass SOS text message, two FOB kids with lawyering aspirations caught wind of my "rare opportunity" and jumped on board my one-wheeled wagon to Chinese justice. I'll never forget my first sight of them on the night before the meeting—so bright-eyed and bushy-tailed, so full of youthful conviction and enthusiasm, so much like me when I first rolled into this town.

At 8:50 A.M., my adversaries arrived.

"I am vice president of operations for GUNS," the short and balding forty-something introduced himself.

Much to my surprise, he did not wear white socks with his black shoes or keep the brand tag on his suit sleeve. But he *did* clutch a man-purse underneath his armpit.

"And you, madam?" I greeted the older, bespectacled lady at his side.

Somehow, she reminded me of Ms. Deng, my third-grade math teacher, who once sentenced me to ten hours of standing in the hallway without food, drink, or bathroom breaks.

"I'm from Harding & Wills," she said. "Counsel to China $ & % × Industries."

"Welcome." I introduced myself and my impressively armored lieutenants. "We represent WIT."

"But you look so young!" The man with the purse tried to put me in my place.

"Well, times are changing." I kept smiling.

"Law-tti-tude?" The opposing counsel studied my card front and back. "Are you guys new in town?"

"Yes." I didn't exactly want to dwell on the subject. "And your English is excellent."

"Thanks." She attempted a courtesy grin. "I have an LLM from Harvard Law School."

"Wonderful." I nodded in actual reverence. "Is Harding & Wills from the U.S. as well?"

"No, it's a local firm."

"Then who is Harding and who is Wills?"

"There is neither Harding nor Wills. It is just a name that we use."

Wonderful. Now I didn't need to feel so guilty about anything.

Thirty minutes later, I concluded my presentation of the facts by offering peace. "But in the event that we cannot arrive at a reasonable settlement, we will proceed immediately with arbitration in Hong Kong in accordance with the contract and then enforce the judgment in mainland China."

"But what makes you think you can actually pull it off?" The lady actually snickered.

"Would you like to see a list of all the arbitration awards against Chinese companies in the past five years?"

"But don't forget that China is a civil-law country." She kept to her clanging monotone. "Past cases have no precedential value here, meaning that one court need not follow the past decision of another."

"But even so, the contract in this case speaks for itself."

"You mean this thing?" She slid across the table a copy of the purchase and sale contract.

Or more precisely, three pages of typos, run-ons, and cross-references that pointed nowhere. Being an American-educated lawyer, I'm used to contracts so thick that I could sell them by the pound; in China, contracts are so short that they could float like a feather. Instead of fleshing out what can go wrong before signing on the dotted line, the Chinese like to keep the writing to a minimum and dismiss every what-if with *"mei wen ti,"* "no problem."

Except that there is *always* a problem.

"As written," the lady continued, "Article 11 says only 'arbitration in Hong Kong.' But it doesn't specify *where* in Hong Kong."

"So?" Anyone doing business in Asia should know that "arbitration in Hong Kong" means arbitration by the Hong Kong Interna-

tional Arbitration Center (HKIAC), which is a well-respected institution that has been the industry standard for years.

"Well need I remind you, sir, that this is China?" She crossed
her arms. "As written, the clause does not designate a specific venue
for the proceeding, so it is too vague, and thus void, which means
that we don't have to show up for anything at all."

"Oh, quite the contrary." I honestly couldn't believe what I was
hearing. "There is a presumption under Hong Kong law that if a
contract provides for arbitration in Hong Kong, it is to be held at the
HKIAC even in the absence of a specific reference. My associate
confirmed that with the HKIAC yesterday."

I turned to my male intern-of-the-day to confirm something that
I had just completely pulled out of my ass. He had no idea what the
HKIAC was; but he still nodded beautifully. The kid hadn't gone to
the Ivy League for nothing.

"But even so. There is no mention of governing law in these
pages." The lady pointed to another flaw in the contract. "You can
argue whatever presumption you want under foreign law, but we say
that Chinese law should govern this contract; and under Chinese
law, if you don't specify the venue of arbitration, there is no arbitration. Trust me, I am a Chinese lawyer. I know."

"But don't forget." I immediately thought of an American legal
principle that *ought* to also exist in China. "It was GUNS who
drafted this contract, which means that if there is ambiguity in the
language, it shall be construed against GUNS. And the fact that the
parties provided for arbitration in Hong Kong implies that Hong
Kong law applies even without a specific reference."

It never feels good to bullshit in a situation like this. But I had to
make up for my lack of research.

"Be that as it may." The lady didn't flinch. "Even if you go to the
HKIAC and spend all that money, so what? You still need the People's

Court in Beijing to enforce it before you can actually collect. Where do you intend to file your application? I worked at the Ministry of Justice for twenty years before private practice. Most of the judges in this town are my friends. May I be of some assistance?"

"Well, you know what?" I didn't want to resort to the most elaborately deceptive intimidation available. "China is in the WTO now. Lots of eyes are watching. If I were a reporter, I just might wonder, How did a company that makes military optics end up selling coke? Did your board know about this? Or was it a 'side project' by someone in the management? Maybe someone signed the contract without anyone else knowing; maybe he even took something from the man who brokered the deal. How do you feel about being on TV, sir? Or in the newspapers? 'State-Owned Behemoth Preys on Tiny Singaporean Trader'—wouldn't you love to read that in the *South China Morning Post*?"

I turned to my female intern-of-the-day for a confirmation. She did not speak much Chinese and probably did not understand 90 percent of the things that had been said during the entire conversation. But she had graduated from Cambridge; and she could nod with a naturally aristocratic flair.

"Some more tea?" I smiled at the VP, whose forehead glistened as if it were on coke.

And he had reason to sweat. To protect its one-party rule from subversive forces instigated by its own minions who live on graft, the Chinese government is now lynching scapegoats with increasing frequency in order to appease the angry public. Every day, there are stories of provincial bosses getting ten years for skimming off construction grants and police chiefs sentenced to twenty years for taking bribes. While these are just the tip of the iceberg when it comes to the amount of corruption actually going on in China, no one wants to be the chicken that is killed to warn a hundred monkeys.

"We of course hope to arrive at a peaceful resolution." I almost felt bad seeing the VP looking so uncomfortable. "Shall we discuss a settlement?"

"Look—" The opposing counsel was clearly ready to play hardball.

Until the man with the purse zipped her up in a snap and said, "Let me report to our board and get back to you shortly, okay? Sir?"

Why, of course.

On our way out to the elevator, the VP asked me out of the blue, "Is there any chance that you would work for us instead?"

And betray a lawyer's most fundamental principle? I could totally get disbarred for switching sides like that, which I guess actually happens in China or he wouldn't have asked. But it was kind of cool, especially when I replied, "Wouldn't that require you to let go of Harding & Wills first?"

Shortly after the meeting, I called the Captain.

"How did it go?" he asked anxiously.

"To be honest, I don't know. They might be willing to settle, but it'll probably be small."

"How small?"

"Three hundred thousand dollars?" Maybe?

"But that's only one-fifth of our damages!" The Captain must have had some salt water permanently lodged inside his head. "We absolutely need the whole thing, all one and a half million dollars!"

"But sir—"

"Please, we are about to go out of business because of this. Is there anything else you can do?"

His voice was cracking like that of a man on the verge of losing his life's work.

"Set aside a budget for some networking expenses. . . ." I gave him my best advice under the circumstances, despite the oath I once took. "Without it, even that three hundred thousand will be a stretch. This is not Singapore, sir. There are certain people here that the laws won't touch."

And that was the last time I heard from either him or GUNS.

But that's all right. In life, you win some, you lose some. Even though WIT didn't work out as I had hoped, at least I made that VP sweat a little bit. And that makes me feel *niubi* (pronounced "new-bee"), which shares the same *bi* with *shabi,* translates literally as a cow's genitalia, yet stands for "cool" or "awesome" in the local lingo. I know, there is still a lot of law that I have to learn; but I also know that I have what it takes to be a great lawyer. As unbusy as Lawttitude has been lately, it'll just be a matter of time before my big case breaks.

24

"Hey, I must be having some really good *yuan fen* with lawyers these days," says the nameless girl sitting across from HH and DD. "You are like the third one I have met this month."

"Well, isn't your fiancé in construction?" interjects DD with a jealous vibe. "Doesn't that make a lot these days?"

Ah, but of course. Now I remember this girl—I met her in Houhai a few weeks ago, together with a few other girls and her fiancé, who introduced himself as being involved in the construction business and seemed like a pretty nice guy. She had glasses on that time, rimless ones that made her look like a madame. No wonder I didn't recognize her just now.

On second look, I quite like the silk Mandarin dress she's wearing, which has black and white checkers, hand-sewn ornate buttons, and side vents just above the knees. It's a shame that the Chinese women of today don't wear more of these dresses, which are perfectly designed for their slender Chinese bodies. Seeing one always reminds me of Madame Soong, who was first lady of the Republic of China before Mao made the Republic his *People's* Republic.

But still, what is her name?

Maybe I'll just call her Madame for now.

"So how long have you been engaged?" I ask the obvious.

"A few months." She doesn't sound all that excited.

"That's nice. And what do you do for a living?"

"Lately? Not much." She sounds a little embarrassed. "But I did run a club called the Velvet Room once."

"Hey, I know that place. Wasn't there a cigar lounge downstairs? And a lot of velvet curtains?"

She grins.

"Then you must know where to go for some ripe fruits." Lethal turns on the charm that has left him dry for months.

"Why don't you just go traveling instead?" Madame politely tells him to "get lost."

"Actually, that's not a bad idea." I haven't left this town in ages; maybe that's why I've been so easily stressed lately.

"Then go to France," DD suggests. "I just spent three months in Provence. It's a different world over there."

"Or how about Thailand?" HH adds. "It's closer, and always sunny. And the food . . ."

"But I don't know about traveling abroad." Lethal squints. "Rather see more of China, you know what I mean?"

"Then how about we take a road trip across country?" Like the way I always wanted to in America but couldn't afford to.

"Great idea! Where can we get a car?"

"What car?" I cannot believe he even thought about the two of us needing a steel cage. "We go by two wheels. I've got a bike. You go buy one."

"You mean like *Easy Rider*? *Wo cao ta ma de-niubi!*"

"That's right, buddy. We'll ride all the way across China."

"From Harbin to Hong Kong?!"

"Why the hell not?!"

"I don't think that's such a good idea." Madame frowns. "Do you know how dangerous it is out there on the road?"

"Yeah, of course." I ride every day and have almost died about ninety-nine times.

"But does he know?" She glances at Lethal. "And what if your bikes break down? Do you know how to fix them? And what if cops pull you over? Those guys aren't too civilized out there."

"Well, actually, I *am* kind of broke." Lethal gets only 7,000 *kuai* a month from his network, plus taxi reimbursements.

"Fine, give me a minute." I borrow DD's lighter.

Finally, my own Zigarette. It's amazing how this thing smokes. I don't mean to brag, but I have gotten so good at it lately that I can now roll the whole thing up without looking. The challenge now would be to roll with just one hand and actually do a good job, so I could conceivably eat with one hand and roll with the other, type text messages with one hand and roll with the other, man the steering with one hand and roll with the other, or even do something ten times as unstable with one hand and roll with the other, like, I don't know, riding a horse, for example.

"Hey!" I love how much smarter I get when I am high. "How about we do it on a horse?"

"On a what?"

Oh yeah. Just picture it—Lethal and me all geared up with ropes and whips and packs full of Zigarettes riding into the sunset. I might be born a rabbit in the Chinese zodiac; but in my heart, I'm a mustang.

"That's brilliant! But where?"

"Where else? Inner Mongolia, of course. Compared to Beijing, it's practically a different country, and no need for a visa."

"*Niubi!* So what's the plan?"

"What plan?"

With any luck, we'll befriend some nomads, tame some stallions, eat some delicacies, pick up some babes, get into some trouble, and maybe, just maybe, find a good place to grow some quality big numb.

"And how about this?" Ideas just keep coming when I'm high. "Let's go search for Xanadu."

"Xanadu? Sounds familiar."

"It's the legendary capital of Kublai Khan," Madame interjects.

"Who was the grandson of Genghis Khan." I thank her with a wink. "You know Kublai. The first emperor of the Yuan Dynasty? The biggest empire in the history of mankind? He had Xanadu before he built the Forbidden City."

"But is it gonna be expensive?" Lethal is always strapped for cash.

"No way. I heard you can buy a full-grown horse up there for less than two thousand *kuai*. Rent it by the day and it'll be even cheaper."

"So are you going to ride every day?" Madame squints.

"Oh yeah, at least fifty kilometers a day, right?"

"Like cowboys," Lethal seconds.

Welcome to the Wild Wild East.

"Do you even know how to ride?" Madame chuckles in disbelief.

"Of course." I have ridden ponies up and down Fragrant Hills at least twice.

"Well, do you?" She turns to Lethal.

"Sure. When I was a kid."

"How old were you?"

"Fourteen? Maybe."

"Then have you considered the weather?" She stays one step ahead. "It gets a lot colder up there."

"Oh don't you worry about that, sweetheart." Lethal pumps up his magnificently sculpted right biceps. "Boom! See these guns?"

"But where are you going to sleep? There is nothing but grass up there."

"Well that's the whole point, isn't it?" Lethal shrugs. "We'll bring tents and sleep under the stars. It'll be *wo cao ta ma de* romantic."

"Then how about food? I hope you guys like lamb."

"Sure I like lamb. We all eat 'em skewers, don't we?"

"But every day? Every meal?"

"I'm sure they have other stuff, right?"

"Oh, sure, like sheep's milk and goat cheese. I bet you'll love the blood sausages, too."

"What's that?"

"Sheep intestines filled with sheep blood, then boiled."

I nearly cough the Coke out of my nose.

"We'll just bring plenty of milk and cookies then." Lethal makes a brilliant comeback. "Or just cookies. Sheep's milk can't be that bad, right?"

"Well what about shower and toilet? How are you guys going to stay clean?"

"Who is going to be there to smell us? I'm sure there will be streams and bushes."

Besides, after a few days without showering, you'd totally get used to it.

"And even if something happens, there is always this." I raise my trusted Nokia. "Even if you get stranded with a flat tire in the middle of nowhere in Tibet, you can get a clear signal. Trust me, I've been there. I know."

"I still think this trip is too harsh." Madame shakes her head. "Why do it to yourself?"

"Cultural differences, baby." Lethal giggles like he's about to bust out Sir Mix-a-lot again. "Cultural *wo cao ta ma de* differences."

25

"Please help . . ." A pitiful chant intrudes from a few meters away.

Once again, time to be reminded that China is still a Third World country.

Like all of his colleagues, Sloppy comes from the villages. With a shaved head and slouching back, he looks as diminutive as any beggar in Sanlitun. While it is impossible to tell his age until he washes off the fifty layers of dirt on his face, I'm guessing that he's about sixteen years old. And given how he wiggles his head from side to side while slurring, he must also be a little retarded.

But he is not blind.

"Benevolent auntie with a Buddha's heart." The smelly juvenile goes after the pretty girls first. "I just want a bowl of noodles, please auntie, please."

This kid has got to work on his technique. While it may be proper to call an older woman "auntie" when you are ten years old, doing the same here just ain't gonna cut it. Women hate to be reminded of how old they are, Chinese women especially. Instead of asking "How old are you," always ask a Chinese girl "What's your zodiac," as each of the twelve Chinese zodiac signs corresponds to a given year. It sounds silly, but out here, being direct about a woman's age is just rude, and to call a single woman in her twenties "auntie" instead of "sister" is even worse.

"Well, in that case"—HH snickers while DD "ew's" at the gray mucus running from Sloppy's nostrils—"what would you do for a bowl of noodles? Can you dance like a monkey? Sing like a chicken? How about a cigarette butt instead?"

No wonder Lethal calls these girls "fruits." Heartless ones too.

"Take this." I pull out 10 *kuai* from my back pocket and make sure Sloppy doesn't touch me during the handover. "Now, go buy yourself something to eat."

I don't mean to brag, but 10 *kuai* is a lot. With this kind of dough, he can get two large bowls of beef noodles, half a dozen sesame pastries, three cans of Coca-Cola, two and a half packs of Oreos, five forty-ounce bottles of Beijing draft, a pack and half of Zhong Nan Hai cigarettes, or—if he wants to stay a beggar forever—a cheap and deadly bottle of *bai jiu* called Red Star 52.

What can I say? THC makes me a generous man.

Besides, if HH and DD keep on toying with him the way they do with their more hygienic suitors, I'll never get to smoke my Ziggy in peace.

"Thank you, uncle! Thank you so much." Sloppy bows repeatedly like a chicken picking rice from the floor.

Yes, I am benevolent, and I'm not fussy about being called an "uncle."

"Say, uncle." Sloppy stops for a second whiff. "How come your cigarette smells so good?"

"Why? Do you want some? It'll only make you hungrier." I really crack myself up sometimes.

"Is this what you are smoking?" He hunches over for a closer look at my stash on the table. "I have never seen anything like it. How do you use it? Is this opium?"

"Whoa." I turn toward Lethal. "Did he just say what I think he said?"

"Sure did."

"Well then, I guess he is not so retarded after all!"

And I'm not just saying that to be facetious. Here in China, no one (other than the users) seems to know what drugs look like, yet Sloppy seems to know. Granted, he said "opium" instead of "hash," but in terms of appearance, the two really look the same. I guess the old saying is true: You can't judge a book by its cover. Had Sloppy been born in America, he might even be on *Jeopardy*.

So perhaps his handicap is really just a show; and he is so good at it that everyone thinks he is retarded. Maybe that's why he dares to walk the beat in Sanlitun all by himself. And if there really exists an underground triad of beggars like all those in the know keep on telling me, then the one, two, three patches on his garb should mean that he is already ranked rather highly for his age. So who knows? My little charity might just have bought me some good face.

I like it best when the giving also benefits the giver.

26

"Hey, where are you going?" Lethal asks.

"Time for a stroll, buddy. Time for a stroll."

Because here and now, I am loving what I am feeling. The day may have started out slowly with a *shabi* in a Mercedes and the firing of an employee, but that is all in the past. Time to get up, stretch out, and let the neighborhood know that I am ready for action.

Looking in the window, I'm loving what I see. With muscles like these, even a plain white T-shirt looks great, especially over my faded 501s that have ripped beautifully in all the right places. After riding all season long, my vanilla racing jacket is looking positively vintage; and I absolutely adore my black Bally lace-ups that are perfectly comfortable even without socks.

Looking ahead, I've got plans.

First, get the bill on Foodiez and cash out. It was fun for a while; but it's just not worth my time anymore. Managing a small company is a pain in the ass to begin with, and doing it with a Third World staff just makes it that much worse. Now that the company is profitable, I might be able to sell it for some cash and start something else, one that would go at least national, if not international, and fast.

As for Lawttitude, no more small potato under the table. Assuming that I become one of the 5 percent minority who actually pass the Chinese bar exam, I'll leverage my *guan xi* in various places to scope out something juicier than WIT. With any luck, I'll get to represent some high-profile political dissident, or maybe even handle a scandal involving big names in the Communist Party. That way, I would have an angle to infiltrate Chinese politics and lay the foundation for the day I run for president.

That's right—president. I didn't feel it was appropriate to tell the Kid when he asked about it earlier, but I chose to retain my Chinese citizenship over getting an American passport for a reason. All things considered, if people like me don't end up running this country, even Mao's spirit would be upset. Now, you may think that I have a big ego. But unlike some fluffs out there, I actually have the stuff to back it up. And that makes me a Superego. Certain things are just born in the blood. As early as five years old, I already knew I would one day do something great with my life; now at twenty-eight, it's time to really get on with my mission.

But first things first. After that dinner on Ghost Street last night, I haven't eaten anything all day on account of the nasty burps from *bai jiu*.

Fortunately, there is the Kiosk. Tiny kitchen. Strictly takeout. Brilliant. My favorite thing on the menu is the Big Bite: a patty of ground beef, lamb, and pork stuffed with gooey mozzarella, grilled just right, and served with leafy greens and marinated jalapeños on a toasted baguette bun. The sucker takes two hands to hold and many napkins to help finish, and I always get the broad-cut fries on the side. The last I heard, the owner is already planning to franchise this alternative to McDonald's all over the city. Perhaps he'll need a lawyer to help put the deals together.

And best of all, it is conveniently located in the *hutong* next to Café 44.

Up ahead, the owner of the Kiosk is chatting with some cute blonde I have never seen before. She must be new. Maybe I'll introduce myself and invite her to dinner at Café Sambal later. She even looks like a hasher.

I love my life.

27

" 'EY! Stop right where you are," someone hollers from behind me.

Now whoever this *shabi* is, he'd better not be talking to *me*. It's not as if the phrase "excuse me" doesn't exist in the Chinese language. He's lucky that I'm not done with my Ziggy yet; or I'd teach him how to behave like a . . .

Oops. Instead of just one, it's a gang of six *shabis*.

Of the four boys in this scrum, none is over five feet seven inches tall, one hundred thirty pounds, or 20 years old. And they all look like Sloppy, just with more hair and without the drippy mess under their noses. Though armed with batons, these malnourished kids in bluish green uniforms just don't look like the intimidators that *bao ans* (meaning "security guards") are supposed to be.

As for the two adults in the middle, they might as well be Tweedledee and Tweedledum. Wearing navy suits a size too fat, navy pants an inch too short, cheap silver ties over gray shirts, and white tube socks inside dusty black faux-leather loafers, these two are just another pair of Spit 'n' Squatters, except that they are also wearing polished number tags on their lapels and crests on their rimmed hats that say POLICE.

Together, this half dozen of Beijing's finest waddle toward me.

Okay, maybe it is time to ditch the Ziggy—even with the various privileges I enjoy, blowing hash smoke right into the cops' faces can't be a good idea.

Okay, that wasn't nearly as smooth as I intended. I definitely meant to flick the roach farther than two feet away. Stupid wind.

"Where do you think you are going?" Tweedledee scowls.

He is about forty years old, with a dark complexion and very yellow teeth.

"Getting a bite to eat."

D'oh! What the hell did I speak Chinese for? Why must I be so honest when I'm high?

"What's this?" Tweedledum picks up the roach that I just discarded and takes a whiff.

"What does it look like?" I hate cottonmouth.

"What's in it?" Tweedledee stares at me in the eyes.

Which are not red, of course. "Tobacco, obviously."

"Are you sure?" Tweedledum is snickering.

"Of course I'm sure. What else could it possibly be?"

That was not a very intelligent rhetorical question.

"All right." Tweedledee signals the four *bao ans* to sandwich me in a two-plus-two formation. "Let's walk."

Crap. Talk about a One A Day. What are they gonna do? Make me watch a pirated DVD on why drugs are bad for me? Some people just love to waste time. Maybe I can skip the speech and just pay a fine. How much would it be? Two hundred *kuai*? Maybe 250?

"Back in twenty minutes." I signal Lethal and the rest as my entourage parades past Café 44.

Better make it quick, *shabis*. I'm starving already.

28

Trekking southward on Sanlitun Road, we pass the coffee-sipping crowd on the sidewalk.

Oh, get a life—what on earth are they looking at?

This is just great; where did I go wrong? How come I never saw these pigs coming? Was I too high or what? I just hope I have enough on me to cover the damage.

But hey, it's only money. And what's a few hundred *kuai* for an experience that most people can't even talk about? For anyone who actually believed the film *Red Corner,* getting arrested in China is no tourist attraction. But I don't have to worry about that, for I come from America. These pigs just don't know who they are messing with yet. But they will. By this time tomorrow, I'll be the hero of Sanlitun.

As for being paraded in public, well, just another page in my illustrious log. Just as Mao himself would have instructed, I'm rebelling with reason. In my book, the big numb is no drug. It's natural and nonaddictive, and should therefore be perfectly legal. If anything, I should get a medal for sticking to my hobby, as it makes me a kinder, gentler, and more generous person, especially around here, where *everything* can be a One A Day.

So keep smiling, Superego. This has been a good day, and I have been a good citizen.

29

"Sit down." Tweedledum points to the dark green sofa.

We are inside a shabby trailer parked about three hundred yards south of 44.

"Let me ask you again." Tweedledee holds up the roach. "What's in it?"

"Are you stupid or are you drunk?" I know only two types of Chinese cops. "I already told you it's tobacco."

I mean, seriously, how many times do they have to ask the same question? Do they really expect me to fess up and say that it's made up of 35 percent hash, 65 percent tobacco, one-sixteenth of a business card, and some imported rolling paper? Come on, I didn't go to law school for nothing. In times like this, just deny, deny, deny.

"Are you sure?" Tweedledum frowns. "You know that we have laboratories with very sophisticated equipment."

"Well then unless your very sophisticated equipment proves otherwise, it's tobacco. Okay?"

If these losers want to play, I'll play. Go right ahead and tell the labs that they should drop every twisted forensic task that spawns out of this city's fifteen million inhabitants and analyze the content of a roach picked off the Sanlitun floor. Do they understand what priority means?

"So where did you get this stuff?" Tweedledee switches angles.

"Get what stuff?" I know his game.

"This stuff obviously didn't come out of a box. So where did you get it?"

"You want me to tell you the store where I got the tobacco from?"

"Yes."

"Well, I didn't buy it from a store. This is Sanlitun, isn't it? You must know how many peddlers sell cigarettes on this strip. Or do you?"

"So which one did you buy it from?"

"Who said I bought it? Did I say I bought it? Don't try to put words in my mouth."

"So you didn't buy it?"

"Of course not. It came free."

"Just like this, all rolled up?"

"Just like that."

"You mean you didn't have to fiddle around to make it yourself?"

"I'm not so good with my hands." I so crack myself up.

"So someone just gave this to you."

"You got it."

"How come no one ever gave me something like this?"

"Well . . ." I almost laugh out loud. "Maybe it's because I'm better-looking."

Tweedledee's pupils are shrinking. I am really enjoying this now.

Tweedledum lights up a cigarette, takes a long drag, and says, "Show us your identification."

"Sorry." I shrug. "Don't have it on me."

"Don't you know that you have to carry your identification with you at all times in China?"

"Oh please, you Chinese have so many rules." Like the rule against spitting in public, which is not enforced, the rule against driving on the sidewalk, which is not enforced, or the rules against jaywalking, random parking, and cutting in line to buy subway tickets, none of which is ever enforced. "How can I possibly know all of them?"

"What do you mean by '*you* Chinese'?!" Tweedledee scowls. "Aren't you Chinese as well?!"

"Well yeah." I love being who I am, don't get me wrong. "But I am just not Chinese like you."

"So then what are you?" Tweedledee had to take a deep breath.

"American!" Of course. Can't he tell?

"But how come you speak Chinese so well?" Tweedledum squints.

"It's called a brain." I squint right back. "Ever heard of it?"

"Then do you have identification to prove it?" Tweedledee doesn't sound so obnoxious all of a sudden.

"Well of course I do. Ever heard of *the* green card?"

But *of course* they have. It's what "being American" means to most people in this country. Of course, technically, a green card is evidence only of my American residency, not of American citizenship; but given how few Chinese individuals (relative to the entire population) have ever been able to get out of China and live elsewhere, I'd bet a million dollars that the Tweedles don't know the difference.

"Hey, *ge-men'er*." I hear Lethal Weapon talking to the *bao ans* outside. "What's happening in there?" He sounds charming, like he is on television. "May I speak to my friend for a few minutes?" He gives Tweedledee his prime-time smile as the latter opens the door.

I never thought I'd say this, but here and now, I am rather envious of my friend. Even though he was smoking right alongside me and is even higher than I am after having smoked an entire Ziggy instead of just the two-thirds that I took, he doesn't have to worry about being questioned at all, for there is no doubt that he is a foreigner, and hence about his privileges.

"So what's the deal, man?" Lethal can't stop giggling.

"They want some identification." I shrug. "Got to prove that I'm American."

"What have I been telling you all this time?" Lethal raises his voice to make sure the cops hear him, in Chinese. "You are American just like me!"

"Yeah, yeah. Just go to my place and fetch my green card, will you? I have to wait here."

"Sure thing, buddy." His voice sounds so reassuring. "But will it work?"

"What do you mean?" It's a piece of plastic for crying out loud, not some gadget out of a James Bond flick; of course it works.

"Uh, *ge-men'er*." He squints. "Don't you remember last week?"

"What about it?"

"You were supposed to leave China last week, but didn't. Remember?"

D'oh!

This must be a special day for the One A Days.

At 9 A.M. last Wednesday, I was standing in line at the Beijing International Airport. On the night before, I had rounded up all my friends at Café Sambal and told them that I was leaving China for a while. After three years, a break was in order. Time had come for unpolluted air, girls from California, and good hydroponics that just don't grow around here. It was a great turnout, with almost too many women, some of whom even got misty-eyed when I said I might not return. And as I waited in line with my ticket in hand bound for New York's JFK, the only thing on my mind was where to have my postflight surf 'n' turf followed by New York cheesecake topped with chocolate fudge.

So imagine my chagrin when the customs officer said, "Sorry, sir, but your green card has expired already."

"What are you talking about?" I laughed at the man. The card was good for ten years and wasn't due to expire until . . .

06-17-04.

Wait a second—I must have smudged it with something. So I rubbed it with my thumb. Then again. And again.

But unless the Americans write their dates in the sequence of year, day, and month instead of month, day, and year, or there is a seventeenth month in any given year, my indicia of Americanness had become just another recyclable piece of plastic.

I was seriously peeved. I had paid almost $1,000 for my nonrefundable ticket and now had to tell everyone that my farewell was a big case of crying wolf. Talk about embarrassing! And what about my American residency? Do you know, or better yet, do *I* know how hard someone from China would have to work to get something like that? How could I have neglected to renew the goddamn thing?

So of course I smoked a Ziggy to calm myself down. Yeah, it was a big loss, and certainly a big hassle; but it wasn't the end of the world. Without a green card, I am still who I am. On a philosophical level, being American needs no physical connection to the territory of the United States, whether via a passport, a green card, or anything else. Instead, it is about having the spirit of freedom, equality, and the pursuit of happiness. After all those years in America, I am just as American in spirit as any American citizen, and probably more so than any passport-wielding Texan who likes to bomb other countries for their oil. To fix the mishap, I'd just call up Homeland Security with a made-up story so they'd let me replace my card without too much red tape.

So a week went by. And nothing happened. I apparently had other priorities that I can no longer remember.

This really *wo cao ta ma de* sucks.

"Now, I'm no lawyer," Lethal says, scratching his forehead, "but isn't permanent residency just a status?"

"Yeah, so?"

"So you don't lost a 'status' just because the card expired, right? Like a driver's license."

"Then why don't you try to explain that to the cops?! I'm sure they'll buy it." NOT!

"Then how about borrowing someone else's green card?"

"Like whose? This is not America, bro. The cops ain't gonna think that all Chinese look the same!"

But what else can I do? Given the circumstances, there isn't even time to fake a green card.

Well then, how about just act normal and pretend the card is good? An old Chinese maxim says, "Good metals don't become nails; good men don't become soldiers." And cops are not much brighter than soldiers. With the economy growing so fast, why would any smart person sign up to be a cop? The pay is crap, there is no respect, and the uniform is a downright disgrace. The chances are that these guys don't even read Chinese well, much less English.

And just so that we can make everything seem more believable: "Go into my storage closet, find the black Coach briefcase at the far end, and bring everything you can find in it, driver's license, Social Security card, even my college ID if it's still there."

"Well how about I call in Plan B as well?" Lethal looks all revved up for action.

"Plan B? What Plan B?"

"Oh, you'll see."

"Whatever. Just hurry the fuck up!"

31

"Let's go." Tweedledee says, fingering me to get up as he puts down the phone.

"Where are we going?"

"Sanlitun Station."

"What for? Are you arresting me?!"

"No more questions, okay? They will deal with you next."

What the hell is that supposed to mean? Who is "they"?!

Oh, okay, I get it—these two *shabis* just want to dump the responsibility on someone else. And I don't blame 'em—why risk being the one who arrested the "wrong guy" when there is a whole precinct to take the fall? Everybody knows that the Chinese government is way past gigantic, and the police must be one of its biggest fat deposits. With two departments for everything unnecessary, the folks there probably do nothing outside of two-hour lunches, two-hour naps, and frequent cigarette breaks in between; yet, unlike robots, they still make mistakes.

So yeah, let's go to the precinct. What have I got to be scared of?

32

"Eh, *ge-men'er.*" Someone hollers for the Tweedles as we walk into the *hutong* opposite Café 44.

Sitting on tiny wooden stools, three middle-aged men are playing a mean game of *dou di zhu* next to a newsstand. Unlike the regulars at Café 44, who settle scores only in private after the game is over, however, this drunken gang has opted to play with real cash piled at the center of their huddle.

Now I don't mean to be a party pooper, but shouldn't the Tweedles do something about that? Isn't gambling illegal in China? And while they're at it, why don't they do something about the migrants selling fruits without a license, too? Oh, not big enough? Well then how about I give them something that is?

Here in China, just like everywhere else, every cent that a business earns is potentially liable for income tax. To lower the tax, one can deduct expenses that are substantiated by *fa piaos*, government-issued receipts that can be procured from the payees of the expenses. To encourage accurate reporting, there is even a scratch 'n' win game built into every *fa piao* that entitles the lucky winner to cash prizes. Sound respectable? It's a complete farce. Instead of making legitimate deductions, people simply buy the *fa piaos* themselves so they can claim false deductions for goods and services that were never actually purchased.

But how is that a big deal?

Well, let's say that you have a business that generates 100,000 *kuai* of extra revenue without incurring any extra expenses. At the end of the year, that 100,000 *kuai* in extra profit could lead to as much as 40,000 *kuai* (US $5,000) in income taxes. Not a small price to pay for doing business in China.

But if you are frugal, you can stroll down to any local bank and spend five minutes with one of the many purse-clutching men prowling the entrance. Then, after paying him approximately 6.5 percent of the amount that you wish to deduct (say the entire 100,000), or 6,500 *kuai*, you will have a government-issued *fa piao* that "proves" you have just spent the entire 100,000 on office equipment, thereby saving yourself 33,500 *kuai* (US $4,300) in taxes. Now how do these men come to possess all those *fa piaos*? Well, let's just say they've got *guan xi* that I don't got.

So what does this mean? For one thing, it makes China the easiest place on earth to launder money. In places like America, people actually have to set up fake businesses in order to launder dirty money and evade taxes; in China, on the other hand, all one has to do is buy fake *fa piaos.* And if that's not bad enough, consider the cumulative effect. If every businessman in China saves 33,500 *kuai* through fake deductions (and we all know how many businessmen there are in China these days), how much could the government actually collect to build better roads, better bridges, or maybe even schools that don't collapse in an earthquake?

And what does the law do about this? As far as I see—nothing; not as long as cops like Tweedledee are still around, who just returned his gambling *ge-men'er*'s greeting with "Don't forget to buy me dinner when one of you hits two thousand."

I don't know why I even bother.

33

So this is it—four stories of post–World War II Soviet-designed concrete across from a shack that sells Korean ramen. All these years on the strip, I never even realized that the police station was right here. Sure, I had seen many cruisers parked outside the building before, but I always just assumed that it was a brothel where cops hung out after work.

Behind the wide strips of heavy semiclear plastic draped over the entrance, an uncomfortably long room is divided into two sides: a row of steel-barred teller windows on the left, a row of plastic bus-station benches on the right.

I pick the seat closest to the entrance. The cold of the plastic goes right through my jeans.

How long do I have to wait? For whom? For what?

The Tweedles disappeared before I got to ask.

Behind the teller windows, three men are talking about the latest football scandal in the Chinese Premier League. I can't see their faces; so they can't see me either. Less than two yards away is the entrance, the heavy plastic drapes barely budging in the autumn breeze. There is no one guarding the entrance.

Should I just make a run for it? The chances are that no one is gonna notice until it's too late. In terms of speed, I should easily smoke everyone in the building.

But how long would I have to run? Would I even make it back to my Yamaha? Should I try to lose them in the *hutongs* around here, or would I get lost myself? Any chance that they'll pull a gun on me? What's China's protocol for opening fire in a crowd?

The linoleum floor looks cheap and dirty. The white walls are yellowed by cigarette smoke. The clock on the far-end wall says 5:45 P.M. Right above it, eight pizza-sized red plastic characters:

"Leniency if you confess. Severity if you resist."

34

"I doon know nutting, I swear." A man's voice cuts short my shut-eye.

It's 6:15 P.M. Already pitch dark outside.

I heard several people coming into the station, but I didn't expect them to be foreigners. Just a few yards away, a local girl is having a heated conversation with two African men in their early twenties, one of whom is wrapped in a head bandage soaked with blood.

From what I can gather, the two Africans were in a brawl between two rival African gangs; and the guy who inflicted the head wound is still on the run. It is unclear what the fight was about, but my guess would be a turf war over drugs.

Being the big brother of all developing countries in the world, China has been rather generous to Africa in recent years. Day by day, more and more Africans come in from impoverished countries like Nigeria and Somalia. But as they speak no Chinese and have little training in anything technical, a great many of them become loiterers in the drug trade. Though I usually go to Prince out of habit, I could ask any young African male in Sanlitun for some "black stuff"; and within thirty minutes, he'd have it. As a result, competition has become increasingly fierce. In this regard, it is probably a good thing that China does not allow civilians to keep firearms.

"Listen to me!" the Chinese girl snaps at the injured African in a rather girlfriend-like manner. "That guy in the basement is either going to prison or getting deported. And unless you tell the police what they want to know, you are going to prison too!"

Poor girl, she must be hysterical. Foreigners don't do time in China unless it is really, really, really serious. I'm positive.

But what if? I'd hate to go the race route, but maybe there is a sliding scale when it comes to the foreigner privileges; white guys from the First World get the most benefit, while darker guys from Africa get deported?

And I am not really a foreigner.

Do these guys have to talk damn loud?

When Is Lethal coming back with those IDs?

Maybe if I just count to three.

One . . .

Two . . .

God damn it, why is it so stuffy in here all of a sudden?

And it's only . . . 6:17?

35

Finally, Lethal crashes through the plastic drapes.

"Did you get it?!" I don't recall ever being so serious with him.

"What do you mean, did I?" He tugs on his T-shirt. "See this? It's Superman, okay? And in case you had any more doubts . . ."

Another figure pops out from behind his back.

"Moneypenny?" I'd better rub my eyes.

Is this what Lethal meant by Plan B?

Unlike the 007 original, this Moneypenny is a tennis-skirt-loving ABC from Los Angeles. For an ABC, her Chinese is superb, which partially explains why she is already a star in her extremely competitive firm despite being only twenty-five years old. And she is cute, too—five four, immaculate skin, a very healthy figure with a dress code to match. So when a mutual friend first introduced her to me some eighteen months ago, he thought we'd make the perfect couple.

I, on the other hand, wasn't about to get tied down no matter how great the girl was.

So before long, it became apparent that the idea of "us" had no future. In her words, I am a real-life 007 who needs only a maid and not a girlfriend, which naturally made her my imaginary boss's secretary.

Except that I don't think the original Moneypenny ever caught 007 in any precarious situation as embarrassing as this.

"Holy shit!" she cries out while rushing to my side. "Are you okay?"

As usual, she still has her company ID card hung around her neck; presumably she was pulled out of some important client meeting.

"I'm fine, sweetheart." I hug her with both arms and kiss her cheek as I never had before.

Her bosom feels snugly soft. Her hair smells like strawberries.

"What happened?" She punches me in the arm. "I thought you guys were getting an early start on Halloween!"

"Yeah, well . . . uh . . . I like your sandals." Which are red and very cute with her skirt-suit and dark nylons.

"Yeah?" Her eyebrows ease up a bit, but still look far from easy.

I am gonna hear about this one for ages.

"What's going on over here?" She snaps her fingers at one of the cops, who is standing around doing nothing. "Why are you holding him? You can't just keep him here. He's American!"

The cop frowns. "Who the hell are you?"

Good question. Well, she's American, bona fide, too. If I were Moneypenny, I wouldn't even be here; not that she would ever be as stupid as I was in the first place. If I could swap one attribute of mine for one of hers, what would it be: her good sense or her passport? Hell, if I'd just taken her seriously, maybe I would have . . .

Moneypenny turns to me with her eyes fluttering.

I know what I want her to say, even *prayed* for it a thousand times in the last two seconds.

But maybe it's not such a good idea. Why drag her into this mess? She has done enough for me as is. Maybe I should just tell her to tell the—

"I am his fiancée!" she announces, staring down the cop. "We are getting married next month."

Telepathy! I can't believe it!

"Identification!" the cop grunts.

"Here!" she roars back. "American passport, see that? And this green card is for him."

I hope I am not squeezing her shoulder too hard.

The cop walks off with our papers, visibly perturbed by having been yelled at by a girl half his age.

"So . . ." She rubs her upper chest while letting out a long breath. "What now?"

"Oh . . ." I doubt that 007 would say "I don't know" under similar circumstances. "Don't you worry. I'm sure it ain't nothing but a chicken wing. What do you say we go for a drink after this?"

I could use about six.

"And some food, too," she says, managing a grin. "Knowing how much you eat, you must be hungry."

"So are you gonna make dinner for me again?" It's hard to be charming in moments like this, but I'm trying.

"Yeah . . . Well, tonight we do Transit. I need a Long Island. And don't you worry, I won't be fighting for the bill on this one."

36

"Hey." Moneypenny nudges me in the arm. "Snap out of it. You were zoning out again."

"Sorry." Like I said, this stuff is pretty strong. "Hey, what's that in your bag?"

"Cosmopolitan."

"For this month?"

Okay, I know. Once upon a time, I actually read books—even if just kung-fu-fighting fantasy novels that I call "kungfutions."

"What are you looking for, anyway?" Moneypenny seems agitated by my rummaging through the pages.

"Horoscopes, babe. Where the hell are they?"

"I didn't know you were so into those things."

"Hey, when in China, do as the Chinese do."

And there is nothing weird about checking one's Western horoscopes when living in China, okay? This is where communication and development have led us—to a handful of glossy pages that can be purchased from any newsstand *and* foretell one's future. Now if that's not a practical spiritual outlet, then I don't know what is!

"Young man." A middle-aged cop interrupts my quest.

Judging by the lone star on each shoulder, he ranks above all of the other cops I've had the displeasure of meeting so far today. Could he be the captain?

On a closer look, he is a rather handsome guy. Tall, broad, not at all fat. The same cop uniform looks much better on him than on Tweedledee and Tweedledum (whom I have not seen at all in the past two hours, by the way). He is not exactly smiling, but his face looks nice and soft nonetheless. In a way, he reminds me of the cops I used to call "Uncle" when I was a little kid in Shanghai, the kind who'd hold my hand to cross the street, the kind I respected and looked up to.

Maybe those cops still exist.

I haven't stood up so straight in years.

"Here you are." He hands Moneypenny and me our respective IDs. "Sorry to keep you two waiting."

"Oh no. Really, it's okay," I eagerly reply, never having thought that "sorry" could be a part of the police vocabulary.

"Young man," he repeats, looking at me with a smile, "you know that you shouldn't have done what you did. *Don't* you?"

Well, of course. I'm a lawyer, for Mao's sake. Even if I don't care about the adults around me, at least think about the children. There are lots of schools in the area, like the French school just down the street; and their students walk by all the time. What if they ask me for a Ziggy one day? Would I refuse? And what's gonna happen after that? While the big numb is not addictive like heroin, I cannot completely refute the argument of its being a gateway drug either.

The fact is, nothing in life is all good or all bad. In the case of my Ziggy, I always focused only on its positives without acknowledging the negatives. But now, I know better.

Starting today, I will smoke less, and definitely not in public places.

So: "Yes, sir. Of course, sir. I'm sorry for what happened."

And I even pat the cop on his right arm to show my remorse.

"So then, tell me the truth," the cop whom I shall remember fondly as Lone Star continues. "Are you really Chinese or American?"

Ha, déjà vu. Normally, I'd be really ticked off by such a question twice in a day. But now, I am actually glad he asked. The truth is, I feel rather guilty about declaring myself an American, for I am not (at least not in the Republican sense). Instead of being either Chinese or American, as if those two identities were mutually exclusive, I am a combination of both. To be perfectly honest to myself and everyone else, I just have to tell it like it is.

"I was born in Shanghai, then moved to America as a teen."

"So are you an American citizen now?"

"No sir, I'm still Chinese." And proud.

It feels good to get that off my chest.

37

Honesty is so very, very overrated.

I'd love to destroy that flickering lightbulb in the ceiling. But I am afraid to.

There are no windows in this room.

Not even a second after I told Lone Star the truth, I was led to the end of the station lobby, down a narrow staircase, past a roll of small rooms with closed doors, and voilà. Into a chamber at the end of a narrow corridor.

That was three hours ago.

For company, I have one folding chair and a small wooden desk. The ceiling is pressing down closer by the second.

If I really look hard for a silver lining, I was right about at least one thing: the inefficiency of the Chinese police. Counting Tweedledee and Tweedledum, I have already been handled by eight different cops, and four of them did not say a word. What I failed to account for was the fact that, as inefficient as the police may be, they can also immobilize you for as long as they want.

"Where he now?!" Choppy English penetrates the thin walls.

Some cop has obviously been taking Chinglish lessons. I hate surprises.

Ever since ten minutes ago, a lot of commotion has been going on in the next room. My guess is that the cops have caught one of the African brawlers on the run.

"I doon know nutting, it's the troots, please!" The African voice sounds like it is about to cry.

"Where you flom?!" the interrogator keeps shouting.

"Nigeria."

"Than where your passport?!"

". . . Home."

"You lie!"

"No, it's true. I swear. I call my wife."

"No call wife! Tell me now or deport tumollow!"

"No, no, please, I beg you, please, I call my wife, please. No! Wait! WAIT!"

The voices stop.

A loud bang on a wooden table.

The sound of a chair dragging on cement.

Then a door slams.

38

"So where did this 'cigarette' of yours come from?" asks the cop across the table.

I can smell the garlic from his last meal, as well as the *bai jiu*.

"It was given by an acquaintance, sir."

With my cover blown, I must now avoid being labeled a habitual user. Maybe there is some special leniency program for rookie dumb-asses.

"From an acquaintance?" he snickers. "How?"

"Well . . . I was having coffee at the Starbucks in Oriental Plaza. And this guy Ivan gave it to me."

"What was that? Who?"

"Ivan?"

"What's his Chinese name?"

"I don't know his Chinese name."

"Why did he give it to you?"

"Well, he said that I looked stressed . . . from work, so he gave it to me as a, you know, to help relax."

"Did you know what was in it?"

"Did *I* know what was in it?"

"Other than tobacco?"

". . . I had a vague idea but wasn't sure."

"You mean you guessed it was some form of narcotic?"

". . . No?"

"Are you sure?"

". . ."

"Is that a yes or a no?"

". . . I'm sorry, what was the question?"

"Need I remind you of what happens if you don't tell the truth?"

"No!"

"So again, did you know if there was any narcotic substance in this cigarette?"

"I . . . suppose."

"How come?"

"I've seen him around before and he smokes that stuff pretty regularly."

"How did you feel after smoking it?"

"Uh . . . a little paranoid?"

"Was it your first time?"

"Oh, yes. Absolutely."

"You mean you never used it before?"

"No. Never."

I can feel his stare.

Keep breathing. Everything will be fine.

He's writing something down on a clipboard.

Everything will be fine. I know it. Nothing bad is going to happen.

Keep breathing.

What could he possibly be writing?!

"Now tell me again, where did this 'cigarette' come from?"

"But didn't we just cover that?"

"What? Do you have somewhere to go? I said: tell me again!"

Fucking asshole . . .

"Now, read it over." He hands me the statement. "Anything I missed?"

Well if he did, he is an idiot. I've repeated the same story four times already. "It's all here. Word for word."

"Then write down at the bottom, 'The above statement is true in its entirety.'"

"The whole thing?"

"Word—for—word."

Fucking asshole.

"Now sign on the dotted line and stamp your right index finger over your signature." He hands me an ink pad.

"And what happens after I sign?"

"No." He is actually laughing. "I ask the questions, you answer. Got it?"

"Well, can I call my lawyer?"

"Excuse me? This is China. You don't have the right to a lawyer at this time."

"Then when *do* I have the right to a lawyer?"

"Again, and listen carefully this time: I ask the questions, *not* you. Now sign!"

*Fuck*ing asshole.

39

Dear Buddha, I know this is a case of *lin shi bao fo jiao* (holding on to the Buddha's foot in last-minute prayer), but I have been meaning to visit you at a temple for quite some time. *Journey to the West* is one of my favorite books of all time, and all the vegetarian noodles I have eaten in the past surely account for something, so how about showing me some love?

Allah, I know I have been bad, but I don't really eat that much pork, really, I don't. Living in China makes it hard to swear off the swine. But I will do my best from now on. Just get me out of this jam first, please?

Jesus, even though I have never read the whole Bible, I have seen a lot of movies about you, and I really think you are a pretty cool guy. All those years in America, gosh, I must have prayed to you countless times without even realizing why. So how about a little grace in return?

And if that's not enough, I do hereby solemnly swear, if any one of you nice gentlemen help me out, I will go to your house of worship the first chance I get, buy the longest incense available, and donate all of the 124.5 *kuai* I have in my pocket!

Cao, what's the use? When you are going up shit creek, ain't no statue is gonna hand you a paddle.

Then how about applying to someone who is more powerful?

Back in April, I read something about an *ernai* of a provincial Communist Party boss who rammed her BMW X5 into a horse-drawn flatbed, killing the peasant on the flatbed instantly. When spectators gathered at the scene, the woman yelled, "What's there to look at? There are too many of them as is!" Then even before the victim's family sued her for wrongful death, she blamed the victim for committing suicide by running deliberately into her path and damaging her X5 in the process. And amazingly, the police agreed with her. In the end, there was no arrest, no prosecution.

The moral of the story? *Guan xi* solves everything in China, especially *guan xi* high in the government.

So whom do I know in the government?

Crap, I don't think I have given any Chinese government official enough face in the past to be able to call in a favor now. Back when I was still with the firm, I had to deal with those guys all the time. Take away their polyester button-downs and condescending attitude, and some of them were just as ignorant as the Spit 'n' Squatters and maybe even more closed-minded when relativity is considered. On paper, they were "Chairman" this and "Minister" that; but could they ever measure up to the merits of my grandfather? After all, it was the Nationalists who actually overthrew the emperor and thrust China into the modern era. Had my grandfather's fellow Nationalists been a little smarter and a little less corrupt, they might still be ruling China instead of a tiny island called Taiwan, and I'd be a prince, certifiably.

Hey, wait a minute, that reminds me—why don't I call on the Princesses? Being granddaughters of some of the oldest Communist Party bosses, these girls are about as close to Chinese royalty as it gets!

Off the top of my head, there is TT—an architect, American-raised. Rumor has it that we made out once, but I don't recall. There is also CC—a lawyer, UK-educated, and quite possibly the most lavishly dressed girl I have ever seen. Then, finally, beautiful SS, the fairest of all aristocrats, almost an identical twin to Sunshine Sunshine, but even cuter. She spends most of her time throwing parties, often inside the Forbidden City.

All I need is for one of these lovely girls to call someone, and boom—I'll be chauffeured home by Lone Star himself, with an apology and a fruit basket. Yes, it could be that easy. . . .

If I can just find their *wo cao ta ma de* telephone numbers!

Why the hell aren't they here?! Did I delete them?

Why the hell did I do that?!

Oh, I know, could it be because they never have to work, never have to cook, never drive anything less than German, never wear anything less than Italian, never pay for tolls or parking by virtue of their military-plated vehicles, and were therefore never cool enough to deserve my holier-than-Mao friendship?!

But now, it's different—now, I need to use them. What a nice guy I am! Yes, these girls have too much relative to everyone else in China; but don't hate the player, hate the game. The last I heard, the parties that SS organizes actually benefit orphanages all across China. Isn't that pretty nice? Maybe some of these girls are really sweethearts, and all I had to do was to make an effort to . . . Ah, keep scrolling.

Hold on, who is this?

A Chinese name saved in pinyin. Two characters. Should be pretty easy to identify.

Man, I really do this too often. Why even take down the number if I don't bother to remember the person? And it's probably a girl, or I wouldn't have saved the number in the first place. . . .

Hey, wait a second, could this be Madame—the Mandarin-dress-wearing know-it-all who tried to talk me out of Inner Mongolia?

She did say she owned a club once.

Any chance she knows some cops?

She has to!

There is only one way to find out.

Nokia should really add a panic button for messages like this.

40

"Get in there!" A party suddenly crashes into my room.

In walk four plainclothes cops and three girls with their hands tied behind their backs.

They must be prostitutes.

According to an Internet bulletin, over one-third of all prostitution-related arrests in Beijing take place in Sanlitun. It's no surprise considering that every time I walk down the street after sundown, at least a half dozen pimps of all shapes, sizes, and sexes will take turn soliciting me with "sex, sex" or "pussy, pussy" in broken English (and lately even in French). And if I retort, "I like boys, so leave me alone!" they'll come back with, "Not a problem, we have those, too!"

Of course, being a male outsider in a developing country, I am no saint when it comes to happy endings—even when I go out with friends and colleagues who look perfectly respectable, the night might still end up at a special karaoke bar. And no matter how much we like to present ourselves as gentlemen, certain memories are harder to erase than others.

If I can still remember correctly, it was a Friday afternoon in late 2001, barely a week after I had moved from Hong Kong. To give my weary bones some much-needed finger pressure after working for the previous thirty-six hours straight, I instructed a rickshaw driver to take me to the nicest massage place nearby. Being a veteran of such establishments, I made it clear that I wanted a real massage instead of some naked girl rubbing me down with her breasts.

"So, *da jie*"—I figured it was safe to call the masseuse "big sister," as she was already in her forties—"what's there to do in this town after dark?"

"What are you in the mood for, handsome?"

"Girls, I suppose." As in girls I didn't have to pay for. "Any suggestions?"

"Well if I were only fifteen years younger." She giggled. "But if you want, I can arrange."

"Yeah?" I pretty much knew what she meant. "But I don't really want girls from, you know, here."

"Oh no, of course not. I am talking about very nice girls. Ones who don't work in the business."

"Don't work in the business? Then what do they do?"

"Oh, you'll see. I can send her right to your room."

"Really? But . . ."

"Relax. *Da jie* will take good care of you."

"Oh . . . All right"—as she was literally twisting my arm—"China World Hotel, room 2812 . . ."

The doorbell rang right on time.

A fine specimen from the Northeast, she stood at an impressive five feet ten. Her nose was sharp, suggesting part Russian blood, and her skin was light with faint freckles. Wearing a red leather jacket, tight black jeans, and three-inch stiletto heels that probably cost her her last three tricks, she was a role model of a call girl. Given the resemblance in eyes and measurements, I had a feeling that she was related by blood to the *da jie* who arranged this whole thing; but I didn't ask.

Shortly after the deed, a Chinese pop song went off in her purse. Pacing around naked, she started a telephone conversation that became a shouting match (at the end which I heard the word *"shabi"* for the very first time).

"Are you okay?" I waited to ask until she threw away her rhinestone-encrusted gizmo.

"Just some guy I was living with." She stood in front of the TV with her breasts heaving.

"Was? What about now?"

"Are you looking for a mistress?"

"Beg your pardon?"

"Give me three thousand *kuai* a month and a place to live, I'll cook, clean, and service you whenever you want."

"But . . ."

"But?"

"But I am only twenty-six. I don't really need . . ."

"Did you like what we just did?"

"Well, but . . ."

"I am good at what I do, aren't I? I used to be a model, you know. It's a good price. Will you think about it? Please tell me you will think about it. . . ."

I admit that I actually thought about it. Even for days after.

But in retrospect, I am glad I just gave her the 1,200 *kuai* to end the night, including a bit extra that was both a tip for her and a severance for me.

The truth is, I was tired of it already. In the beginning, I was curious because it was taboo, especially if it was a ring of Japan Airlines flight attendants who worked a different shift out of Hong Kong's Kowloon Hotel. But after enough times, I didn't want to count money after ejaculating anymore. Somebody once said that you don't pay for prostitutes to come, you pay for them to leave. That's what I did with that pretty woman from the Northeast, except on that night and forever since, I have been the one who left.

Funny thing is, I still wonder where that pretty woman with the rhinestone mobile ended up that night.

In the room, the leader of the four cops begins to pace. He is almost a whole head taller than everyone else, his shoulders thick enough to break walls.

"Tell me where he is." He stares down the trio of streetwalkers.

Looking as emaciated as they do, they'd be lucky to turn 200 *kuai* a trick. Yet the pimp still takes. Sadder still, they wouldn't be doing this if they could make more money doing something else.

"You, did you hear what I said?" The giant singles out the one girl who dares to look away.

He pushes on her chest.

"Cao ni ta niang chou bi! Ni ya ta ma de zhao si ah!"

No, she should not have done that.

With his giant bear palm more than covering her face, the cop proceeds to thrust her head straight into the wall behind her. Over and over again.

For what it's worth, I hope that pretty woman has learned to do real massages.

41

Bzzz-Bzzz!

Please, not another "Where u at" party message. Don't these people do anything constructive on a Wednesday night? The *bao ans* have already warned me about using the phone twice! I'm amazed they haven't taken it away yet—maybe it's a sign that they actually want me to find some help so that they won't have to deal with me.

"What happened to you? I've been waiting to hear from you for hours!" The message reads.

Could it really be Madame?

This is unbelievable!

"I'm still at the station. Had to sign a statement. Don't know what's next. Can you help?"

Please say yes. Please say yes. Please please please . . . I know, I barely know Madame and might even have been rude to her at one point or another, but I didn't know any better then.

"Why are you still there? I thought you were American."

"It's a long story. Have to tell you about it later."

And I will, I promise. In fact, once this is over, we'll have coffee, drinks, dinner, whatever she wants. We can discuss life, politics, and whatever else interests her. She does seem to know a lot about, well, whatever.

"So what have you told the police so far?"

"Just whatever they wanted to hear."

I don't expect them to believe any of it; but they can't disprove it either. At least I *think* they can't. There must be someone who can throw out this whole wrap even after my "confession," or at least re-duce the punishment, or something, anything.

"Okay, give me some time. I will update you soon."

"You have no idea how much I appreciate this."

Indeed, how am I ever gonna pay her back for doing me this favor?

"Don't worry about it. What are friends for?"

42

1:15 A.M. on the dashboard clock.

It was nice to finally get out of that basement chamber—if I only didn't have to be sandwiched in the backseat of a police cruiser be-tween two *bao ans* who reek of burned garlic.

"Cigarette?" asks the cop in the driver's seat.

"No thanks."

"You know, I'd be driving you home right now if you just had an American passport."

Yeah, go ahead and rub it in.

"So do you handle a lot of these things?"

"Urine samples in the middle of the night? No. Overnight shift? Every three days."

"Well then, how about, you know, drugs? You handle a lot of those?"

"What do you think?"

"..."

"You know, there was a time when drugs were everywhere in Sanlitun."

"Everywhere?"

"It changed by the year too. '97 was ecstasy. '98, LSD. Then heroin, coke, methamphetamine . . ."

Really? "So what did you guys do?"

"Rehab. Sent them by the busloads."

"Where to?"

"You mean where they actually go? Never seen it, to be honest. All I know is that it's pretty far away and in the mountains."

I heard the same thing before.

He glances at me in the rearview mirror.

"There used to be a lot more of you guys," he says.

"Used to?"

"About five years ago, I'd say about forty percent of Sanlitun was getting high, maybe more."

"And you arrested all of them?"

"Not all. Just enough. So now we don't have to."

"Why not?"

"Well, people got smart about it. They stay home to get high now."

"..."

"Seven years on the force, I've never seen a case quite like yours."

"..."

"For your sake, I hope your test results come back negative."

OCTOBER 14

43

Back to the police station in Sanlitun.

Different room

Different chair

Same emptiness.

Damn, is the basement always so cold and damp this time of night? My toes have been numb for hours; the leather jacket snuggles like a rayon tank top. It's supposed to be autumn, for Mao's sake!

"I've found someone!"

Really? I can't believe Madame is still awake.

"Fantastic! How much longer do I have to stay here?"

I don't mean to be a crybaby, but it's been ten hours. My back hurts; my butt hurts; my battery is down to its last two squares.

"Looks like tonight is out. He and I will have lunch tomorrow."

Right, lunch. When did I last eat?

"So is this 'he' a sure thing?"

I just want some sort of assurance.

"I think this guy has what it takes. Will find out soon enough."

Right, soon.

"And in the meantime?"

. . .

"Nothing. Just try to get some rest."

Right. It's only 3 A.M., which means that it's only gonna get colder before warming up again for daylight.

Come to think of it, in just a few more weeks it will be my third Beijing winter. Soon there will be no more bike weather. Every day the world will be gray, with nothing but wind, dust, and subfreezing temperatures to make me wonder what the hell I am doing here. And the more I complain, the longer hell will stick around, with last year's being almost five months long.

How am I gonna spend all those lonely nights this year?

I really should have worn some socks.

44

" 'Ey, *ge-men'er*."

I know, I'm not supposed to be talking to anybody (or the *bao ans* outside might get upset), but it's pushing 9 A.M. already and I haven't exactly slept.

He is a good-looking kid, with hair slicked back neatly and immaculate, pale skin. A little bit too thin for his five-seven frame, however; the clothes he has on look two sizes too large.

As I overheard from the cop who smacked his head while ushering him in, he is a "duck," meaning gigolo.

"So where did it happen?" I'm referring to his bust.

As far as I've ever known, all the gigolos are in huge dance clubs like Kiss and Banana. And those places never get raided, as they are owned by cops anyway.

"Chang Hong Bridge," he says with a smirk.

"Isn't that just down the street? What happened?"

"You are not a cop, are you?"

Yeah, funny.

"Well, I was working at Rock 'n' Roll last night," he speaks softly while rubbing his bloodshot eyes. "Then this guy picked me up. He looked pretty normal, said I looked like a model and bought a few drinks. I told him that I could only do a 'flute job,' you know, given my period and all."

"Wait, you mean you dress up like a woman?" This is definitely a first for me in China.

"You should have seen me." He grins. "I had this new outfit that I just bought. The *shabis* took it all away and made me change into this—"

"So he picked you up," I urge, needing to stop him before he goes off on a tangent. "And then?"

"Well, the guy took me to his car, brand-new Audi A6, lots of room. But he was obviously in a hurry—told me to get started as soon as we got on the road."

"In a moving car?" Ouch.

"And he was driving like a madman, probably half drunk, too."

"So what happened at the bridge?"

"Well, you know how the traffic light there takes forever. So there I was, not even a minute away from getting it done, the *shabi* had to go for the reach-around, from behind, and in between!"

"*Cao!*"

"Then he grabbed my wig, which tore off. Then he pushed my face. I screamed. He screamed."

I cross my legs.

"Then he slapped me again! Right on the face. See these marks?"

"Did you fight back?"

"You bet I did!" He brandishes his faux fingernails, at least half of which are roughly broken off. "I just kept clawing him and clawing him until he was swerving all over the road. So some cop pulled us over."

"But he arrested only you?"

"No. There is more. When the cop came over, the *shabi* flashed his own badge."

"You mean he's a cop, too?"

"Worse, a *wu jing*." A term that means "armed police" and refers to China's inner-city military, specifically trained to put down urban insurgencies like Tiananmen 1989

"So was the cop just gonna let him slide?"

"Certainly looked that way, so I yelled, 'This *shabi* tried to rape me!'"

"You did WHAT?"

"Hey, a man can't just hit a girl and get away with it!" The pretty boy raises his larklike voice. "This is not the Qing Dynasty anymore. We have laws now. Right?"

"But is he actually going to get anything for this?"

"Who knows. But I swear, if they lock me up, he's coming with me!"

45

On the road again in the backseat of a blue-and-white police cruiser, this one being an even earlier model of a Chinese-made Volkswagen Jetta.

"Read this." The driver hands me a piece of paper.

There are two lines of text in the middle of the page, plus a very faint red chop at the bottom.

"What is it?"

"A search warrant."

"It is? For what?"

"Wherever it is that you live."

"What for?"

"Coz you hit the jackpot." The younger navigator turns around with an annoying grin and reads from a report: "It says here that your 'cigarette' had morphine and a whole bunch of other chemicals."

"I beg your pardon?"

Have I been shot? Who the hell uses morphine outside of a war zone? And isn't it derived from opium—China's favorite drug to hate? How the hell did this happen?!

"Do you ever read the news?" the driver asks.

"Yes?"

"Then you know about the war in Afghanistan."

"Yeah?" So?

"Then you should also know that the Taliban have been flooding the market with opium in order to finance their war. It's in everything coming out of that region now. Was your stuff very black and oily?"

"So what if it was?"

"Then half of it was probably opium. By the way, morphine is Class A." The navigator keeps on grinning. "Which means we have to search your place inside out. It's protocol. So, why don't you be a good sport and tell us how to get there?"

46

Located off a side street just inside East Second Ring, my flat is a far cry from the "villa" where I once lived.

Thanks to a city ordinance that exempts buildings under seven floors from having elevators, I must climb twelve flights of stairs, or a total of ninety-six steps, to get to my apartment. Though I live on the top floor, which is theoretically the most sound-efficient, I can always hear my neighbors coming in and out of their places, which probably means they can also hear every squeak and shout coming out of my bedroom.

There is not much inside my apartment. The floor is bare cement; the walls are unpainted stucco; and there are no French mugs, German cutlery, Japanese electronics, or Italian appliances anymore. Of course, I could spend some time and money sprucing it up, or at least fix the bathroom so I don't have to shower standing next to the toilet. But I'm single, and in China, comfort is never a priority.

Early every morning, some noise will wake me up long before my alarm goes off. Sometimes it is the old men in the communal garden downstairs practicing "Lion's Growl," a form of breathing exercise so loud that they should really be having some fantastic sex while doing it; other times, it is just the drills, saws, and nail guns that some inconsiderate migrant laborers decide to use as part of some home-improvement assignment before their midday nap.

To enter my building, there is a security code that I should key in. But some ghost will always prop open the entrance with a piece of wood or brick, causing break-ins, which in turn prompt all those who live on the ground floor to install heavy metal enclosures around their windows and heavier metal doors outside their existing doors, effectively turning their homes into large prison cells.

Located at the front and back entrances of the compound are booths for a corps of *bao ans,* who are usually under twenty-five and never seem to do much besides sleep. Twice I have had my motorcycle stolen from right outside of my building, and neither time did the *bao ans* notice anyone shady pushing a large two-wheeled vehicle suspiciously out the front gate in the middle of the night, unless, of course, the thieves are the *bao ans* themselves.

Immediately to the right of the back entrance, there is a hair salon/massage parlor that cuts hair for 5 *kuai* and gives massages for 10. After that, there is another hair salon, and another, and another. Across from them is a string of eateries, where the tables are wiped with the same dirty towel all day long and whose barbecue pits shroud the entire neighborhood in cumin-scented smoke from dusk till dawn.

The biggest military hospital in town is just 100 yards away, and throughout the day, vehicles bearing military plates continually drive against the flow of traffic on this narrow one-lane, one-way street. When I first moved into the neighborhood, it was still rather run-down, but recently it has been completely rebuilt, with fountains and benches for all the children in the neighborhood to play right outside the emergency room.

And thanks to these lovely surroundings, I now pay less in rent for the entire year than for a month at the "villa." Besides, this lets me see how the other 99 percent of China lives. So when I actually run for president one day, I can at least say that I have lived among the masses.

47

Sixty-nine stairs to go. The cops are already huffing and puffing.

This is such a waste of time. It took us twenty minutes to get here; and it's gonna take another ten for these dodoes to pick up their pace. And for what? What could I possibly have in my place that would warrant a search? I probably don't even have an unexpired condom in the whole damn place, now that I've been dry for months. And bottom line—I don't deal. Never did; never will. Unlike my buddy Marley, I don't even buy more than one chunk of hash at a time, ever. Helps with staying in control.

Speaking of the devil, I haven't seen Marley in a few days. An American who moved to Beijing in 2001 with his wife, he is what I consider a China convert. Upon first arrival, he hated Beijing—the pollution, the inconvenience, all the "cultural differences." But after I introduced him to Prince, and local girls introduced themselves, he fell in love with this place. Of course, I warned him not to overexercise his foreigner privileges and betray the vows of marriage. But it went in one ear and out the other. Two weeks ago, the wife moved back home for good; Marley went into hiding.

For a week I didn't hear from him. Then, last Saturday, Marley called me to meet up at Café 44.

"You look like shit!" I hugged him, "And smell like it too."

"I know," he croaked, having lost his voice. "You don't want to know what I've been doing all week."

Let me guess. . . .

"No, bro." His bloodshot eyes blinked slowly. "I've been doing coke again."

"By yourself?"

"Yes."

"How much?"

"Not much."

"Dude?"

"Okay, just an eight-ball . . . This morning."

"Dude!"

"I know what you're gonna say, and that's why I called you out today." He stuffed a FedEx shipping box into my lap.

"Is it my birthday today?"

"You have to keep that away from me. It's everything I have."

"As in IDs and money?"

"No. Hash, Valium, coke, MDMA, everything . . ."

"But this damn thing weighs a good five pounds! What the hell do you expect *me* to do with it?"

"Keep it until I can pull myself together."

"Why don't you just throw it away? This is like a ticking time bomb!"

"Are you crazy?!" The devil in him had an MBA. "Do you know how much this stuff is worth on the streets of New York City?"

So out of friendship, I accepted the box, and that ticking time bomb is . . .

SOMEWHERE IN MY APARTMENT RIGHT NOW!!!

Okay, where the hell did I put it?!

Living room? Kitchen? Storage closet? It's been almost twenty-four hours, but by God I am still high!

Wait, the computer desk. I left it between the monitor and a stack of paper.

The bomb is in plain sight!

I've got to get some new friends.

48

The cement floor is still wet.

The cleaning lady must have just left.

The desk is upstairs in the bedroom. It's the only furniture up there besides my bed and a chair. No one can miss it. Not even these guys.

If I run upstairs right now, the cops will surely get suspicious, chase me down, find the stash, ship me off to execution, and send my father a bill for the bullet.

If I don't somehow get to the stash before they do, they will just skip the first two steps, and still send my father a bill for the bullet.

If there is a God, and I don't care if she is Muslim, make the box disappear. I'll do anything she wants.

"Go right ahead, look all you want."

I had actually thought it would be nice to be back in my own place after the last twenty hours.

The two cops walk into the kitchen as the two *bao ans* left guarding me get busy picking their noses.

"Sit still," says one of them, his finger still up his left nostril. "What you got to be so nervous about?"

This is such payback. The night before last, I came home late after drinking at Transit. When the taxi pulled up to the main gate, the *bao an* refused to let us in. It's the rule of the compound not to let cars enter after midnight so as to minimize noise; but I didn't want to hear it, even though it would have meant an extra two-minute walk at the most. So when the *bao an* refused to remove the plastic cones blocking the entrance, I got out of the car, picked up the cones, and threw them as far as I could.

And now that I think about it, it's not just the *bao ans,* but also the waiters, cabbies, supermarket cashiers, subway token ladies, and pretty much every individual that I have ever yelled at in China as if they were monkeys. Man, I bet they would pay money to see me now.

"Hey, how much do you pay for this place?" someone asks.

"Come again?"

"Your rent." One of the cops sticks his head out of the kitchen. "How much do you pay for rent every month?"

"Uh . . . twenty-five hundred?"

"Twenty-five hundred *kuai?* Are you kidding? How did you manage to find it?"

"In the classifieds. I can show you the lease if you want."

"You live here by yourself?"

They walk up the staircase to the second floor.

"Yes?"

They are entering the master bedroom.

"All this space just for yourself?"

"Mmm-hmm." Is there a law against that?

This is all my own damn fault. Had I been a good friend to Marley, I would have smacked him over the head when he told me about all those girls; and I should have thrown away his package when I had the chance, or better yet, made *him* throw it away. A true friend is not someone who always says "Oh, that's cool" but someone who tells you off when you are behaving like an idiot—like me!

Shit, they are there. I can hear them—right in front of the desk. By this time tomorrow . . .

Please. Please. Please. Please. Please.

"Hey!"

"WHAT?!"

I can see the duo's feet descending the staircase. Here comes the end!

"How long have you lived here?" the older one asks.

"You mean Beijing?" Three years too many.

"No." He frowns. "I said, how long have you lived *here*?"

"Oh, you mean this flat? Six months, just about."

Keep breathing.

"And your rent is how much again?"

"Twenty-five hundred. Paid annually."

The cops look at each other.

The younger one says, "Any chance your landlord has another one like this?"

"I beg your pardon?"

"I mean just look how high the ceiling is." He seems way too impressed. "How is the building security, by the way? Is there underground parking?"

I guess one person's ghetto just might be someone else's paradise. Maybe I haven't been so grassroots after all.

"Well if you gentlemen really want to know, I can ask the landlord once we are . . . you know."

"Oh yes, of course." He signals the *bao ans* to escort me back to the car. "I just can't get over your place. It's spotless. You must have a really good cleaning lady; even the desk is so neat. I mean, all those files and yet she stacked all of them. I wish my wife could clean like that. . . ."

Yes, I must give my cleaning lady a big, big raise.

49

Lone Star is looking a lot different today than yesterday. Dark blue T-shirt, light blue nylon shorts, white socks, black sneakers. If I didn't know he was the station chief, I'd say he looked too cute for his age.

"Here." He hands me a tied-up plastic shopping bag and a pair of disposable chopsticks. "This is for you."

Chilled Korean ramen from across the street? For me?

"Someone called for you." He sits down across the table.

"Oh yeah? Who was it?"

He doesn't answer.

But let me guess—was this Madame's *guan xi* at work? It's 1 P.M. She probably just finished her very important lunch, which is why I'm now having mine. I have never eaten noodles straight out of a plastic shopping bag before, but what's left of my stomach is not going to make a fuss about it.

"So is it casual Thursday, sir?" I am eyeing Lone Star's get-up while chewing.

"Oh this?" He spit-cleans a stain off the tip of his Beckham Adidas. "Weekly football match. Starts at two o'clock. Everyone is going."

"Everyone?"

"Yeah, the entire station except for the interns."

Wonderful, why didn't they have a game yesterday afternoon as well? These cops just work too damn hard.

"It's too bad that you don't work here," he says. "I'd love to have you play for us if you did."

Yeah, right, what a contrived ringer that was. But still, "You are too kind."

"I'm not joking. You look like you are in great shape." He squeezes my upper left arm. The act might have felt a little too close had this not been China, where men seem to have no problem touching each other on the thighs or arms when there is no objective need for doing so (and yet never hug when there is arguably a clear need for having one).

I guess Madame's *guan xi* must be pretty high up in order for Lone Star to kiss my ass like this.

"So, tell me." He crosses his legs, his right foot swirling at the ankle. "What does it feel like exactly?"

"What does what feel like?"

"You know, the thing that got you in here."

"You mean . . . to get high, sir?"

For the record, the stuff was really good this time. In fact, it's been pretty good for a whole month. I know, some of the effect this time was actually due to opium, but no harm done. I'll just find a dealer of normal big numb, and only once in a while. That's right, I will make a conscientious effort to cut down. In fact, I have decided not to smoke for a whole week just to detox, which means that the next time I light up a Zigarette rolled with some good clean hash . . .

. . . "It'll feel like a really good cigarette that makes you relax and crave ice cream at the same time."

It's as hopeless as explaining climax to a virgin, but I've at least tried.

"So when do I get out of here?" I hate to break up this heartwarming conversation so quickly, but all things considered.

"Oh, soon." He nods. "As soon as the paperwork is done, you're ready to go."

I *love* Madame.

"Well, thank you, for everything." I offer my handshake to the two-face.

"Oh, don't worry about it." He waves it off.

Okay, don't say I didn't offer. Of all the things I have learned in the past twenty-four hours, nothing tops staying cool. So be cool and keep smiling. Pretty soon, I shall have my Long Island iced tea at Transit—make that two—as well as the sliced smoked duck served with fresh apple slices and sweet maple sauce. I can feel my clenched jaws relaxing. I can almost smile.

"And once you get there," Lone Star continues, "just lie low and . . ."

I know, the sofas at Transit are really quite too low. But then, if they weren't, I just might sit there all day and never leave.

Wait a second. "Once I get where? Where am I going exactly?"

"Up to the district office," Lone Star says. "There is a van waiting outside."

"What? Why?" But I've learned my lesson already!

"The phone call came a little too late." He shrugs. "Once we start our paperwork, we have to follow procedure."

"So what does that mean? What's going to happen at the district office?"

"That's hard to say."

"Hard to say?!" What the hell?

"Well at least you don't have to go there on an empty stomach." Lone Star stands up and begins to walk away. "Gotta go. Time to kick some balls."

I feel like kicking his.

He turns around all of a sudden. "By the way, do you still have your mobile phone?"

Why? Is this another one of his trick questions? My Nokia is all that I have left!

"Then use it wisely." He exits the room with that ambiguous grin of his.

50

Prior to leaving Sanlitun, I managed to spend a few minutes with Rockette, who had heard the news from Lethal Weapon and had been waiting outside the station for hours. It was very nice to see the closest I have to a little sister, but also a little weird to see her cry as the van slowly pulled away.

But as consolation, I have never been inside a "bread van" before. Once the taxicabs of Beijing before the Volkswagens and Peugeots hit the streets, these white, loaf-sized tin cans come with half-liter single-cam carbureted engines, drum brakes that lock up without fail, tires no wider than four fingers, and ergonomics too basic even for the Flintstones. Now relegated mostly to newly licensed peasants who use only the high beam but never the turn signals (and utterly disregard the blind spot), these road lice pose a chronic threat to China's already congested road system. But as annoyingly retro as they are, their pint-sized dimensions still make them the fastest mode of transportation during Beijing's unbearable traffic hours—so much so that even the cops still use them.

"*I'm in a van going to the district station.*" I must make full use of my Nokia before the battery completely dies. "*We just crossed East Fourth Ring. Any update?*"

I still can't believe this thing has dragged on for so long. I don't mean to sound ungrateful, but whatever happened to Madame's *guan xi*?

The city is now more or less behind us: no more sleek high-rises with neon billboards, only brownish gray warehouses and cement-block chimneys. For now, I can still see construction sites with giant cranes.

"He says it will take some time."

Okay, that's not the answer I wanted. Isn't twenty-four hours enough incarceration for one pesky joint? I know China is inefficient, but come *on*!

"So how many more hours?" I seriously doubt I can take another twenty-four.

"Try a few days."

WHAT? *"Why so long?!"*

I haven't even packed!

"We got too late a start. Too many people got involved before I found my contact."

"So I have to stay overnight at the district station?"

Is there any chance I can take a shower there, maybe even use the police gym?

"But you are not going to the district station."

"I'm not?" But that's what Lone Star told me. *"So where am I going exactly?"*

"The district prison."

"???" Is this her idea of a bad joke?!

"It's only temporary."

"Temporary?! Prison is prison no matter how long it is!"

I can't go to prison! I just . . . *can't*! Do you know what they do to . . . I haven't even seen a lawyer yet!

"So how many days is 'a few days'?"

Like two? Three? No more than three, right?

"Don't know yet. Have you ever heard about compulsory rehab?"

As in up to eight months, like somebody once told me? Why

don't I just throw myself into the path of that oncoming coal truck and get it over with right now?!

The driver glances in the rearview mirror.

"I'm working on at least getting the rehab waived. Just behave yourself in there and wait for my update. And DELETE ALL MY MESSAGES!"

If I could only do the same with history.

On the cracking cement of what was once the only route to the old airport, a short, shaggy, grayish black donkey of a horse trots along in the same direction as our van. With one leg hanging off his throne and dangling nonchalantly in front of the left tire, a brown-skinned farmer in a green army surplus trench coat steers leisurely from the two-wheeled flatbed being pulled by the weary Mongolian breed. Behind him, a pile of watermelons that he will probably try to sell again at the hawkers' market tomorrow starting at 5 A.M.

What I wouldn't give now to be him.

VR-o-o-o-o-o-m!

A jet stream drafts our midget van halfway into the next lane.

The turbulence of a speeding yellow Ferrari.

Only saw this model once before, in magazines.

That guy probably won't do time no matter what he puts in his mouth.

51

About an hour ago, we pulled into this giant compound surrounded by twenty-foot-high concrete walls. The parking lot itself is the size of two football fields. To the east, rows of two-story buildings that look like offices. To the west, a few boilers and ground-level structures that are presumably warehouses. To the north stands another wall with still another gate—an inescapable compound within a compound.

Judging by the line of police cruisers in front, we still have a while to wait. The van is getting smaller by the second.

"Hey," says the young cop who has his naked feet propped up on the dashboard, "I heard you are from America. Is that right?"

"Yeah." Whatever. It doesn't seem to matter.

"What did you do there?"

"I was a lawyer."

"Is that right?" He peeks again through the rearview mirror, this time more surprised than teasing. "Is it legal to smoke dope in America?"

"Not really. But a lot of European countries allow it."

He nods. "So what do you think of China's legal system?"

"How do you mean?" I want to be as polite as I can. Or maybe I'm just getting paranoid.

"Well, would you have to do time if you were in America?"

"No way." I'd be more than happy to Google this one if need be, but something tells me that I am right.

"You know . . ." He tunes the radio to a Chinese pop song that sounds exactly like a Cranberries melody. "You are about the un-luckiest guy I have met this week."

"Tell me about it."

"There are a ton of potheads in this town, but I've never seen anyone get busted the way you did."

"How is that?"

"Well, some beggar came into the station yesterday afternoon asking to see someone. At first we thought he was just stupid enough to be begging inside a police station. But then he said that someone was smoking opium at Café 44."

Huh?

"We all thought he was kidding, of course, given how he was retarded and all."

Does he mean Sloppy?

"But then he said he had witnessed the guy smoking it, and the guy confirmed it was opium, even gave him ten *kuai* because he guessed it right. So then we started asking him about how the stuff looked and smelled, and all the answers fit. . . ."

And then boom, here I am!

52

"It says here that you didn't admit to your crime at first." The lady sitting across the table could teach Margaret Thatcher a few things about looking mean.

Keep smiling. A bit more genuine. That's better.

"Do you know the consequences of not admitting to your crime?"

Drop the head lower. Just like in third grade. And purse those lips. It helped then.

"It also says here that you came back from America. Is that right?"

"Yes?" Whatever helps.

"What the hell for? To sleep with our virgins and defy our laws? Is that all you have learned in America? Is it not enough that the foreigners here live like royalty? That you have to exploit this country even more than they do?"

"I am sorry. I know I was wrong. I shouldn't have. There won't be a next time."

"Oh, trust me." She shakes her head. "There definitely will not be a next time."

This chair is getting colder by the second.

Would begging help? How about crying? I'd be happy to do either, or both together.

"Empty your pockets," she says.

"All of them?" Why? "Are you confiscating my stuff?"

Her look makes the hair on the back of my neck stand up.

"Can I at least keep my mobile phone please?" It's my only means of communicating with the outside world. What would I do without it? How could I possibly carry on?!

"Shut up and put it in the basket!" she barks at me with obvious disgust.

"Take him in." She flags down a deputy walking by in the outside corridor. "And hand over this joker to them."

Not "them" again!

Bang! The lady chops a piece of paper with her big round, red seal and slings the paper across the metal tabletop.

Four ominously bold characters at the top of the page read: "Assessment of Penalty."

What is this? My sentence? Just like that? No lawyer, no trial, no nothing? Really?

And what's that handwritten number in the middle of the page there?

FOURTEEN days?!

As in BEHIND BARS?!

That's not a "few days"; that's *wo cao ta ma de* two fucking weeks!

Wake up! Wake up Now!

FAAAAHCK THIS IS NOT A DREAM!

"Will I at least be free again after this? Please tell me I'll be free after this. I've learned my lesson already, really, I swear. Auntie . . . I mean, miss, no . . . I mean, AUNTIE . . . PLEASE?!"

"Get the hell out of my office!"

53

I never thought a gate could get much bigger than the front gate of the Forbidden City.

But then, I have never been to the gates of hell before.

On both sides of the hulking gray metal, cement walls that rise more than twenty-five feet tall extend east and west for at least a hundred yards more; on top of what is already an unsurmountable barrier, barbed wire and shrapnel glass.

In front of the gate stand two soldiers in long, ivy green army trench coats, green crested army caps, and black leather combat boots. Strapped aross their chests, none other than big, cold AK-47s.

"SQUAT BEHIND THE YELLOW LINE!" An unidentified voice rocks the ground that I walk on.

Maybe I am just too tired, but that loudspeaker on top of the guards' booth looks bigger than Lady Liberty's torch. And a lot less inviting.

Like too many antiquities in this country, the "yellow line" on the ground is really just a scrappy remnant of something that used to be there. How many others have been demeaned in this spot in exactly the same way as I am now?

And who in the name of Mao has been feeding on anchovies and Swiss cheese? And rotten, too! When the hell did they ever become part of the Chinese diet?

Never mind. It's just the bloody body odor of these three guys in front of me. Squatting with their feet shoulder-width apart and their heels digging into the ground, they are in the same position as they would be when eating and relieving themselves. In the one minute or less that it took me to walk up to them, one has spit twice, two have spit once, and now the wind is conveniently blowing some errant spittle into my face.

Since my very first day in Beijing, I have tried to avoid their kind. They're the ones who litter on China's streets, pee into China's bushes, and sleep on China's sidewalks. Nine times out of ten, they are migrants from rural villages. Ninety-nine times out of a hundred, they have never studied beyond primary school. And 99.99 percent out of eternity, they would never be seen in the company of an outsider like me. But now, I have been ordered to squat behind the worst Anchovy 'n' Swiss I have ever smelled.

On various occasions, I have made attempts to understand the Spit 'n' Squatters. After all, I did not invent the term just to put down someone for spitting or squatting once in a blue moon; rather, it is because they do it all the time. When it comes to the spitting, I can almost understand—the pollution is so bad and the weather so dry here that, eventually, everyone has to clean house; and if you were never taught to not spit in public by your parents and teachers, you just might have to do it, well, "sometimes."

But why the squatting? Is it for pleasure, leisure, or comfort? On several occasions I've tried to mimic the maneuver, only to find myself either out of balance or out of breath after twenty seconds (and if you think I'm exaggerating, try to squat without lifting your heels off the ground and see how long you can last). If someone is too tired to stand, then why not just sit on the ground instead? I know the ground might be dirty from all the spitting, but considering where the spit came from, it's not really a valid excuse.

"Stop fidgeting!"

One of the two soldiers breaks from his stoic stance.

"Squat still!" He has no sympathy for the burning in my thighs. "Do not make me tell you again!"

Thanks, asshole. Now I know why there are so many squatters in China.

It's just a theory, of course, but when you squat a lot, it's hard to have dignity; and when you have no dignity, you are more easily controlled. After five thousand years of kowtowing to the emperor, confidence and self-respect are not exactly characteristics associated with China's poor, so much so that a great many of them will squat in self-degradation even without being ordered to do so.

Then to help perpetuate such servitude, I have become no better than those snobs who mocked me upon my first arrival in America, a time when I was just as relatively poor—and thus, in their minds, ignorant—to them as my neighboring trio are to me today. Except that back here in China, I became the one criticizing with holier-than-thou authority.

Why must an epiphany always come at the most unlikely moment?

54

Sorry, 501s. I really am.

It's been almost eight years since we first met in Boston; and you have seen more action than I can remember. Girls sure loved those rips and holes—must have been some psychic connection you have with the washing machine. I'm sorry all of your fly buttons have to be ripped out with a wrench, but they say I might commit suicide later by swallowing them; and it makes no difference that yesterday was laundry day and I left the apartment without wearing any underwear. For the safety of myself and others, I have to remove all strings, buttons, zippers, and anything metallic or sharp from my body and clothes. Those are the rules.

"Now use this." The jailer guarding the fresh bloods hands me a screwdriver.

"On what?"

"Your shoes." He says, "Dig out the metal bridge in the sole."

"But I threw away the shoelaces already. Isn't that enough?"

"Just shut up and do what I say. We wouldn't want you to slit your own wrist with that little metal piece later on, now would we?"

Does that mean there will be things in there that might make me want to slit my own wrist?

Also, Bally probably doesn't even make this style of shoe anymore. If I had only known better, I would have taken these shoes to a local cobbler and had twenty copies made. Too late now.

"What's taking you so long?!" the jailer barks, brandishing his baton.

"They are European!" I almost dared to raise my voice.

"Oh yeah?" he snarls. "Then pull out the nails in the heels too. And your leather jacket, take it off."

I can hardly wait for my mug shot.

55

"Walk inside the yellow line," the man wielding the baton points to a narrow strip running alongside the left-hand wall.

Past the metal detectors, a long corridor keeps going without an end in sight. As the ring of keys jingles in the jailer's hands, our steps echo across the cold cement floor.

Now where else have I seen this corridor before?

"Imagine you are swimming in the ocean all by yourself." So began the story as Guru, the resident computer whiz in my Beijing crew, asked everyone at the dinner table a few weeks ago. "Then suddenly, an undercurrent pulls you down. Just as you are about to drown, a hand reaches into the water and saves you. As you come to, you realize that you are inside a boat. Quickly, how many people do you see?"

"Three," I replied.

The answer turned out to signify how many people I considered to be my true friends.

"Upon reaching the shore," Guru continued, "the captain tells you that you must cross the desert ahead until you reach the city. Without knowing how far you must travel, how many pairs of shoes would you bring?"

I looked down at my Ballys and said, "Two."

Which suggested that I would have to fall in love twice before finding true love.

"Then after many days and nights of trekking through the desert, you are all out of food and water. In the distance, you see the silhouette of your destination. But given desert conditions, you don't really know how far away it really is. Then you spot an oasis, which is in another direction, but also much closer. Do you take a detour to the oasis? And if you do, how long do you stay?"

"Oh, hell no." I thought this one was pretty obvious—what would you do when distractions got in the way of your goals? "Just keep going, man. I know what I want."

"Then upon arriving at the city gates, two vicious Tibetan mastiffs are waiting to eat you alive. To gain passage, what do you do?"

"Throw them my old shoes." I didn't have to think about this one at all—always better to elude your obstacles than to tackle them head-on.

"Then once inside the city, you come upon a castle. As the door slowly opens, you are greeted by a woman. What does she look like?"

Now this was a question I liked. After a long journey like that, I'd definitely need a fine-looking woman—tall, voluptuous, with smoky eyes, crescent brows, glowing smile, full lips, natural cleavage, shapely waist, long legs, small ankles, delicate fingers, straight hair if Asian, wavy hair if white, short hair if black. . . . But to keep it simple, I just answered, "Audrey Hepburn." She wasn't really a good fit for my taste, but it was an answer that gave everyone good face.

"Then, following the hostess, you enter a long corridor where frames of pictures are hung on the walls. As you walk through, what do you see in those pictures?"

"Myself."

"Yourself?"

"Yes, you know, as a kid, as a teenager, graduation, first bike, past babes, so on and so on."

"But inside someone else's house?"

I didn't know at the time that the content of those pictures would be interpreted as my understanding of love.

Here and now there is no picture of me, myself, or I on the walls of this real life prison corridor.

Up ahead, I see a staircase going up. But unlike the one at the end of Guru's test, which I ascended as a symbol of my destined-to-be-illustrious career, this one looks more like the creaking death trap outside my family's first apartment in the American Midwest.

Back then, when I was thirteen years old, life felt like prison too—being the only child of a traditionalist Chinese father, I had to live up to all the expectations associated with my lineage, obey all the rules that supposedly "protected" me, and yet overlook the fact that my father never knew my birthday or said that he was proud of me. And thanks to all the Americanization that followed, my relationship with family has only grown worse since. The last time I saw my father, we practically disowned each other. In fact, one of the reasons why I am all the way out here in China is to get away from him.

Now, I wonder if he'd visit, if he only knew where I was going.

"Then once you finally make your way up that staircase"—Guru saved the best for last—"you walk across a pier of clouds, at the end of which you come upon an old man. What does he look like?"

"007."

"Which one?"

"Doesn't matter. It's whatever I want him to look like, right?"

Because he would of course look like me at the end of my pier. For I am that man.

Or was.

I am really starting to hate this déjà vu business.

56

Steel gate. Painted white. Much shorter than I expected; uncomfortably cramped like a shower stall in a Bangkok hotel.

"Thank you, Officer!" A dark, mustached man in his thirties salutes from inside the cell.

Through the bars, he reaches for the supersized padlock hung on the outside latch and tilts it up horizontally for the jailer to open.

This is it—my cell, number 801.

And I thought 8 was supposed to be a lucky number.

It's not a big cell, roughly twenty-five feet long by ten feet wide, with an oddly high twenty-foot ceiling, which only makes it seem more confined. The stucco walls barely retain their white beneath the myriad fingerprints and smudges, while a portion of the left-hand wall is recessed to create space for a series of storage shelves that have a pileup of IKEA plastic bins. Running from the bottom of the right-hand wall and spanning two-thirds of the floor space is a lacquered wooden deck almost a foot high, with the rest of the floor made of gray cement dotted with random spots of black and brown. At the far end of the deck, piles of dark green military blankets sit beneath the lone window that measures roughly three feet by two.

Facing the blankets and with their backs toward the entrance sit rows of men.

And there are two . . . five . . . ten . . . fifteen . . . twenty-four of them, all crammed into a space half the size of a budget motel bedroom.

The Communists couldn't possibly have done better with their communes back in the days.

"Squat by the gate and put your hands over your shoes." The mustached fellow turns to me after thanking the jailer yet again for locking the gate in his face.

"Pay respect to our *da ge*," he commands, pointing to an older man to his left.

Reclining on a roll of blankets pushed up against the wall, *da ge* ("big brother") is probably in his late forties or early fifties. Thin, sunken shoulders, black hair with a sprinkling of white and gray. His face is round and clean-shaven, with single-fold rice eyes that look lethargic, a flat nose that tips up slightly, and bags under his eyes from either sleeping too much or too little. This guy looks more like an accountant than a prison-toughened "big brother."

"How do you do, sir?" I manage a humble nod.

Da ge dips his chin without taking his eyes off the evening papers.

"Now, the rules," the hairy face continues. "One, tiptoe when you walk on the deck. No stomping allowed. Two, you can use the toilet only twice a day, and you must ask *da ge* first."

"But what if I get diarrhea or something?" Which is just bound to happen.

"Hold it." He frowns. "And no walking in the room without permission. Got it?"

"So what do I do during the other times?"

"You sit."

I feel a hemorrhoid coming on already.

"Now go wash your feet," he orders.

"Why?" My lower body is too breezy as is without underwear and socks.

"Who said you could ask questions?" The hairy face clearly means business.

At the end of the left-hand wall is a cubicle measuring six feet long by three feet wide. On the right, a cement washbasin with a single-pipe faucet. On the left, a raised tile platform with a toilet bowl buried into the ground. To use it, I'll have to ascend the platform, squat over the throne with my pants at my ankles, and flush my royals by pushing a metal button on the wall, straight into a visible swamp that collects just a meter or so below ground, the smell of which has a color and shape of its own. Where there should be a door to separate the space inside from the space outside, there isn't. Everything I do in here can and will be heard by everyone, or worse.

"I just took a shower before I came," I try to plead my case.

"Everyone has to wash his feet. That's the rule." The hairy face looks annoyed.

"But I don't have a towel or soap."

"Use those." He points to some black and gray rags piled next to the basin. "And there is soap in there too."

He must be referring to the bag of white powder that looks like rat poison.

In the background, I hear a couple of inmates chuckling.

57

"Welcome aboard," whispers the man to my left as I find an empty spot on the deck, as far away from the hairy face as possible.

He is a few years older than I am. Thin, dark skin, dull gray jacket over dull blue pants, medium-length hair that contains a good amount of dandruff. Judging from his accent, he is from the Yangtze Delta, probably not far away from Shanghai.

"So what are you in for?" he continues.

I tap two fingers on my lips. "And you?"

"Gambling."

"Really? What kind?"

"Dou di zhu."

"Seriously? But . . . have you been to Sanlitun lately?"

"I guess I was just in the wrong place at the wrong time."

"Underground casino?"

"Not exactly a 'casino.'" He grins in embarrassment. "Just an abandoned warehouse with twelve-year-old dealers and crappier security."

"What's the damage?"

"My pay for this month. And last."

"Ouch."

"Yeah. I didn't even finish one round before cops sacked the place."

"So what do you do? Before this, I mean."

"Carpentry," he says. "I made doors in a furniture factory."

Which I suppose would make him Doorman.

"What's that guy's story?" I ask, pointing my chin at our *da ge.*

"Oh, he is the *tou ban* in here."

"What's that?"

"Means 'first on deck.' "

"So you mean he is Chairman?"

"Yeah, I guess you can call him that. And he doesn't do anything either."

"Then what about that *shabi*?" I refer to the hairy-faced man.

"You mean Scruff? He is the second on deck. I heard he has been in and out of prison for almost four years, this time for petty theft. Unless the *tou ban* says something, his word goes."

And I can see why—with those giant fishlike eyes and thick-as-silkworm eyebrows, he just might qualify for a rodeo, as the bull.

"Is there anyone else I should watch out for?"

"Well, that one over there." Doorman points to an even grislier figure. "He is the third on deck."

Maybe this is not the time for a bad joke, but what do you call a fat Chinese guy?

Chunk, of course.

At a modest five feet seven but at least 280 pounds, Chunk is 50 percent wider than anyone else in here. In a country where any girl who wants to have a boyfriend cannot possibly weigh more than 130 pounds, Chunk is a behemoth. With pockmarks all over his face and random stains all over his ribbed white long sleeves, he is about the most uncouth person I have seen in a while—and that counts beggars.

"And the fourth on deck is Sun." Doorman points to a thin middle-aged man. "He actually just got in today too, right before you did. But I heard he is a regular in here, so he's got automatic seniority."

With prominent cheekbones, a sharp nose, and beautiful silver hair, Sun would be quite photogenic if not for the heavy eye bags and a missing front tooth. He's thin and frail; my guess is that he is more of a counselor than an enforcer.

"So what's your rank?" I ask Doorman.

"Not sure. Probably in the twenties." He scans the other men in the room. "It doesn't really matter once outside of the top four. In here, they are the Government; we are the People."

"Then what kind of work do you . . . I mean we . . . have to do?"

"Everything." He shrugs. "Wipe the deck, wash the laundry, clean the toilet . . ."

"Who gets the nasty stuff?"

"You do."

"Me?"

"Yeah, because you are *mo ban*."

As in "last on deck."

5 8

As a bit of consolation, the TV hung above the cell gate actually works. It is at least a fourteen-incher and perhaps no more than twenty years old. The thing even has color.

Unfortunately, the signal is not too clear, there is no remote, and the channel is locked on CCTV.

On screen, three couples are put to a shopping contest: each is given a budget and a shopping list, and the couple who fills the shopping list first and under budget wins. Sounds bland enough, even boring to the point of no return. Well, there is a twist.

Two of the three couples consist of a local and a foreigner. And out of the two foreigners, one is blond, two are females, and both are cute when fumbling in Chinese. So by default, the camera has been fixated on these two exotic zoo animals since the beginning, including close-ups, fast-forwards, and every sound effect that can possibly make them look funnier than they really are. Chances are, they never signed up to do the show that they ended up doing. But that's how it is: television equals face; and a foreigner can only give China good face on its own television.

Come to think of it, I really should have told Lethal Weapon a long time ago what a great thing he is doing at his network. He has a different type of China dream than many other foreigners in this country. Given his talent, he could live a lot more comfortably than he does now if he would just conform to the "cultural differences" a little bit. The problem, however, is that Lethal is a cowboy; and cowboys don't like being comedians.

So will he succeed? Instead of having a foreigner discuss embarrassing topics such as why every successful Chinese man keeps an *ernai* (mistress) outside of marriage, would his employer prefer him to don ancient Chinese costumes, play ancient Chinese music, perform ancient Chinese opera, or simply put on an "I wish I'd been born Chinese" circus? As a foreigner, Lethal can get many opportunities in China that the locals do not, but there is a cost. Even though a lot of what he wants to say will have to be said if Chinese media are to stop being the laughingstock that they are today, such things can be said, if at all, only by a person with a Chinese face.

So who is this Chinese face?

As a returnee, I too get many opportunities in China that the locals do not. While I may not get the modeling or English-teaching
gigs as easily as some foreigners do, given my Chinese features,
those same features make it much easier for the locals to relate to me
at first glance and from a distance. As a result, I can appear on a
CCTV show that is broadcast nationwide to 1.3 billion people
without being made into a cartoon figure, whereas Lethal's program
is broadcast only via satellite to a much smaller urban audience and
with twice the headache. In terms of its potential for influence, my
opportunity is arguably even greater than Lethal's. But have I given
my opportunity the same amount of effort that Lethal has given his?

Back in April, the producer of *Happy Heroes* gave me a lecture
on why Chinese television is the way it is; and I was upset by how
the restrictions made me look less "cool" than otherwise. Now I
wonder: Could I have somehow turned my resentment into something positive? Could I have taken the time to give the crew some
constructive criticism, such that future installments of *Happy Heroes* would include unrehearsed emotions, unscripted interviews,
and maybe even some individuality?

Of course, there is no guarantee that any of my ideas would have
been accepted, or if accepted, would have caused enough change in
the last six months to make even a few of the People realize just how
badly xenophobic the show they are hooked on right now really is.
But even attempting a baby step is better than nothing: someone
else just might take a giant leap from the baby step that I helped
make happen. After all, my *Happy Heroes* turned out to be the most
successful reality show that CCTV has had to date. And not
everyone—not even a foreigner as deserving as Lethal Weapon—
gets opportunities like this.

But, I blew it. After staying in this shit-hole long enough, I just
might like CCTV as much as the rest of them.

59

The wall-mounted clock chimes 9:30 P.M. No more CCTV.

Simultaneously, the People swarm toward the blankets stacked next to the window, each one jostling for the newest and presumably warmest in the pile. Once successful, each inmate lays down one blanket as a cushion against the hard wooden deck, uses another for cover, and rolls up his own outer wardrobe to form a pillow. They lie side by side with barely an inch of space between the bodies and wrap themselves from head to toe in the smell of hundreds of other men who have previously sweated, farted, and done Mao knows what else inside these faded green fabrics.

If I want any warmth tonight, I better follow suit pronto.

But I have never even cut into a subway token line before.

"Stop." Scruff gets in the way of my survival as a conformist. "Make the bed for *da ge* first."

But what the hell for? His blankets are already laid out one on top of another and neatly rolled into a pile that is kept separate from all the rest. All he has to do is unroll it. And unlike all of us, he has a virtually brand-new set of blankets with his own name written in black ink and a small pillow that he keeps in a private plastic bin at his end of the deck. Whatever happened to being one with the People?

"Straighten out the corners!" Scruff smacks my head. "And press out those wrinkles!"

I keep tripping on my sliding, buttonless Levi's.

"There are too many people in here to fit on the deck," Scruff continues. "Some of you will sleep on the floor."

Which of course referred to me, right next to the bathroom no less. And by now, the only blanket left is a rag that has been worn down to a paisley white despite having been, I believe, dark green once upon a time.

A few feet above my head, the window glass rattles arrhythmically to the evening winds. Through cracks in the window frame, a harsh draft ices down my face in sync with the cold cement on my back. The white fluorescent lamp hanging off the ceiling is never going to be turned off, while the twenty-four other inmates continue their chorus of snoring and flatulence. About four feet to my right is the squat toilet; I can almost hear the percolating of human feces in the swamp below.

If I only didn't care about my face so much, maybe I could actually cry myself to sleep. . . .

OCTOBER 15

60

D'OH!!!

What the hell is that dripping down my neck?!

And why the hell is my face all—

Did this smudge-faced, runny-nosed, monkey-looking bag of shit just douse my head with icy cold gunk from Mao-knows-where?

WHAT THE FUCK DID HE DO THAT FOR?!

"Get up!" He glances at the surveillance cameras high on the wall. "Five o'clock. Your turn."

"My turn to what?!"

"Stand watch."

"Watch what?"

"Watch us sleep." He throws a plastic orange jersey into my chest.

The neon yellow characters read "Prisoner."

Outside, it is still pitch dark. Other than the inmates' snoring, the only sound I hear is the swiveling of surveillance cameras.

It's Friday morning; or, rather, still Thursday night. Ordinarily I'd still be up, just done with the day's last Ziggy with Lethal Weapon and walking home from Sanlitun. I like that walk. It's two miles long, crossing three big intersections, the Second Ring Road, and an overpass. At this time of night there are few cars on the road, and almost no people. Even though there is usually no star to be seen given the thick pollution, it always feels cleaner at night than during the day. As one cannot see the dust at night, either.

If I were in some big city in the West, like, say, New York, I probably wouldn't walk such a long distance all by myself so late at night. But here in China, I have never felt unsafe. Countless times I have taken this walk, right through what is probably the most heavily trafficked area in all of Beijing after working hours. Yet I have never come across anyone who scared me in the slightest. Sure, there are pimps and hookers and the occasional drunks (some of the last group being obnoxious foreigners), but they are always just annoying, not scary. Most of the time, I felt like I was the baddest man in the whole neighborhood.

When I spoke to Doorman earlier, he said that other than Chairman, Scruff, Chunk, Sun, and myself everybody in 801 got arrested for either gambling or stealing bicycles.

"So there is no serial killer in here?" I almost felt gypped for being locked up with a bunch of really small small-timers.

"Of course not." He chuckled. "This is China—we *have* no serial killers."

Well, actually, there are serial killers in China, just a lot fewer of them, with a lot fewer victims apiece than in the West. Of course, there is a chance that the government is withholding the truth on this matter by virtue of its iron grip on the media, but just based on my own observation, China is pretty darn safe.

But why is that? There are fifteen million people in this city; how can the streets be so safe and quiet? Well, could it be because the police lock up people for up to eight months just for getting high—that everyone is so intimidated by overly harsh sentences, far harsher than the weight of the crimes, that nobody dares to commit crimes?

As an American lawyer, I had always been skeptical of the Chinese legal system. Now that I have actually made it into Chinese prison, I'd like to go ahead and declare it completely unconstitutional. Unlike America, China has no Miranda warning, no Bill of Rights, not even the right to an attorney. I have no idea what is happening next, nor where to find out. Had this happened in America, I would have at least seen my lawyer by now; even in the worst-case scenario, I'd post bail within a few hours and make up for everything with a week of community service. For China to actually become the country respecting the rule of law that it constantly advertises itself to be, it'd better learn something from the Americans pronto.

Except that in exchange, I'd probably have to at least give up the 5 A.M. solo walks that I enjoy so much.

It is unfortunate really, but compared to China, America is almost a war zone; and thanks to its system, criminals seem to know a lot more about their rights than law-abiding citizens know about theirs. As a believer in human rights, I of course champion the doctrine of "presumed innocent until proven guilty." But when one hears the ad on American radio that goes, "Been arrested? Fight back!" it is easy to question whether a system that purports to place individual rights and freedom above all else actually delivers on its promises.

So could there be a middle ground—a system that combined the preventive rewards of China's harsh punishments and the equitable safeguards of America's due process? China is now developing; everything is changing. So if there is a place on earth where such a system might come into being in the near future, it could arguably be in China. Yet with all the skills that I have been blessed with, what did I do to help make this happen?

Thinking back to the WIT case, could I have done anything more to help the Captain? Granted, my adversary had way more arsenal than I did, and a full-on engagement would have likely dragged on for months if not years; but at the end of the day, the law—at least as written—was on our side. As unreliable as its enforcement may be in China, the only way to improve the system would be to keep on pushing our just cause. Considering how badly cash-strapped WIT already was at the time, maybe I could have offered to handle the case on a contingency basis or even gone as far as *pro bono*.

But in my heart, the case never had a fighting chance against GUNS's ballistic *guan xi* and my time would have been much better spent on some "big case" that I was destined to win.

Here and now, that "big case" is staring at me right in the face.

And I seem to have already lost.

Ahh-hrrrrrrr-*shhh-toot!*

Brilliant. Judging from the echo, it must have been one thick loogie.

With all the China hype that has been going on since the new millennium, one would think that all these uncivilized habits would soon cease. Otherwise, how would the world see China as anything but a nation of Gucci-loving spitters? Two thousand years ago, the Great Wall was built with mortar made out of congee and saliva; how much longer will the same technique be used to hold together China's increasngly futuristic facade?

In today's world, building a skyscraper is no longer a big deal, nor is blowing holes through mountains to build highways or filling in the ocean to reclaim land. For all those are just material progress. Here in China, the latest technology is readily available to most urbanites. From mobile phones to laptops, the gadgets that China has are no different from those found in America, and in some cases are even newer, cheaper, and better. In terms of materialism, the gap between China and the outside world is closing rapidly.

But in terms of social consciousness and everyday civility, the gap is hardly diminishing. Since as early as the 1980s, the Chinese government has been urging its people not to spit in public. But even now, more than two decades later, a lot of locals still spit whenever and wherever they like—on the sidewalk, on the bus, even on the floor between their feet while eating in a restaurant. Why? I'm no sociologist; but maybe it is because the government itself stands at the forefront of China's spitters, as so viscously demonstrated by the prison guard who launches at will inside his own workplace.

And here he is, a middle-aged man with a paunch, not particularly worthy of a description. In China there are millions upon millions just like him, who not only constitute the backbone of China's economic revolution, but also embody all of the bad habits that come with growing up in a Third World country. As recently as yesterday, I would have called him some derogatory name and blamed him for making China the homeland that I have become embarrassed to embrace. Now, I don't know what to do.

But fortunately, he is already middle-aged. Give it another thirty to fifty years, he will be history and China will be free of spitters. We can't teach old dogs new tricks, but there is always hope for the next generation, like these teenagers spread out on the deck and pavement right now. Indeed, maybe this kid who is waking up as we speak knows better than to spit like the prison guard who could be his father.

Or maybe not. The rumble in the kid's esophagus did not have as much gusto as the prison guard's, but the technique was virtually identical; and the loogie landed no more than an inch away from the head of another inmate sleeping on the pavement.

"Hey!" the suddenly vigilant guard yells at the son he never had. "No spitting! Don't let me catch you again, got it?!"

Well, that sure sounded familiar. Not too long ago, I heard it from someone else, only much louder and more menacing, and ending with something like, "Do it again and you are fired!"

Yes, it was me; and I was yelling at my Foodiez boys for spitting on the office floor. Now that I look at some of the younger People a little closer, they really do look like some of my employees before I whipped them into shape.

But here and now, I wonder if they have really learned their lesson. For sure, my delivery boys don't spit in front of me anymore, but do they go on a spitting spree as soon as I turn my back? The fact is, no one likes to be yelled at. Instead of coercion, it is always persuasion that gets the job done in the long run. According to a Chinese maxim, "Those who are close to rouge turn red; those who are close to ink turn black." In other words, people change by osmosis. In order for good changes to happen, there has to be a good influence in the first place. So have I been a good influence to anybody?

For two and a half years, I have owned Foodiez. I have a dozen employees, yet I can name only two of them at the most and have no idea where any of them live. Looking and smelling the way they did upon our first acquaintance, they were always just going to be my pawns and thus kept at a distance. On the rare occasion that I actually spoke to those who remain nameless, I was either yelling at them for not smelling right or threatening to fire them if they failed to comb their hair again.

Granted, I don't spit on the office floor and have never stunk like a skunk, but without giving any additional attention to these kids, how could I expect them to drop all the bad habits learned in the only environment they've ever known? And during those times away from the office, what was I doing? Getting high? On several occasions I even had my boys pick up the stuff from Prince and deliver it to where I was rolling up, while they were still working!

So what happened? Once upon a time, I actually treated others with manners and respect. Why did I change once I got to China?

Well, believe it or not, part of it had to be the ease of living here—there is no need to tip in a restaurant no matter how fancy it is, no need to park your car, for cabs are so cheap to take, and not even a need to wash your own dishes as everyone has a cleaning lady. In the blink of an eye, many First World responsibilities ordinarily associated with being an adult simply disappear.

Then, slowly but surely, the headaches of living here get to you—the pollution, the construction, all the MSG and lard compelled by "cultural differences." An otherwise calm and amicable you becomes angrier, more easily agitated, a prime candidate for all the One A Days that consumed me for the three years leading up to this moment.

And finally, the amount of praise, envy, and opportunity that you get just because you're an outsider is the perfect recipe for an ego trip. Everywhere you go, you draw instant attention, whether because of your skin color, hair color, eye color, or just having something other than Chinese coming out of your mouth. Whatever it is that you want, someone will help you just so that you can teach him or her a phrase or two of English. If you are anything like me, your superiority complex might get worse than it already is.

So you start to think that the world—or at least China—revolves around you. You'll ride the biggest motorcycle in spite of the moto-ban, sleep with three different girls at different times in one day without always wearing a condom, and expect to get more pay than any local employee in a company other than the CEO himself even though you have zero working experience and your native tongue is French. If there is a clash of opinions between you and China, it is China who needs to change, not you. And if something does not go your way, just give the ignorant local your middle finger and call him *"shabi."*

So now that I think about it, my employees have really had it tough. For barely 1,200 *kuai* a month, they must take not only the attitudes of my demanding customers but also my expectations of their being punctual, efficient, and even well groomed. For two and a half years, I have been an elusive dictator who either never showed up or yelled and screamed when he did. No wonder I have such high turnover in my staff and lose company properties to disgruntled employees.

And now, I might just be gone from Foodiez for good. With my mobile confiscated, my staff has no chance of locating me. After a few more weeks of my being incommunicado, they just might assume that I have forgotten all about the start-up that I once whipped into shape. Would they be saddened by my mysterious disappearance? Or would they just hold a spitting celebration right there on the office floor followed by a looting of the office safe?

It's only 5:45 A.M. This watch is gonna drag on like a bitch.

62

OUCH!

That's the second knuckle drilled into my skull since daybreak!

"Shabi!" Scruff stabs my cheeks with his beard while his spittle irrigates my ear. "Are you deaf or are you stupid? I said, *'No moving around!'"*

Which apparently includes dipping my sleepy head.

At 7 A.M. I woke from my standing sleep to a scratchy tune played through the intercom. Surprisingly, it was Beethoven's "Für Elise" instead of the Chinese national anthem.

Yawning with morning breath outstinking the latrine, the People put back on the crumpled clothes that they used as pillows and piled up the blankets at the usual place on the deck. As only those in the Government have toiletries to brush and wash; the People simply wiped their dirty faces with their hands, combed their oily

hair with their fingers, and cleaned their yellowing teeth with their
tongues.

Then, three in a row and up to eight in a column, we sat down on
the deck with our faces toward the window.

"Sit up straight!" General Scruff paces up and down the narrow
cement pavement in his orange prisoner jersey. "Keep your heads up!
Do not lean against the wall! Do not speak! And don't you dare sleep!"

And so this is our daily activity, the one and only. I asked Doorman in a whisper if we ever get to go outside to get some sun, run a
few laps, or even play some soccer, just like the way they do in prison
yards on television. He giggled.

Piled less than two feet away are the urine-scented blankets we
slept in last night, any one of which would be ideal for cushioning
my burning ass right about now. Other than the occasional dragging
of shackles down the hallway and Scruff's drubbing of human
skulls, the only sounds are of jailers launching loogies as they patrol
the blocks.

Unless given permission by Scruff, I must sit with my legs crossed
like a Buddhist monk, with no pivoting, no twisting, no slouching,
no talking, no standing, and definitely no farting (which brought on
my first knuckle). At any given time, there can be no more than three
people standing in the cell, with each one required to put on the orange prisoner jersey, and I have no shot at that privilege anyway as
the rookie punching bag. As for latrine privileges, the no-crapping-
before-dinner rule is enforced rather strictly—so far, two kids have
already been sentenced to squat over the toilet for fifteen minutes
each without actually being allowed to relieve themselves.

In a way, this is like primary school, only much worse. Back
then, I had to sit upright through six hour-long classes each day.
Sure, I had a chair with a backrest, but I also had to sit with my arms
crossed *behind* my back. Along with wearing the little red scarf to

school every day, this was one of many ways the Chinese government instilled obedience in its future citizens. Being the most restless sitter, I got my palms slapped by Ms. Deng's iron ruler all the time. Here and now, instead of staring at a blackboard, I get the pleasure of staring out an almost decent-sized window high up on the wall. Unfortunately, Ms. Deng's iron ruler has been upgraded to Scruff's bare knuckle.

From behind, I hear Chairman's flipping of the morning paper, which he came into possession of after being let out of the cell for an hour. His job, as much as I have gathered since last night, really consists of nothing. Unless, of course, you consider sitting, pacing, reading his newspaper, sitting, pacing again, sitting again, rereading his newspaper, pacing, and pacing again to be a job, while we the People just sit and sit and sit.

Out of the three executives in the Government, Scruff is the toughest. Since daybreak, he must have called me *shabi* five times, and the amplifier in his belly is only getting stronger.

As for Chunk, he is really a symbolic presence. If Scruff gives an order of "Sit up" or "Shut up," Chunk will repeat it. But he never initiates any command: he is just not quick enough to catch anyone misbehaving. If their looks weren't so different, I'd say he is an older version of Sloppy, maybe a little smarter, but almost sloppier. Given how much fatter he is than everyone else, he automatically commands a little extra respect, even if just for the will to keep lugging all that weight around. Right now, he is talking to Sun about how to lose some weight. His plan: to eat absolutely no meat and to stand more.

So far, Sun has been the nicest. Maybe it is because he just arrived, but he has yet to bark out any orders at me. Unlike Scruff and Chunk, he doesn't look like a bum, but a step above, right where bums and blue collars connect. And compared to the rest of 801 (excluding me and Chairman), he looks cleaner, which leads me to suspect that he is one of the few local Beijing-*ren* represented in our happy little family.

Around me, the People continue to sit, and sit well. On the surface, none of them seem to be bothered by ankles jarring against the hard deck, knees throbbing from prolonged bending, or any shooting pain in the tailbone. But I bet they all are. They just don't show it, for they can suffer more—there must be a correlation between poverty and endurance.

So far, I have counted twenty-two iron bars in the window. Forty-three cracks around the window frame. And fifty-two rings of swirls in my middle finger.

Looking out the window, there is nothing but blue sky, not a cloud in sight, the most glorious day yet since my last Zigarette. All this color is making me a little sick to the stomach.

If I weren't stuck here, what would I be doing? Running laps around Houhai? Riding my motorcycle into the mountains? Or perhaps something even freer—like two weeks of horseback riding in Inner Mongolia?

Freedom.

Once upon a time, I looked out another window much like this one, except that it had shutters and was in Shanghai. From the ages of six to ten, looking out the window from my family's third-floor apartment was the highlight of my daily after-school activities. My father never gave me a reason why I couldn't play with my friends before he or my mother got home. It was just a rule I had to follow. It was then that I first started thinking about freedom, which was simply to escape from control and supervision.

Then after college and law school, I came to redefine freedom as the ability to do whatever I wanted, even if it was hazardous, as long as I didn't hurt anyone else. And it made sense, because unlike any definition I might have had before, it required a balance between *I* and the others.

Then a few years later, I moved to China.

Before I got here, I did expect everything to be less "free." After all, ever since witnessing Tiananmen 1989 on CNN, I had learned that a Chinese national can never openly denounce the Chinese government, pay tribute to the Dalai Lama, or practice Falun Gong. And to meet their annual targets under the One Child Policy, some rural village heads can even force abortions by stabbing needles into pregnant women's wombs. Unlike in America, the people of China hardly debate what constitutes "freedom." Instead, the government tells them what it is. And it has the authority to do so by virtue of tradition—for five thousand years, China has been an autocracy.

But then I arrived. And to my surprise, I didn't really feel any *less* free.

Here in China, just like in America, I could buy a house, own a car, open a business, and travel anywhere for pleasure (subject only to the visa requirements imposed by countries like America on Chinese passport holders, not by the Chinese government itself). Given how badly rosy the local media are, I of course kept reading the occasional dissident stories on CNN, and even opened a few missionary e-mails from Falun Gong Central. But when I looked around, none of those alleged persecutions ever happened around me, or around any of my friends or any of their friends.

And being an English-speaking returnee, I had even more freedom to enjoy. From partying till dawn on a Tuesday night to paying one-eighth the U.S. prices for everything, I actually had far *more* material freedom here than I ever had in America. As for the more spiritual stuff such as freedom of speech and religion, I also soon realized that not everything was what CNN had once led me to believe.

Having traveled to Tibet and witnessed just how poor and unde-veloped the region was and how much worse it would obviously be without economic assistance from the Chinese government, I now questioned the merit of the Dalai Lama's quest for Tibetan inde-pendence. Having studied economics in college and then having witnessed firsthand just how economically stifling 1.3 billion people can be, I now appreciated the government's interest in curbing pop-ulation growth and would urge those in China's rural areas to coop-erate with the One Child Policy. As for Falun Gong, I shall reserve my judgment until the day when some sexually charged scandal exposes its founder in the same manner that other religious leaders have been in the past. And even when it came to denouncing the government, the prohibition did not extend to bitching about the Chinese Communist Party inside a taxicab, which was apparently done by everyone (especially the cabbie) on a daily basis.

So when all things are considered, could China really be as free as America, or, Mao forbid, even freer?

From the perspective of any government, freedom is like a jigsaw puzzle. Depending on the specific circumstances of the country, the puzzle will take on different shapes and images. So when I say that China might be as free as America is, I am not suggesting that the two countries are free in the same way.

In the American jigsaw, people get a bigger piece for freedom of speech, but smaller pieces for other things. Whether on paper or in practice, there is little tolerance for driving without a license, fudging of tax records, or unwarranted issuance of prescription drugs for kickbacks from pharmaceutical companies. In the Chinese jigsaw, the pieces are sized just the opposite. In exchange for the masses keeping quiet about civil rights and suffrage, more leeway is given in a great many things related to economics. Indeed, if Enron had happened in China, Arthur Andersen would probably still be in business.

Of course, this is not to say that cheating is legal in China. But due to the national population and systemic inefficiency, the government does not have the economic means to enforce all the laws all the time. Instead, it can enforce only some of the laws once in a while; and a few particular ones (like the prohibition against publicly denouncing the Chinese Communist Party) must be enforced at all times just so that the government can keep itself in power so as to occasionally enforce the other laws that keep this society under control and growing economically.

Today, despite the many imperfections that are still often disguised as "cultural differences," the Chinese can now enjoy cars, houses, and other material freedoms that they never had before. And as these are much more practical freedoms than the freedom to stand on a soapbox and preach, only a select group (namely, the CNN-favorite dissidents) occupy themselves with dissing the government. Indeed, even those students who participated in Tiananmen 1989 have gone on to become lawyers, bankers, and CEOs of new private companies that not only deal with, but in fact rely upon, the government for success.

But for the sake of argument, let us assume that in one fell swoop, China came to allow as much freedom of speech as there is in America, and all of the dissident stories told on CNN (which we all know can never be wrong or hyped) were actually reporteded on CCTV. What would happen then? Would it be enough to create widespread resentment toward the government, spark yet another revolution, set the country back by another fifty years, and allow the Americans to somehow play the big brother again and set up a new colony for the future? And even if that didn't happen, would it lead down a slippery slope where the public would also demand the freedom to bear arms and other questionable freedoms that might or might not have made America the crime-ridden society that it is today? None of these questions have definitive answers, of course; but then, how lucky do you feel?

Plus, through the Internet and pirated satellite dishes, the Chinese are already learning just *how* free countries like America are—not only in terms of the sizes of the individual jigsaw pieces such as freedom of speech, but also the side effects of having the jigsaw being shaped in that way. And given the inevitability of this increased awareness, the government has no choice but to revise continually its own way of defining freedom, as demonstrated by its more and more frequent prosecution of internal corruption and appointment of better-trained technocrats to higher government posts.

So perhaps, once China's construction dust finally settles, its concept of freedom will change as well. On the one hand, the government will have more means (whether through increased funds or increased efficiency) to better enforce the laws it already has while making more laws; on the other hand, the people's priorities will evolve, resulting in a higher demand for things that they currently have less of, such as freedom of speech, freedom of religion, and the right to bear multiple children.

Now, speaking for myself, I never really had much of a beef with Chinese freedom. After all, I am still single, am agnostic at best, and never cared too much about CCTV until last night. Other than the moto-ban, I cared for only one piece that was conspicuously missing from the Chinese freedom puzzle: the freedom to get high. It has been more than 160 years since the Opium War, and a lot has changed. It would only help China for it to realize that not all drugs are bad like opium and not all smokers are bad people. I wanted others to admire my Zigarette not only for its craftsmanship, but also for the "freedom" of the act itself. I wanted them to say, "Hey, there goes a handsome and robust young man who is enjoying some big numb, and he is Chinese; so it must not be so bad for us. How paranoid we have been all along."

But in reality, someone must have been pretty bothered by my daily expression of "freedom." Given 160 years, China's rift with drugs runs deep, with so many ingrained memories that a transformation in attitude and awareness could be fostered only by constructive education over time, not in-your-face violations of the law. Even I myself would not like it if someone lit up a cigar around me, and that's legal, whereas hashish smells twice as strong and looks just like opium.

So why the lapse in judgment? Was it some subconscious urge to make up for a repressed childhood, or the spoiled outsider in me who thought that my definition of "freedom" should apply to everyone else?

Well, probably both.

But more than anything else could it be that my definition of freedom—doing what I want without hurting anyone else—is fundamentally flawed? After all, despite its requisite balancing of opposing interests, it was I, and only I, who applied the test each time.

But then, how should I define freedom if it does not start with "I"?

There are, so far, 423 cotton stubbles on the blanket at the top of the pile. And counting.

Ain't freedom a bitch.

63

"How are you, *da ge*? You look great!" Scruff is sucking up again.

But this time, he is bowing with one knee on the ground to a boy half his age.

The boy, a juvenile inmate who is pushing a water wagon from cell to cell, fits a nozzle through the bars and into a green bucket held in Scruff's hands. The smell of plastic mixes in with that of the latrine as the scalding H_2O melts off carcinogenic particles from our prison-grade container. Judging from a similar exercise this morning, this half bucket will be all the water we get from now (11:15 A.M.) till dinner. To drink it, one must use the only cup that is available for all of us (except for Chairman, of course, who has his own set of everything). But as there are twenty-five inmates to share in this wealth, of which the Government takes at least half, none of the People can actually drink more than half a cup; and the person stuck with the last sip will just have to disregard the unidentifiable sediments at the bottom of the barrel.

"Thank you, *da ge*. You look great!" Scruff bows a half dozen more times as the water boy walks off without acknowledgment.

Upon seeing Scruff's first kowtow of the day earlier this morning (when he did the exact same thing for our breakfast water supply), I almost couldn't believe my own eyes.

"But what are you gonna do?" asked Doorman with a shrug. "Without it, we wouldn't even get half a bucket."

This is just how China works.

Go to any restaurant on Ghost Street, and you are guaranteed to spot (maybe even at your own table) a suck-up-athon involving a bunch of local businessmen. For every such table, there is at least one *zong* (pronounced "ds-own"), meaning "big boss," who gets that honor for being a supposed shot caller in his company and will be addressed as such by everyone at the table. In actuality, Mr. Chen (or Chen *Zong*) might be only third assistant to the VP of marketing. But then, it is his relation to the others at the table that determines who is a *zong* and who is not.

For the duration of the meal, at least one non-*zong* will periodically applaud Chen *Zong* for his long list of special qualities, including his youth, looks, uncanny ability to drink an ocean of *bai jiu,* extensive knowledge of the world without having ever left China, and just generally his being key to his company's ultimate success or failure.

But can you blame them? Now that the economy is booming, everyone wants to be a *zong*. For those who have less-than-stellar résumés but still want to seize the opportunities instead of just seeing them, dream jobs and big breaks have to be earned through ways other than substantive knowledge. To help build the *guan xi* that is necessary to move forward, some have no choice but to suck up, or *pai ma pi,* which means to "slap a horse's ass" (so that the horse will run and take them where they want to go). Indeed, if someone goes through life without ever performing *pai ma pi,* he just might end up as the busboy refilling Chen *Zong*'s teacup.

Or worse.

Shortly after the water boy moves on, a slightly older youngster pulls up with a flatbed holding stacks of bamboo trays piled a mile high. After counting the inmates in our cell, he stuffs a batch of steaming white buns through the steel bars.

Once again, it's *mantou* (pronounced "mahn-tow"), a solid white steamed bun that tastes like nothing and chews like yeast. And unlike the way they might be served outside prison, these *mantous* are neither fried nor dipped in condensed milk.

"Thank you, *da ge*! You look wonderful today, even better than yesterday." The young inmate ordered by Scruff to fetch the *mantou*s seems even better at *pai ma pi* than Scruff is.

"I bet you'd never see something like that in America, right?" Doorman sighs quietly.

"Oh, no way." In America, if a boy his age *pai ma pi'd* like that, the school punks would have a field day on his ass. Over there, people just don't, well, suck up quite the same. Instead, we have Hallmark to help us get the job done. After an interview, send a thank-you card to every person you just met with, not because you care, but because you want the job. In essence, you are sucking up, but to give ourselves some face, we call it "professional courtesy."

So in this regard, I should really correct Doorman's statement. When he first explained to me the necessity of *pai ma pi* over breakfast, I said to myself, "Here's yet another 'cultural difference.' " And the quotes around the term automatically meant that we outsiders would never do such things. But in actuality could I have been blinded by monumental exaltations of my own virtues?

Indeed, if I had just *pai'd* a little *ma pi* in the past, I might not be where I am now.

"*Mo ban!*" Scruff must have caught me thinking too much. "Your turn to fetch the rest."

My knees buckle from sitting too much as I tiptoe for the last bin on the shelf.

A middle-aged man pulls up with an oil drum lying on a two-wheeled trellis. Through a metal siphon placed between the bars, he ladles something into my bin. Upon contact, the thick liquid splashes like diarrhea. As the contents swirl in a whirlpool, I can see yellow and green, plus bits of rust and dust from the drum they were stored in.

If I am not mistaken, it is boiled cabbage instead of yellow cornmeal grits (the latter being what we had for breakfast). Do I have to wait until dinner for some real food? Whoever is running this place sure is smart—deprive us of all protein and hormones so we'll never have the energy to dig a tunnel or stage a riot. Am I actually going to eat this stuff? I'll faint if I don't; I'll probably throw up if I do, and then faint.

Now what? The cabbage man is slowing down his ladling.

I look up. Our eyes meet. His brows seem heavy, the look in his eyes unfriendly. He wants something.

"Thank you, *da ge*." I dig up some gratitude from my empty stomach.

His face looks the same.

"THANK YOU, *da ge*." I dig even deeper.

Still nothing.

What does he want? A compliment? A *pai ma pi* that he looks "fabulous"? Does it have to be this way? He is already out there walking around while I am stuck in here sitting and starving, and he wants me to suck up for some damn cabbage that even real horses wouldn't eat?

But if the bin doesn't get to be at least a third full, someone will end up starving as a result of my unwillingness to play by the rules. And, being *mo ban,* that person is guaranteed to be me.

So why be such a hard-ass? Why can't I suck up a little more with a little less packaging? It's not so hard. Who cares if I tell this cabbage-ladling Quasimodo that he looks fabulous like Fabio? What do I have to lose? Integrity? Self-respect? How much is that a pound, or kilo?

OUCH! I swear if he knuckles me one more goddamn time . . .

"Sorry, *da ge*." Scruff bows to the cabbage master nervously. "This *shabi* is new. You look fabulous, really, you do."

64

I can't believe I'm hungry again already.

Once lunch was over, I was ordered to wrap my hands in some rat-skin-like rags and push them up and down the floor in an ass-in-the-air sprint. The purpose was to wipe up all the crumbs and drippings left over by twenty-five leaky mouths, even though the floor is so beyond Mr. Clean that the entire exercise was more impractical than an Olympic event. And just when I thought I was getting the hang of it, I tripped over my slipping jeans, bruised my chin during the ensuing fall, and shed some flesh when my pinky scraped against bumps in the pavement. Then after that, I had to wash the communal utensils in the latrine basin while Scruff and Chunk exempted themselves from the rules by taking turns crapping into the squat-hole behind me.

Now, back to silence. Just like in kindergarten, we have to take naps.

But there is no sleep for me. Until fresh blood comes in, I stay as *mo ban*, and *mo ban* always stands watch.

"By the way," Sun warned me before dozing off, "stand up straight. No walking. No fidgeting. No funny noises. No unnecessary movements. Don't think for a minute that no one is watching."

So far, I have tried to imagine a meadow. But it smells like pee. For a second, I even thought about a naked woman. But I had to stop, for it just made me horny on top of being miserable. If I could just do lunch all over again (and that's all I ask), what would it be? Would I mind the last dinner on Ghost Street as much? Or the last Korean ramen I had in Sanlitun? Or maybe something warm and sweet, like the *tang yuans* that Mom and I used to make for Spring Festival.

Spring Festival is China's biggest holiday. When I was a child, it was the happiest time of the year, not only for the fireworks that came with the occasion, but also for the good times that I got to spend with Mom. Back then, it was just the two of us. With my father far away in America, I was the man of the house. Come Spring Festival, which lasts fifteen days and thus involves many family gatherings, I had to help her with all the cooking and cleaning around our modest home.

In Chinese tradition, the fifteenth—and thus last—day of the Spring Festival is a time for *tang yuan,* which literally means "circles in a soup" and is a dessert composed of sticky rice balls filled with sweet sesame or red bean and served in warm, clear broth. Today, one can purchase *tang yuans* from any supermarket with dozens of brands to choose from. Back in 1987, they had to be made from scratch.

To get the ingredients, Mom would take me to the farmers' bazaar, where we searched for the perfect sticky rice, black sesame, and red beans. The markets back then were just baskets, cages, and stands huddled along the sidewalk. The street would be littered with loose vegetable leaves, chicken feathers, and even fish intestines; but that was how to tell a good market from a bad one—the heavier the debris, the heavier the traffic, hence the better and fresher the foods were. As everyone would be shopping for the Spring Festival at that time, the whole mission would take hours, for at least ten minutes would be spent on haggling with the farmer over every single item.

After soaking the sticky rice in water for about a day, Mom would somehow procure an old-fashioned mill and set it in the middle of our living room. It was gray, about three feet tall, and made entirely of stone. The wheel was about the size of a large pizza, with a wooden handle on top to guide the turn and a cup-sized opening for inserting the soaked sticky rice. As the man of the house, I turned the wheel to do the grinding while Mom did the scooping. With each circular push and tug, a cascade of rice cream seeped from between the wheel and the base and collected in various cloth bags that would be hung above the sink to drain out the excess water and become dough. In retrospect, the grinding was far more strenuous than playing the violin, but I loved it, especially when I got to grind up the black sesame, which filled our small apartment with a unique fragrance that came only once a year.

By the morning of the fifteenth day, I would already have eaten at least half of the *tang yuans*. Unlike the machine-made ones you can now buy in the frozen-food section, the ones Mom and I made shone with a translucent glow and always tasted sweeter, stickier, better.

Okay, knock it off. This is getting embarrassing. If I were really to think about where the *tang yuans* of my life happened, I'd almost have to admit that I am missing home. But as I've already told the Kid at Café 44, I'm now *si hai wei jia*, meaning that I live among the four seas and that the world is my home—the world!

But what does that mean?

Ever since leaving the family nest at seventeen, I have more or less run the gamut in the types of homes that I have had. From the ghetto to the villas, I've tried them all. Some were very lavishly decked out, as close to "home in a box" as I ever got to. Yet compared to my very first home in Shanghai, where we had neither heating nor air-conditioning and had to share a communal bathroom with two other families on the same floor, none could match the memory of Spring Festivals and making *tang yuans* with Mom.

Then after three years in China, I have become more and more minimalist in the way I treat my abode. As of now, the only pieces of home decoration I own are a vase that is always empty and a stereo that can't play any bootlegs. My kitchen does not even have a stove.

Could this choice just be a reflection of my personality? Or could China have something to do with that too? Maybe I was having too much fun. And when you are having fun, you never think of home.

Until the fun burns you out.

65

"What's going on, *da ge*?" I whisper to Chairman as the two of us are fingered out of the cell by someone I've never seen before.

He ignores me completely, with not even a twitch of his eyebrow to indicate that I have spoken. Maybe his mind is still asleep, even though his nap ended more than two hours ago.

The man who summoned us is quite tall, a lanky six-footer wearing black cloth kung fu shoes instead of the standard police-issue lace-ups. The three of us walk single file: the tall stranger first, Chairman second, and me last. With his chest sucked in and shoulders hunched, Chairman seems half a head shorter than before. Waving his hand behind his back, he reminds me to walk inside the prisoners-only floor strip.

The stranger's office is stark. The same white walls and gray cement floor as our cell's, but cleaner, with the addition of two wooden chairs, a desk, a gray metal file cabinet, and a stack of Disney-print plastic stools meant for toddlers.

The stranger points to the stools indicating I should sit down on them.

"Pay your respect at once." Chairman introduces the stranger with the utmost humility. "This is the chief of our block."

Oh, I see. No wonder he has stripes on his shoulder while the other jailers don't.

"*Nin hao.*" I sit up straight, with my hands on my knees.

In Chinese, the equivalent of "How are you?" would be "*Ni hao,*" with *ni* meaning "you" and *hao* meaning "good." Then, just like in French and numerous other languages in the world, there is a more polite way of addressing "you" than just *ni,* especially when "you" is someone who commands respect, such as an elder, a teacher, or the chief of a prison block. In such cases, "you" become *nin,* as in "*nin hao.*"

Seemingly a few years older than Chairman, Chief is probably in his midfifties. With sunken cheeks, a sharp jaw, and a hawkish nose between deep slit eyes, he has one of the longest faces I have ever seen, and the overcast skin tone does not help. As he taps his left foot in deep thought, the reddish brown sole of his kung fu shoes strikes a series of crisp notes on the gray cement.

"I got a phone call about you this morning." His voice chimes like muffled cymbals.

Yeah? Really? Is that good news or bad? Maybe it is Madame's *guan xi* finally kicking in—it's about friggin' time!

"It seems that a lot of people are concerned about you." He pops a Jade Creek out of his red-and-gold soft pack with one seasoned stroke.

Against the lighter's flame, his hands look dry and wiry, with bony fingers like wilted bamboos and grayish yellow fingernails devoid of luster.

"They want to"—he starts to cough after two puffs, his shoulders convulsing with each torrent of air forced out of his tar-filled lungs—". . . make sure that . . . you have a . . . comfortable stay here."

Really? Does this mean he is my friend? I don't know how long of a "stay" he has in mind or how "comfortable" he can make it, but I am suddenly smiling.

The strong smell of Chinese cigarettes soon fills the room. Like most older and more patriotic locals, Chief prefers 100 percent toasted tobacco over milder blends that are less pungent (e.g., Marlboro Lights). Back in the 1980s, foreign cigarettes were the hottest things on the market. First 555, then Marlboro, then Kent. One by one, they took China by storm. For a long time, a few cartons of Marlboros could get you some good *guan xi*. Now, after every brand of cigarettes has made its way into China, people seem to be going back to domestic cigarettes, and hardly anyone smokes Marlboros anymore, even though some domestic brands can actually cost a lot more.

"It's my first . . . day back from vacation." He keeps on taking long drags despite his chronic cough. "There was . . . no problem when I . . . was gone, was there?"

I naturally glance at Chairman.

A shade of white flashes across his face. His right heel lifts off the ground and starts to bounce uncontrollably. I guess this question has completely taken him by surprise. Fortunately, the desk in front of him hides his nervous tic from Chief's view.

If I am going to take my revenge for every act of oppression the Government has inflicted upon me since last night, here is my chance. And Chairman certainly knows he is guilty—for not stopping Scruff from being a complete asshole. As *tou ban*, he has to take responsibility.

But should I?

"No problems at all, sir." I am not a lawyer for nothing. "*Da ge* has been very nice to me."

I can almost hear Chairman's exhalation.

"Ha, you are a smart kid." Chief's snicker sounds like an average person crying. "So what got you in here in the first place?"

I tap my fingers on my lips again.

"What does that mean?" His dipping chin demands a spoken answer.

"*Da ma.*" I whimper the big numb.

"Are you addicted?" His forehead wrinkles into a scowl.

"Oh no, sir!"

"But then"—he squints—"why do you smoke it?"

Um, because I like it?

Would he smack me if I said it?

The truth is, I have never considered myself a pothead. All my life, I have never even owned a pipe or bong. Back in college, I often mocked my more grassroots friends for smoking resins scraped out of caked-up bowls; and during my first few years after law school, I even put the big numb on hiatus.

Then I moved to China, where grass became hash and the whole trade became only a text message away. Even though I never actively looked for the stuff, the stuff found me. Slowly but surely, I let the old game back into my life. At first it was just a rehashing (as it were) of old times—friends getting together and shooting the breeze after a few puffs. But then, as my professional path took a detour, an occasional activity became more and more of a regular escape.

When I first started rolling my own Zigarettes, SARS had just hit

Beijing. Unlike all the outsiders who fled China to dodge the virus, I decided to stay. But given how slow everything was while the epidemic lingered, the best thing to do was to sit by the artificial lake in Houhai and get high.

At the time, I said to myself, "No more than three Ziggies a day." And I had full confidence that I could stay under the speed limit. Like the imperial Chinese government that had once said no to British opium, I thought I could keep the situation under control.

But recently, I've been smoking a lot more—after a workout, after any extended period of real work (which is rare), or even as the first thing I put in my mouth after brushing my teeth. Before dinner, I smoke; after dinner, I must smoke; and there is no way I'd watch a bootleg DVD without getting high first. Sometimes I even smoke alone.

Then on the morning after, I wake up to a bad case of cotton-mouth and maybe even light-headedness; and everything that happens before my first Zigarette of the day becomes a potential One A Day. And lately, the daily incidence of Third World annoyances has gone through the roof, with each episode lasting longer and longer and being more and more maddening. The only solution I've seen is to roll more Zigarettes, which has made me even more irritable when I'm off the high, thus driving me to smoke even more still.

So why the vicious cycle? Is it really to make myself a nicer person? And if so, why can't I just be nice naturally?

On many occasions, people said to me, "Wow, you can do all this and that and still get high all the time? You must be really smart and capable." And I always enjoyed hearing that. It made me feel cool, for I was doing something risqué with seemingly perfect ease, even though it would have rendered many of my "admirers" incapable of coherent thought and action.

But then, is it cool to be addicted to being cool? All along, I thought I was the smart one, the gifted one, the precociously wise one who could control the high. But here and now, I can only admit that I was too young, too overconfident, and, well,

"Too immature, sir."

Rubbing his mile-long chin, Chief sinks into a deep "hmm."

Keep smiling like an idiot. That's it. Show a little more remorse.

"I hear you grew up in America." The chain-smoking man changes topic.

"Yes, sir?" I suppose Madame communicated that little bit of personal bio with much emphasis.

"My father died in Korea fighting the Americans." His face grows longer. "I was in Vietnam myself."

I hate cottonmouth, especially when I am not even high.

"So you speak English, I take it." Chief takes an extralong drag on his cigarette, the tip of it sizzling like a branding iron. "Do you speak it well?"

"But I had to speak it, sir." I duck my head in a flinch, just in case he decides to hurl his shoe at my face.

And here he comes! His long strides traverse the pavement in fluid silence. I knew it—"comfortable stay" is prison lingo for ritualistic torture; and now he is going to teach me some Chinese!

"Then tell me something." He stops about six feet in front of me.

"Yes, sir?" I look from the soles of his shoes up to the tip of his nose.

It must be the damn stool, but he looks as tall as shit. And he is tapping his feet again. Those reddish brown soles . . . Those damned reddish brown soles . . .

"What's the best way to learn English?" he asks.

"Huh?"

"It's not for me." He dry-heaves a half dozen times. "It's for my son."

"Your son, sir?" I am starting to feel sorry for the kid already.

"Yes. He is nine years old"—he crosses his bony fingers before him—"and he needs to improve his English grades. So tell me how. Quickly."

Oh, brother.

66

For the first time in a while, I learned a new word: *tuo'er*. Pronounced "too-or," it apparently means someone who has been entrusted to carry out a task below the radar screen—or as I would like to call it, deep throat. And after giving Chief the tip of buying his poor son some bootleg CDs to help improve his English, I am being led to see my *tuo'er* at the other end of this giant prison complex.

And there he is, sitting behind the lone desk in an otherwise vacant room that took Chief and me a good five minutes to get to. In his late thirties, he is not a particularly striking-looking guy—stubby nose, medium lips, regular-sized eyes on a round face, plus a very short crew cut gelled to a solid along the front hairline. Judging by the three studs on either side of his shoulder, he is bit of a big shot, presumably higher than even Chief himself.

With his pudgy left hand, he rotates a clear flask on the table. Just soaking up their first pour of hot water, the fresh green tea leaves are slowly making their way to the bottom.

When it comes to the Chinese, tea is in the blood. From taxi drivers to government officials, a lot of men like to bring a flask of green tea to work and sip on it all day. Even though Starbucks has infiltrated as far as inside the Forbidden City itself and more and more people are experimenting with coffee, the vast majority of the Chinese population still prefer their loose leaves in water. My *tuo'er*'s flask looks to be made out of tempered glass and polished metal instead of pedestrian plastic; and judging from the shape of the soaked leaves and the light jade green of the tonic, he is drinking some rather gourmet stuff.

"I am a friend of your friend's." The man signals me to sit in the empty chair.

"Nin hao," I bid with a half bow, and step forward to offer my handshake.

Oops, there goes my presumptuous Americanness again—jailers don't shake hands with prisoners!

"Ni hao." He rises to reciprocate with a warm, sturdy grip before I can retract.

What a nice guy! And he looks rather friendly with his five-seven frame and slight paunch.

"Your friend has told me all about you." He blows away the last few tea leaves still floating on the surface of his tonic before taking a smiling sip.

"So do you work here, sir?"

"Oh yes." He grins. "Twelve years. Ever since I graduated from the academy."

"Then you must know a lot about this place."

"Yeah, more or less." He reclines in his chair leisurely.

"So how do you know my friend?" I figure I should keep Madame's name out of the conversation.

"Well, you know about the business she ran a few years ago, right?"

"You mean the club?"

"Yes. My fiancée was her landlord."

Oh wow, the boyfriend of the ex-landlord of Madame's old nightclub, that's three degrees already, not to mention past tense.

"So how should I address you, sir?" I know my Chinese well enough to know that *tuo'er* is not something I should call a person to his face.

"Well, your friend calls me *jie fu*," he says.

"*Jie fu?*" I swear he just said "brother-in-law." "Oh, I'm sorry, I didn't know you two were related."

"Oh no, not by blood." He grins again. "But you know how China is—hardly anyone under thirty has siblings. So your friend calls my fiancée *'jie'* [older sister]. And once her *jie* got engaged to me, I became *jie fu*. You follow?"

"Well then, how should I address you?" I mean, I can't call this guy *"jie fu"* as well, right?

"Oh"—he waves his pudgy hand—"you don't have to worry about that."

Right, of course. It is not as if I'll be in a position to look for him anyway. Maybe I'll just give him a nickname—like Bill, for example. BIL is short for brother-in-law already, then add another *L* for love, which is something I really need now.

"So, uh, how much time am I looking at?" I ask Bill.

He lights up a cigarette, the label of which I cannot see in the dim light.

"How much Chinese history do you know?" he asks.

"Well, some. But I intend to learn more." If that helps.

"But you do know about the Opium War, right?"

"Yes?"

"Then you must know this country doesn't like drugs, especially opium."

Yes, I know.

"And most drug users are sent to compulsory rehab, especially opium addicts."

I know that one, too.

"And your substance contained morphine, which is derived from opium and typically requires rehab of six to eight months."

Okay, I *know* I am in a lot of trouble.

"Did you know that you have to pay seven thousand *kuai* each month for rehab?"

What? Paying the government to lock me away in an insane asylum? That's as preposterous as being required to donate blood! Although that has already happened to students at some Chinese universities.

"So what happens now?" I gulp.

"Your friend has asked me to do two things." He takes a drag. "One, to get the rehab waived. Two, to get you an early release."

"Now if you don't mind my asking"—I lean forward—"how does it work exactly?"

Bill blows out the smoke with a smile.

As he explains it, for every person thrown into this compound of two thousand–plus inmates, an investigator is assigned to review his file and recommend a penalty. In the event that such investigator feels a more thorough investigation is needed, he will then send the file up the ladder for further review; if not, the file is closed and the person will serve out whatever sentence the investigator recommends. And it just happens that my file has conveniently been reassigned to Bill within the last twenty-four hours.

"So can you recommend that I be released immediately?"

"Oh now," he almost tut-tuts, grinning. "It is not exactly as easy as snapping my fingers. I still have superiors to report to, you know."

"Yes, of course. So, uh, what are my chances?"

"Well . . ." He takes a long drag with a slight frown. "One can never make any guarantee in these matters. Without being overly optimistic, I'd say . . . a forty percent chance."

"Ah?! I mean, huh. . . . And how much is this forty percent going to . . . you know?"

Calmly, Bill writes something on a paper pad and turns it around for me to see.

Fifty thousand? That's not in Chinese money, is it? It is?! But that's practically a new Hyundai in American dollars! Do you have any idea what I can buy in China with that kind of money? My entire year's rent is only 30,000 *kuai*! And the prick is not even modest about this whole *hutong* robbery in the slightest—at least give it a damned Chinese discount, for Mao's sake, like 48,888 or something!

But then, eight months of rehab at 7,000 *kuai* a month, or 56,000 . . . plus pain and suffering.

Mao-fucker! Fifty thousand actually sounds reasonable.

What an expensive Ziggy that last one turned out to be.

"All right, then." I haven't made such a large financial commitment in years. "When do I hear from you again? Tomorrow? The day after tomorrow?"

"Patience, young man." Bill puts out his cigarette. "Our mutual friend will take care of the money for now. You just sit tight and wait. Anything happens, I'll let you know."

"But soon, right?"

"Oh of course." He nods and grins.

"And this is, you know, top priority, right?" I don't mean to press, but all things considered.

"Mei wen ti," he says, "no problem," in Chinese, loud and clear.

I suppose I have no choice but to trust him.

"Don't look so nervous." He chuckles. "Personally, I think this will be a good experience for you."

"Oh . . . ha . . . yeah . . ." I'd like to scrape that stupid grin off his face with a chipped razor.

"Here, take these with you." Bill walks over to a gray metal cabinet beside his desk that opens with a rusted screech.

One after another, he hands me a purple bottle of Head & Shoulders, a white-and-blue Oral-B hard-bristle toothbrush, a small tube of green-tea-flavored Colgate, a pink, coarse, Winnie-the-Pooh face towel, and a big bar of orange-colored soap wrapped in transparent cellophane that smells like it can really kill something.

Maybe I'd better give him some face and just assume that, for 50,000 *kuai*, he'd take care of my other basic needs too, like a real blanket or something.

"Now, is there anything else that you would like to have for the next few days?" Bill asks.

"You mean like for entertainment?"

"Well, obviously nothing electronic, can't allow computers and cameras in here."

"Well then how about just a pen and some paper? Maybe I can doodle and keep a journal or something."

After all, that's what people do in prison, isn't it?

67

The past twenty-four hours have certainly been interesting.

As soon as Chief escorted me back into 801 yesterday, things changed dramatically.

"Fold up a nice and clean blanket for him and put it next to mine." Chairman gave Scruff an executive order. "From now on, that spot is his."

Meaning that I was now second on deck, number two in the Government, surpassing Scruff and all the rest.

I wish I had a camera to capture the look on Scruff's face, especially when he called me *da ge* for the first time.

In terms of variety, the ensuing dinner was exactly the same as lunch—*mantous* and boiled cabbage—but I could now eat as much as I wanted. So I had four *mantous* and two bowls of cabbage, which was not really much considering that dinner happened at 4:30 P.M. and we didn't get anything else to eat for another fifteen hours. Then after the meal, no more cleaning up. Even when I was about to lend Doorman and the rest a helping hand, Chairman stopped me dead in my tracks. As the new VIP, I now have zero responsibilities, only privileges.

To name just a few, I can now lounge with my legs extended using a blanket for a cushion and even lean against the wall to doze off. Not only can I eat as much as I want, but I can also purchase meat dishes usually reserved for lifers housed in another block with a meal card precharged with 1,000 *kuai* (courtesy of Madame, according to Bill). Last night, I slept next to Chairman on the deck instead of next to the latrine and even got two blankets to cushion against the hard wood while everyone else got just one. As for the latrine itself, I can now drop whenever I want, as much as I want, which is really quite important given how easily digestible *mantou* and boiled cabbage are.

"Hey, somebody . . ." I seem to have forgotten something important on my hasty run to the latrine.

"What can I do for you, *da ge*?" A young inmate sticks his head into my space.

I can smell his nervousness even from where I am squatting. He was the one who woke me up yesterday morning by pouring cold water on my face.

"Get me some toilet paper, would you?" I don't know why I feel guilty for asking such a thing, given how Scruff does the same every shit he takes.

"Yes, of course." He nods repeatedly as he talks. "Anything else I can do for you? Wash your clothes perhaps?"

"Right . . ." If only I had something else to change into; for now, "Just toilet paper, please. Thank you."

"Huh?"

"What?" Did I say something weird? Why does he look so confused? Oh right, I said "please" and actually thanked him. He probably doesn't get that a lot, or maybe ever. There is a first time for everything, I suppose.

Strange, all eyes are on me as I come out of the latrine. Was I too loud in there? Or is this what you get for being a VIP?

"I think I am going to wash myself now." Anything would be better than going back to more sitting.

"But . . ." Chairman seems surprised. "Isn't it a bit too cold for that tonight?"

Well, it certainly ain't no Turkish bath where I'm headed. But when Bill handed me my toiletries yesterday, he specifically said, "Keep yourself clean. A lot of things can grow in there."

And I can feel them already.

"Feel free to use the hot water in the bucket." Chairman extends me the same privilege that he enjoys himself.

But given that there is only a quarter bucket of lukewarm water left for all of us until tomorrow morning, using it to wash my privates just seems too much of an indulgence (not that I didn't consider it for an extra second and a half).

A buzz runs through the crowd as I strip down to my Skivvies. It's good to know that my eight-packs can still win me some vanity.

Now, exactly how do I do this?

The washbasin is obviously too small. I guess I'll just have to stand over the toilet in my bare feet and pour buckets of ice-cold tap water from head to toe.

The tiles around the toilet have not been washed for, well, ever. Hair, spit, leftover toilet paper, yellow stain, yellow stain, big yellow stain.

I can see the waste pool below. It's black, syrupy, and reflecting light. One misstep and I'll literally be in deep shit.

Maybe I'm not so dirty after all.

Oh, who the hell am I kidding? Forget the soap, shampoo everything!

As I brush away the suds from my eyes, I find the same young man staring at me from just beyond the half-wall barrier.

"Can I help you?" Even though I meant to say: "What the fuck do you want?!"

He looks flustered, too embarrassed to admit that he was taking notes on my masochistic act.

You know, all those folks out there who keep on ranting about "democracy" in China really ought to stand right here full-frontal and get a taste of this kid—he doesn't even understand "privacy" yet! To him, and to millions upon millions of other undereducated people in this country, freedoms of speech, religion, and anal sex with a pet donkey in the backyard of one's house mean nothing; for they are not even free of the dirt on their faces yet. If all of them got to vote, Jackie Chan would be elected president, and Jet Li vice president.

Then why not just give a lesser vote to these guys and let the "smarter"—more educated, more outside-influenced, more of everything—minority run this country? There could be up to, say, three hundred million of them out there by now, given how fast this country has grown in the past two decades. When America first started its own democracy, woman didn't even have the right to vote. The Chinese democracy at this point could be more generous—give a half vote to every adult with less than a primary education, and a full vote to every adult who is "smarter."

But will these "smarter" ones actually exercise their proportionally bigger votes to take care of those who have proportionally less? In twenty to thirty years, maybe, after the current generation of "smarter" people has made enough economic progress to become more interested in things beyond Mercedes Benzes and vacations to Paris. Personally, I never thought much about those who have less, nothing more than calling them Spit 'n' Squatters anyway; and I always thought I was a rather nice guy.

The water bucket is full. Time to rinse.

Let the shrinkage begin.

68

Mao, I mean no disrespect, but if there were ever a phrase in the Chinese dictionary for "sadistic prick," your balding visage should be right next to it.

Out of this entire year, how many blue-sky days have we had? Does four sound about right? And they all just happen to be today, yesterday, the day before yesterday, and the day before that!

Are you going to keep the weather this nice for as long as I *can't* enjoy it?

Now if I could only join those birds flying across our window right now, the right side of their torsos switching from golden to brown and back again as their V-formation races against sunset.

Is it time to head down south for the winter already?

This means that, pretty soon, all this glorious weather will be gone; everything colorful will go back to being sooty gray; and there will be no more torture by blue-sky days.

Hooray . . .

It's amazing. Even from so far away, I can hear the birds sing. And it even sounds familiar, like . . .

Für Elise?

Damn it. It's the intercom.

Time for *mantou* and cabbage, again.

69

About ten minutes ago, Doorman was released. One by one, he and three other inmates were picked out of the cell and marched out of sight in a single file. But out of the four, only he was set free, while the others had to go someplace called the "Farm." Before I got around to asking what that was, however, a new batch of seven guys checked in. Together with all the others who came and went over the past few days, we are now up to thirty-one inmates altogether.

"What's with the long face?" Sun bumps me in the shoulder.

"Nothing."

"You look nervous."

Nonsense. I am perfectly calm; really, I am.

"First time in here?"

Is it that obvious? "And you?"

"Me?" He chuckles. "This is my vacation spot. I come here once every couple of months."

"Then do you have like, I don't know, a tip for me?"

"Sure. Don't think too much." He rubs his silver-gray hair. "Everything will work out. It's all within your *yuan fen*."

"Within my what? *Yuan fen*?" As in fate? Gee, thanks, that helps a lot.

"Pss!" someone calls for my attention.

"How are you doing?" Bill asks from beyond the bars. He looks almost too energetic for this early in the morning.

"Not bad." I wish I could do a better job of pretending. "Anything new?"

"I just saw your friends."

Really? "Which ones?"

"There was a foreigner, tight T-shirt, cowboy boots, funny as hell."

Lethal Weapon? Yes, he certainly is a character.

"And the others?"

"Well, one of them we both know." He glosses over mentioning Madame's name. "And the other one is quite petite, but big tattoos, really cute."

As in Rockette? But it's only 7:15 in the morning, and the prison is at least an hour away from the city.

I get it. Judging from Bill's big smile, they probably just heeded his call and dropped off my ransom money. I hope they were smart about it, though—a down payment is fine, but not the whole fifty grand yet.

"They want me to give you these." Bill stuffs a vanilla envelope through the metal bars.

A care package? Nice! I haven't had one of these since . . .

"By the way," he says, smiling, "is the little one your, uh, you know?"

"Oh no." I get this way too often. "She is like my little sister. Why do you ask?"

He shrugs with sympathy. "You should've seen the way she was crying."

Shucks, that is already the second time she's shed tears for me in less than a week! I know it sounds bad, but that actually made me feel pretty damn good.

Inside the envelope, two pairs of underwear, two pairs of socks, six small cartons of fresh milk, and four packs of Prince brand sandwich cookies. Wicked!

As a fitness buff, I pretty much shun junk food, greasy food, and even a lot of local Chinese food; but there is one exception, which only Lethal Weapon would know. And Prince is his favorite brand.

"So what about, you know, my thing?""

"Mei wen ti," Bill says it one more time. "I am working on it as fast as I can."

"So is it going to be tomorrow? Or the day after?"

"Well, if all goes smoothly, it should be the next couple of days."

Okay, not exactly the answer I was looking for.

"Don't you worry." He pats my fist clenched around the bars. "You have a very good friend working very hard for you. She calls me practically every hour on the hour. I couldn't put it off even if I tried."

Fine. I guess I have been a little impatient, maybe even a little selfish. All this time, I haven't given any thought to Madame's well-being, yet I expect her to do things that were never her obligations in the first place. Had our fortunes been reversed, would I have ever done the same for her? Before this all went down, I didn't even consider her a friend.

But now, I can't even begin to describe how close she has become.

I know this is China, where paying a "fee" just might have to be the way to get some dumb ass out of some excessive punishment unfitting his crime (and I'm not—repeat, NOT—saying that doing so is anything less than 108 percent legal and legitimate), but come on. By helping me, Madame is taking a great risk, notwithstanding the fact that she has seen me only a few times altogether. So if there is any silver lining to my dark cloud, Madame is it. Life sure is ironic; who would have thought that my brush with prison would have some bearing on my friendship with Madame?

So maybe Sun was right. Maybe I should just relax and not

worry so much. Who knows, something even better just might happen as a result of my current Waterloo.

Could that be what Sun meant by *"yuan fen"*—that instead of just fate and nothing but, *yuan fen* is also a long chain of cause and effect that no one can ever really predict?

"So how many *mantous* for you this time?" Chairman holds up China's punishment for anyone who prefers bread.

It's time for breakfast again.

"Well how about we share these milk and cookies along with the rest?" I offer up my breakfast of champions.

I know my friends wouldn't mind.

70

Since the end of breakfast, I have tried every last trick in my book to find out a bit more about my cellmates, with less than spectacular success.

So far, Chunk has been the most candid about his crime, which was charging his neighbors 3 *kuai* a person to see a porn DVD that he had bought for 30. For that, he will go to the Farm for an entire year. Apparently, disseminating pornography is a serious crime in China, even for a first offender.

Then little by little, Sun told me about his. In a scuffle over who got to claim his deceased parents' one-room flat in a 1950s apartment building, he put his brother-in-law in the hospital. Apparently, now that the city has been on a building rampage, a lot of close family members have been beating each other up over who can claim any property being seized or demolished by the government and therefore keep the compensation money.

As for Scruff, well, I have not really talked to him at all. Ever since I replaced him as second on deck, he has avoided me like the plague. In his mind, I must be planning something sinister to get even, which I suppose is just the right amount of fear he deserves for all that he has done.

When it comes to the People, the discovery process has been tough, especially with the juveniles. Ask them, "What are you doing in Beijing?" No response. Ask them again with very clear enunciation, still no response. And when they finally do answer, it has been either a nod, a head shake, "Nothing," "Not much," "Don't know," "Haven't thought about it yet," or the best so far, "Sorry, *da ge*, I just don't have that much education."

All along, I thought that my Chinese was pretty damn good.

So now, there is only Chairman left. But I haven't found a good way to start with him. Ever since I was promoted, he has given me a lot of face, thus making it more difficult for me to ask anything about who he really is, until now, perhaps, after he has been staring at the ceiling aimlessly for a good two minutes.

"Say, *da ge*. How long have you been in here already?"

A slight frown gathers between his eyes. "Just over five months."

"That long? How much longer do you have to go?"

"Don't know."

"Beg your pardon?"

"Once you are in, there is no telling when."

"But what about the papers?" I pat the "Assessment of Penalty" tucked away securely in my back pocket.

"What about them?" He chuckles. "The investigation can take a long time."

"But what's there to investigate?" I sure hope that whatever he did was a lot worse than smoking a joint.

"Ah . . . It was nothing."

Yes, of course. Wrong question.

"So what did you do before? For work, I mean."

"Business." He says it with discernible pride.

"Oh yeah? Did you have your own company?"

"No, no, not mine," he refutes rather nervously. "It was my brother-in-law's."

"Cool. What did you do there?"

"Oh . . . stuff."

Looks like this one is going to take some time.

"So how old are you, *da ge*?"

"Almost fifty-two."

"No kidding." That means he is twenty-four years, or two Chinese zodiac cycles, ahead of me and therefore also born in a year of the rabbit. "Nice."

"What's so nice about it?" He grins awkwardly. "You must be talking about yourself. At least you never had to live through the Cultural Revolution."

True. Nor have I had to live through the Great Leap Forward, the Three Years of Famine, the early Communist era when China's average male life expectancy was less than forty.

"So what did you do during the Cultural Revolution?" I ask. "Were you like a Red Guard or something?"

Foot soldiers of Chairman Mao, the Red Guards were ideology-crazed students who burned books, closed down schools, destroyed artifacts, and persecuted intellectuals for having any beliefs not on the extreme left. Today, their deeds are universally condemned. Back then, being one was an honor. Young people are always easy to incite, and Mao sure knew how. My mother was a Red Guard herself—Chairman might have been too.

"No." He shakes his head. "My grandfather was a Nationalist in his youth before joining the Communist Party. Not revolutionary from the beginning; not revolutionary enough. My family would have been labeled 'black' if we didn't have *guan xi* to help scratch our names off the list. But I still got sent down."

"Down where?"

"The countryside, of course."

"You mean as a 'youth intellectual'?" Like the sixteen million other youth intellectuals who were sent from all the major cities "down" to the countryside between 1966 and 1968, many of whom did not return to their homes until more than a decade later, including my mom's younger brother.

"Yeah." He smirks. "I was in middle school at the time."

"*Cao!* What the hell for?!"

"To be reeducated by the peasantry."

As opposed to the other way around?

"So any stories? Did you ever go through a struggle session or something?"

From what I understand, if you were for any reason listed as "black" (a category that included landowners, rich peasants, counterrevolutionaries, rightists, and above all, "bad" people), you could be dragged into a "struggle session." There, you would kneel or squat with your hands tied behind your back and be censured, denounced, and sometimes beaten and tortured before a large public audience that included your colleagues and maybe even your relatives. And if you were not tough enough for the torment, which would not stop until you fainted from exhaustion or until the public got tired of spitting on you, you might just kill yourself; that is, assuming you were not too old, too sick, or too injured to die of "natural causes."

"No, I didn't have to do that." Chairman lets out a long sigh. "Someone else in the village always did though."

"All the time?"

"Often enough. There was this one guy who was seeing some girl behind closed doors, even though dating back then was considered bad for the revolution, especially for teenagers. After a while, he grew paranoid of getting caught. So he decided to report his own girlfriend to the village heads, saying that she had said something counterrevolutionary. So of course the girl got 'struggled,' couldn't take the humiliation, and drowned herself in the nearby river in the middle of the night."

"So when did you come back?"

"Nineteen seventy-eight. I was twenty-six."

"Then back to school?" I hope?

"I wish." He chuckles. "My parents were already getting old then. Time to get a job to support the family. Enough reeducation already. No more real education."

Great, just when I thought it couldn't get any worse. What do I ask him next? About his crime? Given the era that he endured, he probably doesn't like to share too much personal information; not that I would know how to ask without picking on any of his scars.

Come to think of it, my father would have been twenty-two years old in 1966. Being the son of a Nationalist general probably got him blacklisted in a jiffy. Any chance he got "struggled" as well? How did he even manage to survive that tumultuous era?

I never asked my old man those questions or ever felt the need to do so.

"So . . ." Chairman obviously does not want to answer any more questions. "What is it that you do?"

"Me? As in work?"

"Yes, for a living."

"Well, I um . . ."

71

Things I wish I had in 801:

Newspapers (but *not* those printed by the police)

Deodorant (for all the Anchovies 'n' Swiss around me)

Game Boy (preferably "unlocked" by the geeks on Ladies Street so that I could play all the cheap pirated games, too)

A string (to hold up my buttonless Levi's)

An eye mask (to block out the twenty-four-hour ceiling lamp)

Zigarettes (I wish I had never given up cigarettes)

~~Melatonin~~

Sleeping pills

Lots of sleeping pills

But since I don't have any of the above, life in 801 is:

Boring
Dull
Monotonous
Repetitive
Droning
Tedious
Tiresome
Wu liao
Fucking *wu liao*!

72

"Looks like it's your lucky day." Chairman breaks aparts one of his dinner *mantous* and stuffs a quarter of it into his mouth.

"How do you mean?" I haven't noticed anything different, and certainly not anything that indicates luck.

"This . . ." He holds up the rest of his bun like a fermented trophy while talking with his mouth full. "This is much, much better than . . . the *mantou* . . . we normally get."

Oh yeah? Looks the same to me. In fact, I think it looks worse—

the skin of the bun is almost light yellow as opposed to white and is nowhere as glossy as the ones before.

"Are you sure, *da ge*?" I hope he hasn't gone cuckoo with boredom.

"Of course I'm sure." Chairman looks to Sun, who is apparently busy admiring his own Godiva of a bun, for a confirmation. "Wouldn't you agree?"

"Are you kidding?" Sun chuckles. "This might be the best I've ever had in here."

"Serious?" This little bun of horror must be laced with hallucinagens or something. "What's so new-and-improved about it?"

"You mean you can't tell?" Sun seems rather incredulous. "Are you Chinese or what?"

"Of course I am." I've been asked that question enough times in China to not be offended anymore. "But . . ."

"But what?"

"Well, I grew . . . I mean I spent some time overseas."

"Ha, whereabouts?"

"America."

"No kidding," Chairman interjects. "So you don't eat *mantous*? Ever?"

"Well . . . Not never." Just not since I was thirteen years old. I mean, where would I have found a *mantou* in a midwestern town where the entire Chinese population was barely two hundred?

Besides, I was thirteen. All I wanted to eat was hamburgers and pizzas. Being the only Asian kid in my high school, I certainly didn't want to stand out as the only Asian kid in my high school. Then with all the TV shows constantly telling me how much greater America was than any other place on earth, I of course saw no reason to actively retain my Chineseness. As far as I was concerned, having a Chinese face was more than enough. Bottom line, I wanted to change and change every habit I could.

"So what about now?" Sun continues. "I take it that you have moved back? How do you like it?"

"Beg your pardon?" This is hardly the time to ask me whether I "like" living in China, don't you think?

Okay, fine; as we are all prisoners here, I am sure he meant no sarcasm. But honestly, being an outsider in my own country can feel pretty odd sometimes.

"Do you have a lot of local friends?" Chairman asks, "as in folks who have never been abroad?"

"Yeah . . . some." But no one I would really consider close.

"Do you read local newspapers?"

"Sometimes . . ." If I ever feel the need for more brainwashing after CCTV.

"How often do you eat Beijing food, as in really *hutong* style?"

"Like stir-fried pig stomach and spoiled tofu?" Are you kidding?

All right, I get it—he is trying to say that I don't live the life of a local Chinese. And he is right. Going to America changed my entire being. In fact, many of the One A Days I suffer from now can be directly attributed to the fact that I am Americanized and therefore cannot stand the things that most locals have lived with and tolerated for life.

But what can I do? I am never going to be like the locals, for I can never undo the influence that America has had on me. Remember that I am not thirteen years old anymore; peer pressure just no longer means that much.

Besides, why would I want to give up my American ways for Chinese ones when this whole country is still trying catch up to the Americans? Relative to the locals, I am already running so much farther ahead, with more exposure, more skills, more options, and a whole lot more . . .

Damn it, I was going to say "freedom."

So am I wrong? All my life, I have considered myself to be pretty smart. So what would a truly smart person do when he moves to a new country? Would he stay set in his own foreign ways and expect every local person to be like him, or at least make an effort to meet others halfway? Indeed, if China and America were swapped in their relative positions in today's world, would I still be so lazy in becoming more Chinese? And more fundamentally, why should it even matter?

"So what *is* so special about this *mantou* anyway?" I guess any change would have to start somewhere.

"Well, first, look at the color." Chairman seems to be able to write a treatise on this. "It's light yellow, which is actually the natural color of the raw material, with no artificial white coloring added. Then feel the weight. It's denser, meaning less yeast; so you won't go hungry again in two hours. And look at these. See the finer pockets of air inside the bun once you break it open? That means someone put more time and effort into rolling this dough. Here, taste it."

He stuffs a *mantou* into my hand.

"Anything different?"

"Mmm . . . Hmm . . . Maybe . . ." I guess the difference is a lot subtler than I can readily appreciate.

"Then have another bite," he commands. "And chew it some more before you swallow. You'll taste the difference. Guaranteed."

Fine, I'll give him the face that . . .

Oh, wait a second. "Are you talking about that extra bit of sweetness on my palate?"

As well as the extra substance and texture as I chew?

"And no more chalkiness as it goes down, right?"

Cao, I think he is right! The difference is not exactly amazing, but hell—there aren't too many things to get excited about around here.

"Well if you like that . . . ," Chairman gives me a wink while scooting toward his private little plastic bin by the end of the deck.

With his back facing the rest of 801, he clandestinely stuffs a vacuum-sealed packet of something into my palm.

"What is it?" I ask.

"Shh!" He frowns. "Read the label. You do read Chinese, don't you?"

It's preserved cabbage, made out of the stalkier parts of the vegetable as opposed to the leafier ones that are already boiled and served to us at least twice a day. Salty, shredded, and dark green, they look as if they have been pickled for longer than I have been alive.

"Hey, I remember these. Used to eat them with porridge for breakfast when I was really little." And I remember not liking it one bit. "Much better packaging on this one, though."

"Times are different now." He chuckles. "I had one of the guards sneak in some for me a few weeks back. Here, break your *mantou* in half and stuff some of this in between."

"You mean like a sandwich?" Does he even know what a sandwich is?

"Precisely. Think of it as a hamburger, just Chinese style."

"*Cao,* you must mean Chinese prison style." Because the color combination of dark green on light yellow is not doing this thing any visual favors.

"Just take a bite." Chairman grins. "Not everything has to look good to taste good."

Fine, here goes. . . . The things we must do to give fa—

Whoa, how could anything preserved turn out to be so refreshing? And it crunches beautifully against the softness of the bun. The savory-sweet combination is waking up taste buds that I haven't felt in days!

"This is . . . brilliant!" I almost wish I had the ability to chew my cud so I could enjoy this thing over again later. "How did you ever come up with this idea?"

"Wasn't me." He shrugs it off. "We've been eating *mantous* like this for ages."

"Really? Then how come I haven't seen you doing it before?"

"Hey, supply is limited." Chairman shrugs. "Only for special occasions in here."

And today is one of them?

Looks like it's my lucky day indeed.

73

Shut up! Shut up! Shut the fuck up!

Scruff's thick hide can sure take a beating.

"What now?!" The startled hairy face struggles to open its eyelids.

"Stop your *wo cao ta ma de* snoring!" I haven't cursed like Lethal Weapon in days, but this is for the head knuckles as well as his noise pollution.

"Really? But I didn't hear anything," he says.

I should really smack him in the face.

"What's the matter?" Chairman is awakened by all the ruckus.

"How the hell do I sleep with a damn Peking Opera going off next to my head?!"

"Well is there anything we can do about it?" He rubs his eyes in helplessness.

"You bet there is!" It's about time a real *da ge* takes charge around here. "From now on, whoever snores again, wake him up!"

"Wake him up?" The boys on night watch look confused.

"Yes, do whatever is necessary. Just shut him up so everyone else can get some decent sleep."

"Do you mean that for everybody?" Chairman is probably new to rules that apply across the board.

"You bet I do!"

Honestly, I never have insomnia, never. But I can't sleep now. Scruff must have turned up his snoring extra loud on this night number four; that wretched ceiling lamp just won't stop flickering; and I am still stuck on Chairman's question from earlier in the day:

What is it that I do?

Foodiez? Lawttitude? *Happy Heroes*?

With a résumé longer than the Great Wall, what is my career?

Okay, I said it. The dreaded *c* word that marks the end of youth and the beginning of responsibility. It is inevitable, I suppose. Confucius said that a boy becomes a man at thirty; and I am almost twenty-nine.

Looking back on the past three years, I have been rather all over the place. At any given time, I had at least three different projects across three different fields. And most of the time, they had nothing to do with one another. It was my way of maximizing the utility of all opportunities. After all, I was young, I was robust, and I had tons of energy.

But not every opportunity worked out. Not every opportunity ought to be taken. Here and now, what do I really want?

Well, money would be a good place to start. It's a material world out there, especially in today's China. Even though this place is still relatively cheap to live in compared to the West, the price difference is shrinking by the day. Foreign cars are subject to 100 percent import duties, and much of the newly developed real estate commands Manhattanesque prices despite its Third World quality. Like it or not, the Chinese are getting rich, and some extremely so. The new millionaires and billionaires are buying up everything the government allows them to, thus driving up the prices for everyone else. If I want to live comfortably in the China of tomorrow, I'd better start making some real money today.

So what can I sell? Well, how about cars? Here in China, people are crazy about cars. It is psychological really—next to a fancy abode, a car is the most prominent show-off piece a nouveau riche can buy. Mercedes is no longer the status symbol it once was. Instead, top prestige goes to Ferrari and Rolls-Royce. In fact, even cars that I have never heard of before are coming to China to get in on the gold rush.

But even so, they are still just brand-new cars that anyone with money can buy. Vintage cars, on the other hand, are different. Just imagine cruising down Tiananmen Square in a red 1962 Ferrari 250 GTO. Nothing else could set one further apart from—and above—the boring Mercedes. Given their utter nonexistence in the Chinese market up to this point, I could set prices as high as the stars. And once I got the attention of all the *ernais* spending their sugar daddies' money in Sanlitun, I'd make millions—in dollars.

The problem, however, is that typical of a nouveau riche, China doesn't like to buy anything used just yet; and the law actually prohibits the importation of secondhand cars, regardless of whether the vehicle is a beat-up Yugo or a sweet-sounding vintage. Of course, there is always a way around this law, i.e., through some under-the-table dealings with folks in the customs services, the tax bureau, and the registry of motor vehicles, none of which should have a paper trail and all of which fall under the dark umbrella of *guan xi*. Sounds risky? Well, I certainly won't be the first guy to pay off the government to get rich.

Until, that is, I get tagged for bribing the wrong government official—when and if the government chooses to actually look—and get sacrificed in the process.

Well then, how about going back to being a lawyer? If I sent out a résumé today, I'd be interviewed by three different international firms in a week; and the salary plus bonus and housing allowance would be a relative fortune considering local prices. It's not bragging really, for my language abilities are that good, and law firms thrive on language abilities.

But then, would I be able to tolerate BlackBerry 24/7, corporate retreats to learn about ethics, and annual evaluations that might or might not promote me from a junior associate to a senior associate, then counsel, then junior partner, then full partner, and eventually, death?

There is a shortcut around this hierarchy, of course: join a local firm, like Harding & Wills. Such firms are not as prestigious as Wall Street's usual suspects, and their offices aren't half as posh, but they sure as hell have a lot of potential. To them, I'd be an absolute gem— young, charming, fluent in English, totally Americanized yet with a Chinese face, instant credibility for the firm even if I had no idea what the case was about. And that's okay. For now, Chinese firms don't get paid because they know the law; they get paid because they know judges and magistrates. So I could just kick back and get paid for being what the Chinese call a "flower pot"—one who only looks great but doesn't do nearly as much.

Right, as if.

In my younger days, there was something that I always wanted to be. It wasn't a real job, however, as the title only appeared in the kungfutions that I read for entertainment; and even the books themselves gave no job description for it.

In Chinese, it is called *da xia* (pronounced "da she-ah")—a kung fu master who travels the underworld of Chinese society to help the good and punish the evil. If I were to translate *da xia* into English, it would be something of a full-time superhero, like Batman (except during the day too and in regular clothes) or a Jedi (but right here on Earth, and no need for light sabers). As a vigilante of justice, a *da xia* is respected and admired by everyone. Being the constant target of his evil enemies, he never lives a dull life. In fact, now that I think about it, *da xia* was probably the original inspiration for my Superego.

But in real life, being a *da xia* sounds rather idiotic. At the most basic level, the books never disclosed one crucial piece of information: what does a *da xia* do for his day job? Surely there is no prize money to be won from his various duels, and even when he robs the rich, he has to be like Robin Hood and help the poor.

So at the end of the day, I still need a career. And unlike Spider-man or Superman or Batman, I don't want to live a double life. Hell, maybe it's time to ditch the Superego altogether and settle for something easy. . . .

Hey, who is that tugging on my toe?!

"*Da ge*," one of the kids on night watch whispers. "You were snoring."

"What? Me? Don't be silly."

"Sorry, *da ge*." Another one among the trio shrugs. "You were the loudest of all of them."

"And we've waited a whole five minutes already," the third one adds.

"But how come I didn't hear anything?"

Never mind. I'd better stop before embarrassing myself any further.

Looks like this is going to be the longest night yet.

74

That's it—*Für Elise* is now my most-hated song of all time!

Without going into the details of my wonderful (and tragically interrupted) dream of the Playboy mansion, what am I going to do about the increasingly dangerous hormonal imbalance that will soon take over my body? Do I somehow self-administer a happy ending—and ignore all the dirty, smelly men around me?

The assholes running this joint sure are sadistic. Have they ever considered, for even an instant, the adverse effect of pent-up testosterone? I am not asking for a dirty magazine here, much less a conjugal visit; all I ask for is for someone to PLEASE turn off that bloody Beethoven!

75

It's Day 6 and Chairman has been a little weird all morning. For ten minutes he has stood by the gate, hands clutching the bars, trying to look down the hallway in search of something.

"Something on your mind, *da ge*?" Sun asks again after a few seconds of no response.

"Oh, nothing." Chairman backs away from the bars reluctantly. "Say, you got any family?"

"Me?" Sun rubs his buzz-cut silver-gray hair. *"Cha bu duo."*

"Cha bu duo?" Chairman repeats the ubiquitous local expression for "give or take"—something that one would say when not too sure about something.

"I have a son." Sun gives in to the squint. "He is, uh . . . seventeen, *cha bu duo.*"

I guess my father is not the only parent who doesn't remember the age and birth date of his only flesh and blood.

"And you?" Sun kicks the ball to me. "Still got family in America?"

"Yeah." Well, technically.

"Growing up there must be nice, right? I mean, all the uh, you know."

"Oh yeah, America is great—as long as you have the dough."

Except that when I first got there as a thirteen-year-old FOB, we lived in a one-bedroom apartment in the ghetto. The staircase leading up to the second floor reeked of moldy carpet, two out of four burners on the kitchen stove never worked, and the pint-sized bathroom could be accessed only from my parents' bedroom. Even though my home in Shanghai had not exactly been grand, at least

I'd had my own bed. In the middle of my first night of sleeping on the floor, I even said to myself, "Wow, Americans really like their firecrackers"; only months later did I realize that what I'd heard was actually gunshots.

Thinking back to the China I grew up in, we had almost nothing by American standards. We had no car, no brand-name clothing, and certainly no real estate. But relative to most locals, we still had more of nothing. After all, we were the first family in our entire building to have a TV. It was black-and-white and had a twelve-inch screen, but it was the newest thing on the block at the time. In America, on the other hand, we just had nothing, period. Practically nothing we owned was new—used car, used furniture, used toaster, even used clothing that certainly didn't qualify as vintage.

In my dreams, I of course wanted to be rich—so I could at least buy real clothes from classy downtown malls instead of shopping at some embarrassing garage-sale-with-a-roof called Schottenstein's, and never again would I have my hair cut in our tiny bathroom by my father's own appalling hands while seated butt naked on a cold metal fold-up chair. With any luck, I would found my own company, make my first million by the age of twenty-five, and buy my mother a big house on the beach, and even let my father live there if that would make my mother happy.

Well, at least I don't have to worry about that big house anymore.

"So what about you, *da ge*?" I kick the ball of pleasant memories back to Chairman. "Got any family?"

"Oh yeah." His face lights up like I've never seen. "I have a son, sixteen going on seventeen."

"That's nice. He must be a really good kid." Especially with the father looking so soft and all.

"Well, he is better now." Chairman shakes his head. "But he was a handful once upon a time."

"Oh yeah? Did you have to discipline him?" But nothing like beating him with a bat, right?

"Are you kidding? Kids are so spoiled these days given the One Child Policy and all. I must have slapped my son hundreds of times over the years."

"How about in public?"

"If that's necessary."

"But . . ."

"Hey, even the best iron won't make a sword without pounding. Trust me, it hurts me more than it hurts him."

"But it's still humiliating."

"Which is precisely why he'll remember not to do the same thing again. Without shame, he would never even have gotten into high school. Now he wants to study in England and be a doctor."

"But isn't that kind of expensive? Have you any idea what London is like?"

"No, but I've been saving up. Worse comes to worst, I'll just sell my flat to help pay for it. Good thing the market has risen."

"You mean all of your money is going into your son's schooling?"

"Every last penny."

Okay, I hate to be a realist, but is that why he is still here after five months—he has no money to pay his own ransom?

"So what about your kid?" I ask Sun.

"What about him?"

"Well, where do you guys live, is he in school—"

"We don't really see each other." He answers unenthusiastically, avoiding eye contact with me or Chairman. "He lives with his mother on the north side."

"Divorced?"

"*Cao*, who has got time for a divorce?" He chuckles self-mockingly. "Say, uh, what's with all this family talk anyway?"

"It's visitation day." Chairman sighs.

"Really?" I didn't even know there was such a thing, especially not for people being held temporarily.

"So is your family coming to see you?" Sun asks Chairman.

"No. I wouldn't allow it," he says.

"Why not?" I thought he had a wonderful relationship with his family.

"I don't want my wife and son to see me like this." His smile disappears.

"But don't they worry about you?"

"I had my wife tell my kid that I am away on business for a while."

"You mean he doesn't even know that you are in prison? After all this time?!"

"Are you kidding? Of course not. It is shameful to have a prisoner in the family. Just imagine what his schoolmates would say if it leaked out. I wouldn't put my kid through that."

"But don't you miss them?" And how long does he expect to keep this up?

"I know." He shrugs. "But that's parenthood for you. Sometimes you just have to, uh . . . How should I say—"

"Suck it up?" Like the way my mom did? All those years in America, she never had much fun. Having had to give up her own career in China, she ended up working as a waitress, a seamstress, and at all the other odd jobs that only paid a pittance and stress. Then, after ten years of struggling, she passed away, partly because we never had any insurance to afford the annual medical checkups that could have caught her cancer before it spread. I am just glad she was able to attend my law school commencement. It was probably the happiest moment in her life.

"So what about your *lao ye zi*?" Chairman asks about my "old man" in the local lingo.

"What about him?" I shrug. "Sun probably talks to his son more than I talk to him."

And frankly, I don't think he wants to talk to me much either. In all of my twenty-nine years, he has never even told me the name of his own mother, much less how he was at my age. All I know is that he was the eldest son of a southern warlord who later became an admiral in the Nationalist navy. His home was in the ritziest neighborhood, just off Shanghai's famous Nanjing Road, and his childhood neighbors were diplomats from America and Europe. In a time when most of China had never heard a foreign language or the roar of a propeller engine, he was already taking English lessons from professional tutors and jet-setting across China on my grandfather's own military plane.

"So what happened to him after 1949?" Sun speaks of the year when the Communists drove the Nationalists out of mainland China and onto the island of Taiwan.

"Not too sure." Those years have never been discussed openly in my farmily. "All I know is that he met my mother when he was thirty-two."

"If I were to guess," Chairman says with a frown, "he probably had a pretty hard time when he was your age. He ever tell you what happened to your grandfather after '49?"

"Actually, I don't think he ever saw him again after the liberation. Some mass exodus right before the Communists took Shanghai; the family got separated or something. I think he was raised by his uncle or aunt or whomever."

"So you mean your old man grew up without a father or mother of his own?"

"He did?" Really? My father was a de facto orphan of the Communist revolution?

Never thought of it like that before. Not even once!

"Funny thing about men from those times." Chairman sighs. "Certain things, we just never talk about."

"But why not?" I mean, had my old man told me more about himself before, maybe we wouldn't be so distant from each other now. Maybe I would have understood why he had to be the disciplinarian that he was. Maybe I would even call him to chat once in a while instead of just "everything is fine" in my rarer-than-a-blue-moon e-mail.

And truth be told, I really wish we could be on better terms. In my younger days in Shanghai, I was often asked by family members, "Whom do you love more, your father or your mother?" Each time, I would say that I loved both equally. And back then, it was the truth. The fact is, I once idolized my old man—he was smart, handsome, dignified; everybody called him "teacher" or "sir" not only because of his profession but also out of respect. He even translated the story of *Robinson Crusoe* into Chinese. But somewhere along the way, a fork separated our paths. For the longest time, I blamed him for taking one road while pushing me to the other. But now that I actually look back from an ocean away, was it really all his fault?

Putting myself in his shoes, had I been born the son of a general, I'd probably have set sky-high goals for myself. But between all the wars and revolutions, history was cruel to my father's generation. By the time he finally got through the turmoil that almost threw China back into the Stone Age, he had already lost his youth and had a family to support. Being human, he probably wanted to pursue his dreams and provide for his family at the same time. And he certainly tried. During those tough months in America, he even moonlighted as a delivery guy for Domino's Pizza at night while pursuing his Ph.D. during the day. As irritable as he was during that time, he never complained and always brought home a pizza for me after his late-night shift.

And all things considered, he actually did a pretty good job. Granted, he was rather harsh with punishment; but given my mischief, maybe even Mother Teresa would have beaten me with a cross. Had it not been for his discipline, I might have ended up in prison a long time ago. And even more important than the smart genes that he passed down to me, it was he who took me to the public library on my second day in America and taught me to say to the librarian, "I would like to check out this book, please." Without him, I would never have become half of who I am today.

And now he is getting old. I think his sixtieth birthday passed in August, but I can't be sure. Just as he doesn't know my birthday, I don't know his either. It's quite sad, really, two fewer occasions for gifts between the two of us, and neither of us is getting any younger. If I keep this up, what am I going to tell my own children when they ask about their grandfather twenty years from now? *Cha bu duo?*

"Well, I hope you'll get to see your kid soon." I wish there were something else I could say to cheer up Chairman a little more.

"Yeah." He nods. "Maybe I'll tell him about this place when he is of age."

"You mean eighteen?"

"No." He chuckles. "Didn't you read Confucius when you were little? A boy becomes a man at thirty. I'll tell him then. Maybe."

76

"What am I doing here, sir?" I ask the guard for the second time.

The middle-aged man walking a few steps ahead of me apparently does not hear too well.

"Uh, *nin hao*? Hello?" I don't mean to be paranoid, but why am I being led into a room with no lights and no windows?

Other than a small table, two fold-up chairs, and a fanned vent hole high up on the wall, there looks to be absolutely nothing inside this eerily damp cement chamber the size of a two-car garage.

Is this guard deaf?

"*Da ge*, you look wonderful today." I'm pulling out all the stops already. "Now would you *please* tell me what is going on?"

With nothing less than an annoyed frown, the man finally turns, walks toward me and—

"HEY! Where are you going? Don't close that!"

Thump! The door slams shut with the force of solid metal.

Okay. What now?

There must be a perfectly logical explanation for this.

Maybe this is some sort of VIP treatment. Yes, they must have felt bad about making me sit all day, so they have provided this little space for me to stretch out and . . .

What the hell am I talking about? This place looks like a damn tor—

No, just because it's cramped and unlit and sealed off like a tuna can doesn't mean that it is used for . . . What the hell is that rusty metal thingy dangling from the ceiling?

Where the hell is Bill? He never mentioned anything like this before.

Maube I should tell the guards that I know him—if I only knew Bill's real name!

Wait a second, did something happen to Bill?

Did he get caught for trying to help me?

Have I lost my *tou'er*

Am I all alone?!

All right, breathe. Hum a little tune, that's it. Anything to help lighten this—

But not *Für*cking *Elise*!

Wait . . . . . Someone is headed this way in a hurry.

And there is more than one of them!

The quick tapping of heavy soles on cement stabs like a sewing machine on spine.

Please, Mao, whoever these people are, let them be gentle. I promise to tell them everything they want to know, do whatever they want me to do. Just let me live to see my next birthday please. It's less than two and a half months away!

The lock is turning.

Close sesame. Close sesameClose mother@#$% . . .

The heavy metal door opens a crack from the outside, sucking out my lungs with it.

Is it better to sit or stand?

Don't think. Just choose:

Come on man, SIT or STAND?!

Against the background light a figure appears in the doorway.

Crap, they sent in a *she*? That can't be good news! What is she gonna use? A knife? A whip? A battery of Chinese prison secrets to make me regret ever being born with a penis?!

Where is the damn toilet when you most need one?!

The door shuts behind her with another *thump*.

The room turns almost pitch dark in an instant.

I really need to go now . . .

"Hey." Her voice echoes from across the room.

"*Nin hao*?" Maybe being deferential could spare me from being turned into a quadriplegic.

She is moving in closer still.

I've got a cold cement wall in my back.

"What are you doing?" she says.

"Nothing."

"Why are you all the way there?"

Isn't it obvious?

"Don't you recognize me?"

Do I want to?

In the cone of dim light shining through the vent, a corner of her wardrobe appears.

My eyes must be playing tricks—where are the leather boots and combat fatigues?

Could it really be?

A Mandarin dress?

"It's me!" Her face appears. "Now would you get over here and give me a hug please?"

77

Seated across the small desk, Madame is looking positively radiant, the glow of her flawless skin quickly lifting the cement off of my idled senses. Now that my vision has adjusted to this dark room, I can enjoy the luminescence of her pink pearl necklace, the fine hand-stitching on her ivory mandarin dress, and even the intricate phoenix carvings adorning her silver and red jade hairpin. For the first time in a long while, I can appreciate a woman for all her:

"How have you been?"

"Are you eating enough?"

"How was your sleep?"

"Anyone harassing you?"

"Got enough clothes?"

"Any aches and pains?"

"Do you—"

"Okay." I guess any type of pure joy would have to come in small doses. "Can we slow down on questions just a tiny bit?"

"Oh, my bad." She grins apologetically. "So, what do you do every day?"

"Well, let's see . . ." How can I put this to make it seem at all interesting? "Today, I sat. Yesterday? I sat. The day before yesterday . . . I sat some more. What else? . . . Oh right, some prison guard asked me to do his English homework yesterday. You should have seen the size of his neck."

"He didn't hurt you, did he?" She grips the edge of the small desk with both hands.

"Oh no, he wouldn't do that." I laugh for the first time in days. "He had to pass some English test to get his promotion. I even got free cigarettes in exchange—now the whole cell comes to me for handouts."

"Well, *jie fu* promised me that he'd take care of you." She refers to Bill by her own code name. "Has he kept his word?"

"Oh yeah, no problem." I give a thumbs-up. "Next time I go to Europe, I'll ask you to make the arrangements too."

"Oh, shut up." She giggles.

"But seriously, I really must thank you for doing all of this."

"It's all right." She straightens up proudly. "What are friends for, right?"

Indeed. Loyalty, friendship—my *yuan fen* with this girl is definitely pretty good.

"So anyway. When am I getting out of here?"

"Well"—a slight hesitation in her voice—"*jie fu* said that he is working really hard on it, so . . ."

"But it's almost a week already." I didn't mean to change my tone like that, but, "Are you sure he is working hard enough? Who is he anyway?"

"You mean his title?" She squints. "I don't know that exactly, but I think he pretty much decides who gets to stay and who gets to go."

"*Cao,* like a god or something?"

"But I am sure he'd rather get paid more."

"How well do you know him?"

"Personally?" She shrugs. "I call him '*jie fu*' because I'm close to his fiancée. So, you know. But he did drink at the Velvet Room often when I still had it, on the house, of course."

"But that was more than three years ago, wasn't it?"

"Yeah." Madame nods, apparently incognizant of my insinuation. "He's been engaged to my 'sister' for longer. Should've seen him back in the day."

"Is he a nice guy?"

"Is he a cop?"

"Okay . . . Have you worked with him before?"

"You mean 'scooping' people out of prison?" She's just taught me yet another new phrase. "No, this is my first time working in this spot."

"But you have 'scooped' before, right?" I hate to be the lab rat for a rookie.

"Relax." She giggles. "I ran a club once."

"Then tell me what's going on!" And pardon my tone of voice, please!

"Well, *jie fu* has to pay off a lot of people." She counts with her fingers: "His boss, his deputy, his backup deputy, all the cops you saw in Sanlitun, all the jailers that supervise you here. That's at least twenty people."

"What the hell?"

"Welcome to China."

"So how much longer do I have to wait?"

"A day? At the most two."

"Still? Some gambling junkie in my cell got out after three days when he was supposed to serve twelve."

"Wow, that's pretty good. Who was he?"

"Some driver for the National Security Bureau."

"There you go. Do you drive for the National Security Bureau?"

"No, but—"

"My dear," she says a little harshly, leaning forward, "don't forget that your stuff contained morphine. Even a good *guan xi* might take a while to work out the kinks."

Okay, fine. "So how are the usual suspects?" I might need to borrow some money soon.

"Well, the ones in the know have been trying to figure out who the rat was." She is obviously referring to Lethal Weapon, Moneypenny, and Rockette.

"Don't bother." I feel a headache coming on already. "It was the beggar at Café 44. Can't believe I actually gave money to that little twerp."

"Oh, come on." She is giggling. "Do you really think it was him? The kid is retarded, for heaven's sake."

"But even the cops said it was him."

"Yeah, a snitch he may have been; the mastermind he was not."

"Mastermind?" What, am I dealing with the Chinese Mafia now? She whispers a name.

"As in the owner of Café 44?"

She nods confidently.

"Get outta here! Why would he do something like that? I'm like his best customer. Do you know how many friends I have brought to his place? I was going to 44 before it was even his. And I've been smoking up there every day for the past two years."

I really appreciate that Madame is trying to help. But this is absurd. Lao Chu is a friend. We may never hang out or talk for more than three sentences at a time, but we do coexist peacefully, and I have never owed him money.

"We thought so too," Madame says. "But why is it that nothing happened to Café 44 when you were arrested? According to *jie fu*, 44 should also have been searched if Lao Chu wasn't in on it."

"But what's his motive? I have never done anything to hurt him."

"I can give you three reasons."

That many?

"Number one, envy."

Really? "For what?"

"Well, let's see." She seems to have given a lot of thought to this. "He is pushing fifty and still runs a coffee shop the size of two bread vans. Competition in Sanlitun is fierce; and now winter is coming. How much money can he possibly make on a fifteen-*kuai* cup of coffee in a place that small? He probably never even finished high school, which is why he has nothing better to do except to play that stupid card game of his. Personally, I think his *ernai* works the night shift at some special karaoke bar where 'happy endings' go to the highest bidder; even if not, how many Viagras do you think he needs to keep up with her?"

Okay, I never felt sorry for Lao Chu quite this way before.

"Whereas you, my dear," she continues, "never seem to work hard, always have pretty girls around, make enough money to travel as you like, ride everything everywhere you go, and even manage to have an American green card."

"Well, not anymore I don't."

"And that's reason number two. Do you think that he actually likes for you to get high inside his place of business? I certainly wouldn't if I were in his shoes. Yes, you bring him customers, but they are all hashers too. Hashers who drive other customers away. He couldn't do anything about it before because you had the green card. You had the power. But as soon as it expired, which I am sure he knew about given how often you hung out there, he had a way to get you."

Well, now that she mentioned it, on the day when my green card debacle happened, Lao Chu was certainly present for my subsequent bitching session at Café 44.

"And finally, reason number three—are you ready? It's face."

"What do you mean? I've never bad-mouthed him or turned him down for a favor. I even translated his menus for free, twice!"

"But what about his *ernai*?" Madame cocks her left eyebrow.

As in the foxy Desire of Ten Thousand Men?

"She gives you special looks, doesn't she? I was at Café 44 only once, and I read them loud and clear."

"Well . . . yeah. But I can't help it."

"Exactly. You made him lose face without even realizing it. Maybe he noticed her looking at you. Or maybe one of his buddies did. Either way, just having you around made him lose face. I mean, how would you feel if the *ernai* you paid for wanted to hump someone else? Personally, I think that's the best reason out of three."

"But it's just a theory, right? You don't have any proof."

"Oh, quite the contrary." She grins. "I think I do."

This is getting weirder by the moment.

"I went to Café 44 yesterday." She winks one eye.

"What the hell for?" I think I have a right to be offended in light of what she has just led me to believe.

"It's the original crime scene." She seemed a little hurt by my reaction. "I just wanted to see if I could pick up some leads."

"Fine." I didn't mean to dampen her spirit. "So who was there?"

"Just Lao Chu, the waiter, and some foreigner I'd never seen before. I heard from people that business has been really bad since you were arrested."

"Really bad?" *Good.*

"Anyway, I just ordered a coffee and sat quietly. But I felt Lao Chu peeking at me all the time."

"Maybe he likes you."

"I doubt it." She giggles. "I think he thinks that I'm with you."

Yeah, that dirty old bastard probably thinks I am with every girl I have coffee with.

"Then he asked me a question," Madame continues. "He wanted to know if you had been released. So I said you got out a long time ago—you know, for face. And guess what? He grew nervous, muttered some nonsense, and left the shop. It had to be a knee-jerk reaction. Right?"

Well . . . Of course! This lady really knows what she is talking about! I know it's all circumstantial evidence at best; but proof beyond a reasonable doubt is not exactly the standard we need to use here. Fucking Lao Chu, all along I thought he was a nice guy. How could I have been such a trusting fool?

So now what?

Madame cocks her right eyebrow. "Get even?"

Hell yeah!

"How?"

Beat him up? Pour sugar into his gas tank? Hire a bunch of smelly migrants to squat in front of 44? Call up the tax bureau to audit his books? Introduce his wife to his *ernai*? Introduce myself to his daughter?

"Anything short of burning down the goddamn place!"

Don't forget that I'm a lawyer—we can make damn good criminals, too, if we just put our minds in the right places!

"Are you with me on this?" I definitely want Madame's help.

"Are you kidding? Whatever you want, I'm in."

She is breathing heavily with excitement. Her eyes sparkle like beacons in the prison darkness.

"So what now?" I wrestle for a way to start my new project immediately.

"Well, how about we . . ." She flicks her eyebrow once again.

"We what?"

"Do something."

"Do what?"

"You know what."

"I beg your pardon?"

"Oh relax. Look where we are. No one else would ever know. Cone on, let's give it a try."

"What are you talking about?"

"Stop playing. Don't you do this all the time in America?"

"This? OH you mean . . . *that!*" As in *it?* Seriously?! "But I thought we were friends?"

"For sure." She stands up with a wink and reaches for the buttons on her dress. "This is only between good friends."

"But I thought you were engaged." I scoot my chair back as far as courtesy would let me.

"So? That's just for society." She shrugs nonchalantly while unfastening the top button out of the three just above her left breast. "I'm twenty-five years old. Got to be at least engaged to somebody or people will talk. Stupid traditions. Well, what are you waiting for? Let's get on with it. *Jie fu* said we can have this room for half an hour."

"But wait!" I fumble for an excuse. "I don't want to give your fiancé the 'green hat.'" Which is what a man wears if his woman cheats on him, a really embarrassing way to lose face, thus explaining why green baseball caps just never sell in China.

"But what makes you think he'd mind? He and I have an open relationship. We can each do our thing on the side. Just don't let it interfere with our engagement."

"But this is not typical of a Chinese couple, is it?"

"It's the twenty-first century already, my dear." She laughs. "Besides, there are so many people in this country, who is to say what's typical?"

"So you don't mind that your fiancé sleeps with other girls?"

"What can I do about it?" She shrugs. "No man likes to sleep with the same woman for the rest of his life. Got to give him some space."

"But what about diseases?" I know for a fact that Chinese girls don't always demand protection, and men are, well, men.

"I don't worry about that." She shrugs it off. "He is actually too busy with work to pick up girls on his own. So I make arrangements for him. Once a month I call up the *mama-san*'s and order a clean girl to be sent over. I was supposed to do that earlier this week. But I've thought about nothing but you since we met."

Really? Why?! This is only the fourth time I have seen her! What the hell did I do to get her hooked? A week ago, I couldn't even remember her name. All this time, I have treated her with the same courtesy as I have every other girl, and . . .

Or could that be it—that I charmed her just by being normal?

Given how commonplace prostitution and *ernais* are around here, China is not exactly a hotbed of feminism. Indeed, a lot of the courtesies that men extend to women in countries like America simply do not exist here. But because I'm a returnee, it is more or less second nature for me to at least hold doors open for the ladies, and they really like that. Maybe Madame thought my nice-to-meet-you routine was more than just simple courtesy. And the fact that I asked her for help in this rather life-or-death matter must have blown her misinterpretation of some cultural diffenences way out of proportion.

"We can use this right here." She rubs the cold metal surface of the junior-sized fold-up table between us. "I've got some things in my purse too."

Damn it, I can feel my erection. It's been seven months, almost eight. I don't even remember the last girl I slept with. I hope she was pretty. But then, I have been smoking too much lately. If I get it on with Madame right here, right now, I'd add another crowd-pleasing page to my illustrious log, not to mention confirming that my pipes are still in working order. And to be quite honest, Madame is easily a 7.0. A lot of guys would kill to be where I am now, especially the FOB foreigners so keen on wild, exotic, Chinese-prison sex.

But the thing with abstinence (even if involuntary to begin with) is that, in some cases, the longer you keep it up, the less willing you become to give it up. It is almost like virginity renewed, which becomes only ten times more precious now that I am older and have been around the block.

And bottom line, I don't want to become some engaged woman's *ernai*.

So what do I tell her—that I am not interested? That would be totally rude. Besides, it's not as if I can't appreciate her situation. Love is blind; infatuation, even more so.

"You know . . ." I'm mincing my words while scratching my head, giving it my best law school try, "I haven't showered in days. Feeling kind of . . . you know. Perhaps we can, uh . . . take a rain check?" Yes, I should be as firm as is the erection in my pants right now; but how do I do that without making her lose face? And I definitely don't want to make her lose face at a time like this—not after what she just told me about Lao Chu! "Instead of . . . *that*, why don't we get to know each other a little more. You know, like friends." As in friends *without* benefits?

"Okay . . ." She sighs. "What do you want to know?"

"Well, where did you go to school?"

"Beijing University."

Damn! That's like the Harvard of China. "And what did you study?"

"Marxist and Leninist theory."

Double damn!

"Are you sure you want to do this now?" She starts to whine. "We've got only twenty minutes left. . . ."

"Well, you know what—get me out of here first. Whatever comes later will come, okay?"

I really hope I don't have to regret saying that.

78

It's been more than eight days since my last Zigarette. That's a grand total of 192 hours. A whopping 11,520 minutes!

I don't feel much different from before, other than occasionally coughing up sticky, yellow chunks of phlegm as part of my body's self-cleansing process (or at least I hope that's what it is). My thoughts still flow at more or less the same speed, which is almost a curse now given that I have nothing to do all day. I can speak more clearly than before, with fewer mispronounced words even when I pick up the tempo. And my handwriting seems to have gotten a lot more legible.

That means I was never addicted to the morphine in my big numb, right?

Earlier today, two teenagers from the neighboring cell were disciplined for fighting during lunchtime over the last remaining *mantou*. Apparently, these adolescents were just hungry. As punishment, the guards chained together their hands and feet and paraded them up and down the block, requiring the pair to recount their offense in front of every cell and apologize for causing a ruckus. For the next three days, they will have to pee and shit in each other's presence.

Moral of the story: Under no circumstances will I allow myself to convulse, hallucinate, or throw up a million pieces to cause any commotion in this cell, whether I'm addicted or not.

79

Chiwarzenegger, the thick-necked prison guard whose English homework I have been doing for the past three days, turned out to be more literate than I thought.

Reading from a roster as part of some surprise cell-block inspection, he called out the names of Chairman, Scruff, Chunk, and Sun, one after the other.

"Here." "Here." "Here." "Here." The gang of four answered with trepidation in their voices.

Then, His Muscularity called me.

"On the toilet, sir!" I answered as loudly as I could while trying to finish the task at hand ASAP. Last night's near-freezing temperature was too much for my thin blankets; and the boiled cabbage from lunch didn't like being eaten.

"Show your face." Chiwarzenegger was obviously not used to waiting on prisoners.

"Hurry up!" Chairman urged in the background, adding his nervousness to my runs.

With no time to spare, I wiped myself half clean, pulled up my jeans, and flushed the toilet while stepping down from the tiled platform. I was going to make it, and dodge what was bound to be an eruption of Herculean proportions by the skin of my teeth.

But the leather sole of my laceless lace-ups had other ideas—with one hasty slip on the wet tiles, my bony ass crashed onto the cement floor with a ring-tone-worthy snap-crackle-and-pop.

As a result, I wound up at the infirmary.

"So what happened to you?" The middle-aged nurse checks my bruise with her gloved fingers.

"It was an accident." I try not to suck cold air too obviously.

Before I forget, I must thank Chairman. Had it not been for his reminder to Chiwarzenegger of Chief's instructions regarding my "comfortable stay," I would not even have been allowed to seek medical attention. But it still was a nightmare to limp down those long stairs with Chiwarzenegger stabbing me with his baton the whole time. So much for quid pro quo.

"Well, there doesn't appear to be anything broken." The nurse has a soft and calming voice. "But this is going to stay for a few days."

"Oh good." Because, no matter what Madame told me two days ago, "I don't think I'm going anywhere in a day or two."

Or two or three, or three or four . . .

"So what are you in for?" she asks.

"Oh . . . just stupid stuff."

She mutters something.

"Beg your pardon?"

"Nothing."

"Go ahead and say it." Anything is better than more prison silence.

"Well"—she lowers her spectacles to hang on her collar—"I was just thinking that you don't really look like you belong here."

Okay, maybe not everything is better than prison silence.

"I mean, for one thing"—she chuckles—"you are far cleaner than the rest."

Oh, right, I used to think so too, until I got wetness all over my hair and clothes from all sorts of cracks and crevices that I really don't want to think about right now.

"So where are you from, anyway?" She takes something out of the medicine cabinet.

"Long story."

"Any time abroad?"

"A bit."

"No wonder." She nods. "I thought there was something different about your *qi*."

Okay lady, I appreciate your being kind and all, but if I really had some *qi* ("chee"), which is what George Lucas decided to rename "the Force" in *Star Wars,* I wouldn't even be here today.

"So why did you come back to China?" she continues.

"The future, I suppose."

"Do you still feel like a Chinese?" She sticks a smelly medicinal patch onto my bruised hip.

"HONESTLY!" I didn't mean to squeal like a girl. "I don't even know anymore."

". . ."

"Well don't get me wrong. I didn't mean it like, you know, that I don't like this place. I mean, I do like it, honestly. I mean, up until last week, there was at least, I don't know, say fifty percent of this place that I liked. I mean—"

"Relax." She saves me from digging the hole any deeper, "I can see what you mean."

"Yeah?"

"Sure. Move to a new place, your *qi* needs to adjust. I've lived in China all my life, but if I left for a while and then came back, I probably wouldn't feel all comfortable either."

Right: China, comfortable—she should be a comedian.

"But look on the bright side." The nurse begins to prep the second patch. "There are a lot of people out there who feel out of place too."

Oh sure, all the foreigners, plus oddball returnees like me.

"You'd be surprised by how many locals are going through the same things you are."

"Yeah? Like who?"

"You are looking at one right now."

"PARDON?!" How can the second patch hurt even more than the first?!

"Well, in case you haven't noticed, everything is changing now." She shrugs. "The China I once knew is nothing like the China of today. Fifteen years ago, there were only two channels on television; now there are two hundred, and everyone is getting a satellite dish on top of it. And the Internet, heavens. Whereas me, I'm pushing retirement already."

"Already?" I thought she was probably in her forties.

"I'll be sixty-five next week."

"WHAT?!" That was not just for the third patch—I know all about Chinese ladies aging gracefully without Botox, but this one is off the charts.

She chuckles. "If this were a real medical facility, I would have retired a long time ago to make room for the younger nurses. But since no one really wants to work here . . ."

I guess it is true what they say—prison really does preserve the body.

"Keep those patches on for a day and replace them tomorrow." She signals me to pull my jeans back up and hands me a new box of my medicine.

"That's it?" I was hoping for more of a soothing, time-consuming treatment.

"Sorry." She shrugs again. "There is only so much I can do here."

But it's been over a week already and this is the first time I've been out of my cell unsupervised. And this lady seems nice. No condescending looks. No cigarette smoke in my face. No I-control-your-fate attitude. I'd give anything to stay here a bit longer, anything at all.

"Hey, uh, can you tell me more about the *qi* thing?"

"What about it?"

"Well." I start, hobbling over to her small desk and sit down on my left cheek. "Does it really exist?"

No disrespect, but I always thought it was just some hocus-pocus used to sell some kungfutions, and now movies.

She grins.

"Then what does this *qi* do?"

"It keeps you alive and healthy."

"But how?" I mean, I know all about vitamins and proteins and all that food pyramid stuff from high school, but *qi*?

"Well, in a nutshell"—she pauses for a second to set down her glasses—"*wu zang liu fu zhi jing qi, jie shang zhu yu mu er wei zhi jing. Jing zhi an wei yan, gu zhi jing wei chong zi, jin zhi jing wei hei yan, luo zhi jing wei hei yan, qi an qi zhi jing wei bai yan. . . .*"

Uh . . . what?!

"Look, there is a whole science behind *qi* that you can one day learn on your own. For now, let me just say that *qi* exists in your body naturally. If you live a healthy lifestyle, you promote good *qi*; if you live like a mess, you get bad *qi*."

"So what do you do for your own *qi*?"

"Not much. Just meditation here and there. Plus tai chi in the morning."

Like those old folks outside Club Mix at 6 A.M.? "Does it really work?"

She grins again.

"So then, can someone actually use *qi* to kill with a finger's touch and jump ten floors in a single leap? Like those *da xia*s in the books?"

I am of course referring to the kungfution superheroes whom George Lucas made into the Jedis.

"Well, anything is possible." She shrugs with amusement. "But to get your *qi* to that level, you'd have to drink nothing but pure mountain snow water, eat nothing but unseasoned organic vegetables, and do nothing but meditate all day; is that what you want?"

Bummer.

"Besides, all those are just the potential benefits of *qi,* not the goal."

"Then why do it?"

She taps her temple.

"As in intelligence?"

"No." She shakes her head. "As in wisdom."

"But don't we get wise with age anyway?"

"Are you wiser now than two years ago?"

"Am I not?"

"Then what are you doing here?"

Okay, that was almost below the belt.

"Look," she speaks softly, smiling as I blush, "when we were first born, our bodies were fresh and pure; so was our *qi.* But as we age, we become exposed; and half of the things we do in our youth tend to be bad for us too. In the process, our bodies get contaminated, thus compromising the natural source of our *qi.* Then pile on all the messy sevens and dirty eights of everyday life, we become irritable and arrogant, and end up making bad choices. Like driving a car on dirty gasoline, we drift further and further away from wisdom. So the point is, good *qi* allows you to achieve clarity. It is not wisdom in and of itself, but it can help you find the way there."

"Well then"—I think I actually understood half of what she said—"how do I fix my *qi?*"

"Fix it?"

"Yeah, you know, like debugging a computer." Or better yet, putting in a new processor to help speed things up.

"But why?" She crosses her arms.

"Well, I mean, why not? Sounds pretty cool."

"But the training would take a long time."

"Yeah . . . but I don't think I'm going anywhere soon."

"Then what about focus? Can you repeat the same routine day after day?"

"Oh, absolutely. I used to work out seven days a week." And all I had was vanity to keep me going.

She is squinting.

Oh, I get it, she must think that I want *qi* for the wrong reasons, that I want to jump ten floors in a single leap and kill people with a finger's touch. But come on—I am an adult, and this is reality. All my life, I have never been in a fight; and I see no reason to start now. To be quite honest, I really just want something new to do so that I won't be so damn bored in the cell. Give me a tip, a chant, something, anything.

She is not responding.

Okay, maybe boredom is not the right reason. But there is more. Given how much the idea of *qi* permeates Chinese culture, learning how it works must be a good way of learning about China. And given all the theories behind *qi*, none of which I ever came across in my high school science class, learning them would help me see nature from a completely different angle. So even if *qi* turns out to be not for me, I would at least acquire some new knowledge; and that is always good, right?

The nurse's gaze could practically etch a rock.

All right, how do I convince her? Purse my lips? Make a puppy face? A few more awkward moments of staring at each other in si-

lence? She doesn't expect me to drop down to my knees and kowtow, does she?

Okay. I have never been good at this type of thing. "But I just
want to do something good for myself."

For a change.

Okay, I admit, fixing something after it is already broken is never
as good as preventing the damage in the first place, and Chinese
wisdom always follows the latter approach. But I am only twenty-
eight, and I grew up with "If it ain't broken, don't fix it." According
to a Chinese maxim, a lost child who finds his way back is worth
more than his weight in gold; and I weigh almost 160 pounds!

Her face eases up finally. "Well then, I suggest you start with
meditation first."

"Terrific! Is there like a book that you can show me?"

She squints again.

"You know, like a manual or something?"

She shakes her head.

"You mean there is nothing to read?"

"Why, you didn't actually think it was going to be that easy, did
you?" She chuckles. "Finding *qi* takes focus. No book can teach
you that. If you have potential, prove it."

"And if I do?"

"Then you'll feel something, at which point you can start reading
the books."

"But where? How?"

"Ever heard of the Internet?"

Touché.

"But a word of advice." She points with her index finger. "Don't
overdo it. Go slowly. No one reaches the sky in a single step. Understand!"

Yes, of course. Everything in moderation, right?

80

Thanks to the supposed "tiger penis extract" in that herbal patch on my butt, I've been getting hot flashes all day. My body kind of tingles and itches at the same time, which only makes everything more annoying than it already is.

Now, counting all the days since this whole prison thing went down, other than firing someone on the day of my arrest, I haven't done a thing for Foodiez in almost a month. Just imagine all the vendor e-mails and customer complaints and messed-up orders and, please, no traffic accidents. I hate to be thinking this way, but is my office still gonna be there when I get out?

And even though I haven't made any big bucks in a while, what will happen to my license to practice law? The bar overseers on those high chairs in the U.S. will be thrilled to find out about this little due diligence of mine inside the Chinese prison system. Any chance they will ask me to write a law review article? Or will they demand that I write an explanation, an apology, an affidavit of some sort, and still revoke my license without the possibility of reinstatement by means of a bribe?

And what am I going to tell my old man? Or when? And how? What kind of archaic corporal punishment will he pull out of his chest of ancient Chinese secrets this time? Given that he is much older now and presumably unable to carry out the task himself, will I possibly have to inflict the pain on myself by myself?

Man, I wish I could see my friends right about now. Have a smoke. Have a chat. Do whatever I want in their company without ever feeling any pressure to bullshit. Maybe it's circumstances, but I really think they are the best group of friends I have had in a long time. Intelligent. Thoughtful. Caring. We share the kind of camaraderie that the first generation of Chinese Communists might have felt in their own time—a time when they were the few, living in a world much different from the one they envisioned and aspired to. As harsh as Beijing can be in terms of weather and pollution, even just a clay pot of the simplest tea shared with one of these guys or gals has always more than compensated for the dust and grime.

So have any of them started to miss me yet? Besides Lethal, Moneypenny, and the few who are in the know, how many have even noticed that I have been gone for all this time? And assuming that they do eventually come to that realization after a few unanswered text messages, how will they react? As Chinese as I may look in person, I'm still an outsider; and outsiders can get homesick easily, with some quick to skip town when things don't go their way. Once I've gone missing for a few days, others just might assume that I've packed up and left. Not everyone likes farewell parties, after all. Some might just go quietly into the night, or in my case, the big house.

So will I become the "forgotten friend"? How many people have deleted my mobile number already?!

That's it. Think about something pleasant!

But what? Women? Again? I am really starting to get sick of those flashbacks. Yes, we did have our good times together. Yes, I even thought I was really in love at the time. But guess what? Nothing. And now, look who's sleeping next to me. What do I say to myself? That maybe I should have compromised a little more? That maybe I should not have set my sights so high?

But then, where would I have drawn the line?

No disrespect to the good nurse, but meditation is meant for folks with no problems!

81

Heilongjiang has got a motormouth that just won't quit.

Hailing from the northeastern province of Heilongjiang and thus called "Heilongjiang" by Chairman, this rather scrawny kid is a regular stand-up comic compared to the rest of the People. Since coming on deck earlier this morning, he has already told two dirty jokes and given beautiful face to the food troupe in return for some extra *mantous* for everyone.

According to Heilongjiang, this is his second stint in prison in as many weeks, both for stealing bicycles; except that this time, he was "helping out a friend." When asked about his age, he said he is eighteen, which would ordinarily make him an adult and thus subject him to a whole year on the Farm for his repeat offense. But he said that because of his migrant status, the cops have no way of verifying his identity, and his short height helps him lie about being only seventeen.

"So do you steal motorcycles, too?" It just occurred to me that my prized Yamaha has already been left unlocked outside Café 44 for nine long days.

"No, only bicycles." He shrugs. "And only when I am short on cash."

"So does that mean you actually have a job?"

"Are you kidding? Of course. I work for a syndicate."

"Really? What kind?"

"Well, in a nutshell, we open locks."

"Oh, good. So I can call you when I get locked out of my place next time."

"Well, not exactly." He squints. "You can call us if you want, as we do keep a few apprentices for customers like you. But you won't see me."

"Why not?"

"Because I only work on 'black locks.' "

"Come again?"

"Well, let's say that you have cased out a joint with some loot. Then I can help you unlock the door to grab it. Sometimes I bring another guy for the safe as well."

How wonderful. I thought cat burglary was still a thing of the future for China. "So how much do you charge?"

"Twenty percent of the pot."

"And how big is the pot?"

"Up to a few million *kuai*. I've even seen a briefcase of American dollars once."

"Well that ought to pay the bills for a while, right?"

"*Cao.*" He wipes his nose. "Everything I make goes to the boss. I am a migrant on migrant pay. Five hundred *kuai* a month. If the boss feels generous."

Well, I don't mean to rub it in, but my Foodiez boys make more than twice that in a month. And they always get paid on time.

But is it enough? What about those who have families to support? Any chance that they also have to steal bicycles to make ends meet? Is that why the kid I fired the other day decided to run off with his company ride?

"So how do you do it, technically?" I ask.

"Special keys," he answers nonchalantly. "If it gets complicated, I use ball bearings and a wire, or just acid to melt off the lock. Most jobs take under fifteen seconds."

"But where did you learn how to do that?"

"Certain people just get it." He shrugs. "The safe expert at my company is only sixteen years old; and he doesn't ever use an earphone either."

"So what about your family?"

"Back in the village. I am the second of four children."

"Four?!" Whatever happened to the One Child Policy?

"It is the countryside." He laughs. "High in the mountains, far from the emperor. Up there, there is no one to monitor. I mean, we don't even have electricity for every hour of the day. What else are you gonna do?"

"Then what about school?"

"*Cao,* I had to trek three hours each way if I wanted to do that. It's a shack with no heat, and the same idiot teaches everything. Might as well come to the city and make some money."

"All by yourself?"

"Well, originally, with a few other kids from my village. We were all supposed to work on this construction site that promised free food and lodging plus a salary. Then some *shabi* up there in management stole all the money and skipped town. I worked three months for nothing."

"Was there anyone who could help you?"

"*Cao.* This is the big city, isn't it?"

"Then does your family know what you are doing over here? Wouldn't they be worried?"

"Not as long as I send money home every month."

Come again? I have never sent a dime home in my entire life. And how does he even come up with the money? "So do you miss home at all?"

"What's there to miss?" He snickers. "I'd eat the same *mantous* there as I do here. And it gets even colder up in the Northeast."

"Then what are you gonna do when you get out of here?"

"Oh"—he pulls on his oil-stained overcoat—"find a sauna, unload my cannon, and definitely get some new clothes."

"Not that. I meant a job!"

"*Ai,*" he says it with a chuckle, waving off my concern with a flick of his wrist. "When the time comes, I'll naturally steer my ship straight."

And of course he will—China is the new Land of Opportunity, isn't it?

But even so, there is yet to be a Land of *Equal* Opportunity anywhere. Regardless of how smart, able, and streetwise Heilongjiang may be, will his other circumstances ever allow him to find a way out?

Come to think of it, the start-up that I almost abandoned on more than one occasion just might have saved a dozen other Heilongjiangs from wasting their whole lives away in this shithole. Granted, Foodiez doesn't make anybody a fortune from month to month, but it's certainly more of an opportunity than slaving away on any construction site; and given time, the rewards might become much greater. Some of the most successful businesses have the humblest beginnings, and having the right people makes all the difference between boom and bust. Could it be that there are actually hidden talents among my staff who can help me take Foodiez (and their own lives) to the next level, and all that I have to do to find them is to talk to them in the same way as I am talking to Heilongjiang?

"Say"—my growling stomach reminds me—"when was the last time you had any meat?"

"What do you mean, 'meat'?"

"As in beef, pork, chicken, lamb. You know: meat."

"Chunks and chunks of it?" Heilongjiang looks up into the ceiling. ". . . Can't remember."

"Well then, how about I treat you to some pork stew?"

Better yet, why don't I treat everyone in the cell to some pork stew? It's been nine days already and I have not used my meal card even once. Maybe it was due to the close quarters in 801; but somehow, it just never felt right to use that particular privilege all for myself.

"Say, *da ge,* can I ask you something?" Heilongjiang looks puzzled. "Why do you have all those rips in your jeans?"

"Huh?" I look at the rips that I call style.

"If I were you, I'd buy some new clothes once I got out of here. There is no need to wear old, torn clothes when you can afford new ones, right?"

Right. The cultural differences.

"Well then, Heilongjiang, can I ask *you* something?"

"Of course."

"It's a little personal, though."

"Ask away."

"How many times do you shower each week?"

"Each week?" He scratches his head, looking rather stumped. "It depends on the season, really. If it's summer, then maybe once a week. In the winter, more like once a month."

"Once a *month*?!" No wonder some of my Foodiez boys smell the way they do! "How can you stand it? Don't you feel uncomfortable? Aren't you afraid of disease?"

"Well, sure." He blushes with an awkward blink of his small eyes. "But I've never had a shower of my own. If I want to get clean, I have to go to a public bathhouse. It's up to five *kuai* a shower now in most places; *and* I have to bring my own soap and stuff; *and* the water is not even hot most of the time. I'm not strong like you, *da ge.* It's easier for me to get sick taking a shower than not taking a shower, and I can't afford to get sick. Besides, I can always just use a wet towel to wipe myself anyway. You'd get used to it. Say, have you ever been to a public bathhouse?"

"Oh . . . pssssh. Are you kidding?" Would I still be asking these questions if I had?

But really, winter is coming any day now. How will my employees cope with Beijing's longest and worst season? Will they be forced to take showers only once a month as well? Can they afford decent winter clothes to keep themselves warm and insulated while riding in sub-zero temperatures across a town full of diesel trucks and newly licensed female Chinese drivers? Do they have helmets? Gloves? Insurance?

Granted, there is no law in China yet—not one that is actively enforced, anyway—that requires me to help them with any of the above; but just because they are laborers in a developing country does not mean they are any less human. Being in business for myself, I of course have to focus on maximizing profit and minimizing cost; but once all the number crunching is done, is there room left between the margins for having a heart too?

82

"So what did you do this time?" Chunk asks Scruff for the second time as he puts down a pair of 8s.

Earlier on this Day 10, Chairman brought back a deck of playing cards after his daily report to Chief. So for the first time in an eternity, 801 has got real entertainment; and even though I have never been a big fan of the devil's game, beggars can't be choosers. During the postdinner CCTV hour, I finally learned to play the three-player card game of *dou di zhu*. And, guess what, I didn't go through all that schooling for nothing. Since none of us had any money, we just kept score. According to the ranking system, the first one to win 1,000 points would be crowned "emperor." Before I decided to sit out this round, I had already made the rank of "second-class mandarin."

"Keep it coming." Scruff hurries Sun for his turn, obviously unwilling to answer Chunk's question.

"Oh, come on. What did you do?" As usual, Chunk is just too slow to get the message.

"Shabi!" Scruff slams his cards onto the deck with a loud bang. "How many times do I have to tell you that it's none of your business!"

Yikes.

Somebody give that poor guy a *mantou* to suck on.

Believe it or not, I was actually referring to Scruff this time.

As much as I still consider him to be a horribly uncivilized ass, I have actually gotten to know Scruff a lot better over the past few days. Whenever his snoring kept me up at night, I made him stay up to shoot the breeze until I got tired enough to doze off. In the process, I finally sniffed out Scruff's story.

Before he was made an enforcer in 801, Scruff was a lieutenant in the armed police. Unlike regular cops, who have only blue-and-white Volkswagens, the armed police are known and feared for their black Audi A6s that terrorize traffic with their sirens and flashers. With the traffic police turning a blind eye to their conspicuous WJ license plates (short for *wu jing*), they are China's undisputed road kings.

For many years, Scruff enjoyed such privileges to the fullest, until karma caught up with him one night four years ago. According to Scruff, the accident occurred on a U-curve section of a narrow, unlit mountain road as he was driving back to the base in his platoon's Audi A6. Rounding the apex of a tight hairpin with the mountain on his left, he came upon a bread van that had not only stopped right in the middle of his lane (presumably for missing a turn immediately before the hairpin) but was actually in the process of driving in reverse. To avoid going off the precipice to his right or slamming into the reversing tin can, he swerved into the opposing lane and the path of an oncoming vehicle, killing the driver and passenger instantly.

The prosecution's case rested on two arguments: one, Scruff was driving drunk, and two, he was tailgating. As for the first charge, there was no Breathalyzer done at the scene, and the only evidence that the prosecution had of Scruff's drunkenness was an on-the-spot observation by a traffic cop that he smelled *bai jiu* on Scruff's body. But as *bai jiu* has such a strong stench, anyone who stays close to an open bottle for an hour would have the smell rub off on him, and Scruff had just attended a group dinner with some friends. Plus, if he is like me and hundreds of millions of other Chinese who have the Asian Flush, his face would have turned lobster red if he was drunk; yet the traffic report made no mention of that telltale sign.

As for the second charge, the tiny bit of law that China actually had on the subject more or less presumed, irrefutably, that any vehicle that collides with the rear of another is a tailgater and thus strictly liable for the collision—even if the vehicle in front deliberately slams on its brakes so as to induce a collision. According to the prosecution, the fact that Scruff swerved to the left of the road implied that he was tailgating the vehicle in front. But since the accident happened at a cliff-side hairpin, Scruff's vision of the road ahead could have been blocked until he was already too close to the bread van. And as a bread van does not have antilock brakes and would have left skid marks on the pavement had it really come to a screeching halt (as described by Scruff), a simple photograph of the accident scene might have shed light on whether he was tailgating at all.

Of course, none of the above questions were raised by Scruff's lawyer. In fact, he saw Scruff only twice before the trial, and no photograph of the accident scene was ever produced. As the bread van that (according to Scruff) was the original cause of the accident had long fled the scene, the armed police simply paid a few hundred *kuai* to make the case go away. This ended up costing Scruff three and a half years on the Farm.

After being released from the Farm eight months ago, Scruff was dishonorably discharged from the armed police and stripped of his Communist Party membership for life. Like a Thai hooker banished to Islamabad, he lost all his privileges and *guan xi*s as a member of China's mighty military. In the time since, he has managed to be arrested two more times—first for snatching a purse out of a hospital waiting room, for which he did another six months on the Farm, and now for stealing his neighbor's used camera, which the police had valued at only 300 *kuai*.

No wonder he is always in such a foul mood.

"Hey, *da ge,* are you ready to come back in?" Scruff turns to me after effectively ejecting Chunk from their game.

"But we've done ten already." During which I relegated him to the lowest possible rank of "eunuch," *castrated*.

Besides, I've got much better things to do.

Okay, I know what I said only days ago—that meditation isn't for me. But as is often the case, the light came on just before I completely gave up.

It happened last night when, as usual, I had no *yuan fen* with sleep. Somehow, my mind wandered onto visualizing the exact way I roll my Zigarette. From making the filter out of a business card to separating the laced tobacco with my fingertips, I was making the Fabergé egg of joints in my mind. Then as I finally finessed off the excess tip at the end of my imaginary escape, something clicked.

All this time, I've been smoking my Zigarette as a means of getting to higher ground. Given our compartmentalized world of logic and materialism, my Zigarette really gives me the elevation I need to "think outside the box." When I am high, I don't worry much about anything: I am in good health, have wonderful friends, am not exactly starving to death, and, well, what else do I really need? Now if only I could somehow get to this state of mind all by myself— meaning without any chemical influence (which is arguably just another box)—maybe I could *really* think outside the proverbial container, even one built of bars and concrete.

Of course, pulling off something like this isn't going to be as easy as hiring a maid to do my laundry, cook my meals, and clean my apartment top to bottom three times a week for the equivalent of US $120 a month. But then, if I could be so meticulous and patient when it came to something as small as rolling a joint, maybe I could learn to do the same with respect to the other aspects of my daily life.

Just take driving, for example. In a developing country like China, where the entire nation just got its learner's permit, being on the road for any reason at all is already a huge hazard. Yet in response to some local drivers' rude and inconsiderate behavior, I often up the ante by leaning on the gas a little more or go as far as turning into the Windshield-Spitting Bandit. But how can I defeat *shabi*-ness by being part of it? To get out of this vicious cycle, *someone* has to take the higher road. Does it have to be me? Well, at least I know what it feels like to be high. Then if I could remember that feeling whenever something bothered me about living in China, I just might be able to brush off the mundane pollution, and there would be no more—or at least fewer—One A Days!

Now meditate on that.

Of course, I haven't felt anything that might come close to being *qi* yet. But all in good time.

"Oh come on, just one more round." Scruff isn't going to let me off the hook without a fight. "I'll be gone by this time tomorrow."

"Really? Where to?"

"The Farm."

"All right, would somebody *please* tell me what this 'Farm' thing is all about?"

"Have you ever heard of 'reeducation by labor'?"

Sure, just not since I was last warned about it by Ms. Deng in third grade.

"So how long are you going for?" I ask.

"Eighteen months. Fifteen with good behavior, maybe."

All just for stealing a used camera?

"What are you gonna do there anyway?" Chairman interjects.

"Depends on the Farm," Scruff answers. "Some work the fields, some make basketballs. I had to grow soybeans and tend chickens the last time I went."

"What are the hours like?"

"Rise with the sun, breakfast in five minutes, work until noon, lunch for ten minutes, then work till dinner at sundown."

"That doesn't sound so bad." I try cheering him up. "What's there to do at night?"

"Nothing."

"What about TV?"

"No."

"Then what about cards? You can at least play *dou di zhu*, right?"

"Yeah, right." Scruff tries to grin. "You can't even smoke ciga-rettes there. And if they catch you causing any trouble, they fit a metal helmet over your head and shock you with electricity till you shit in your pants."

Right, saw that in *One Flew Over the Cuckoo's Nest* once.

"Anything else?"

"Well, you better learn how to do this."

With uncharacteristic enthusiasm, Scruff pulls a blanket from the top of the pile. Amid a storm of dust, he flings it open, lays it out flat on the deck, and proceeds to fold it in familiar Chinese fashion: first along the long side into three layers, then piling up a quarter of a bundle from one end and another quarter from the other, and fi-nally doubling it up to form a stacked block.

"Uh, *ge-men'er,* I can do that too." Don't forget that I'm a lawyer qualified in two American states.

"This is just the beginning." Scruff motions for me to keep watching.

Using his index finger and thumb, he begins to pinch creases out of the block's various edges and corners. As the blanket is by nature soft and limp, however, each crease lasts only a few seconds. Unde-terred, Scruff pinches on. To improvise the effect of a steam iron, he even collects the beads of sweat on his forehead and applies them to the edges that he fastidiously molds.

The People quickly surround the spectacle.

"Hey, *da ge.*" I turn to Chairman. "What else do you know about the Farm?"

"Not much," Chairman says, sighing. "All I've heard is that everything depends on your *guan xi* with the guards down there. Piss them off, and life turns sour real quick. I heard of folks trying to get out of labor by smashing their own kneecaps. It's nothing like here. We have the nicest cell in this entire compound."

Hmm, I heard the same thing from Chief before as well, but, "Seriously?"

He chuckles. "You think this place is crowded? The last cell I was in had at least thirty-five people at all times; and there were no juveniles. Get my drift?"

Okay. "Then would you know anything about rehab?"

"You mean for drug addicts? No, I don't know much about it personally. But there was this one guy in my old cell, hooked on something or another. He wasn't too happy about going to rehab though, kept trying to kill himself by ramming his head into the wall. They had to put a helmet on him and cuff his hands to his feet."

"And where is he now?"

"Beats me." He shrugs. "But if I have to choose between that and the Farm, I'd take the Farm."

"But you don't think *I* have to go there, do you?"

"Oh, don't you worry." Chairman smiles. "You'll be out in no time."

"Really?!"

"Well, you've got your *guan xi* down pretty good." He looks me straight in the eye. "Right?"

"Finished!" Scruff pumps his fist in triumph.

It's a miracle. I can't believe I am that this perfectly rigid cube is actually a blanket. Every edge has a crease. Every corner is ninety degrees.

"Good job." Chairman rubs his chin. "But is there any way you can do it faster? That was rather long."

Scruff is almost out of breath due to an obvious lack of training. "Once you've done it enough times with the same blanket, it'll take only a few minutes."

"But how long before that happens?" I ask.

"Not long." Scruff wipes the lingering sweat off his forehead. "It

took me about a year and a half. Just wake up before sunrise so
you'll have the extra time to get it right."

"And if you don't?"

"Then you don't eat."

And Chairman would still take the Farm over rehab?

I'd better talk to Bill again real soon.

83

Just like that, it dropped fifteen degrees overnight.

For hours, the juvies have been coughing, sniffling, and sneez-
ing. Wave after wave, winds from the barren northwest pound Gobi
sands into the rattling window glass.

Other than our own steaming breaths, there is not a single bit of
heat in the cell. My fingertips are numb; I can hardly feel my nose;
and sitting up against this wall here is practically leaning on ice.

I really, really don't want to get sick in here.

"Are you all right?" I see that Sun has been pacing for a while
with nothing on except a pair of thin cotton trousers and an even
thinner long-sleeve shirt. He is not even wearing socks.

"Oh, don't worry about me." He keeps rubbing his upper arms
vigorously.

"Come on, *ge-men'er,* put this on." I throw him the other green sweatshirt that came with Madame's last care package.

He studies the Polo knockoff for a second, seemingly uncomfortable with accepting handouts from someone much younger.

Until a draft of Beijing's worst persuades him.

"Thanks a lot, *ge-men'er.*" He sits down next to me. "Nice friends you've got. I bet it's a girl, right?"

Yeah, for better or worse.

"A girlfriend?"

"No." I chuckle. "Haven't had one in years."

"Really?" He squints. "But there are so many girls in this town; a guy like you must get tons of action."

"Oh yeah, sure." I didn't mean to be rude by sighing.

Now don't get me wrong, I have enjoyed singlehood very much. In the five years since my ex, I have gotten so good at the game that if I were to talk to a girl with strictly carnal intentions, I'd know her fifth sentence into the conversation before she even began to speak.

Unfortunately, once the game becomes as easy as computer chess, only those who have no desire to challenge themselves want to keep on playing. And that is where things turn sour—it gets damn lonely when you are single and picky. Besides the cold winter nights, there are also holidays, vacations, and the many meals that I no longer fancy eating by myself. As much as I tell myself to enjoy being one of those guys who don't give a damn, deep down, who wouldn't want to take a romantic stroll around the Forbidden City, walk up the Great Wall hand in hand to catch the sunrise, or even just rent a boat for two and paddle around Houhai as the old men in Speedos do their afternoon laps? Millions of people fall in love in Beijing all the time; so why can't I?

"Well, have you considered some of the local girls?" Sun asks. "There are a lot of beauties in this town."

Yeah, but I don't know if I really want another Mirage. And Madame is not giving me much confidence about the local talent either.

"Then how about the foreigners? You like them, don't you?"

"Oh sure."

Thanks to my American influence, race or ethnicity is not an issue. White, black, red, yellow, I find beauty in all of them. But foreign babes tend to be the exact opposite of local ones—they watch a lot of CNN but know almost nothing about China. While some of them can be very attractive and intelligent, being with them would require me to play big brother in yet another way. "I just don't want to have to explain words like *'shabi'* and *'er bai wu'* all the time. You know what I mean?"

Sun laughs. "But aren't *lao wai* girls studying Chinese anyway?" he asks, using a slang term for "foreigners."

"Yeah, just not as fast as I'd like."

After all, given their privileges, a lot of *lao wai* babes still don't need to speak much Chinese to get by. And when there are more knockoff clothing markets coming up every day, where one can spend hours upon hours bargaining for the newest Prada or Gucci that looks exactly like the real deal, it might be difficult to actually set aside the time to study much beyond how to shop in Chinese.

"You mean there is no one in this town who has caught your eye?" Sun doesn't seem to buy my conviction. "But there are fifteen million people here."

"Yeah, sad, isn't it?"

"Or perhaps you have set your sights too high."

"You think? But it's not as if I am asking for a perfect ten."

"Then maybe it has something to do with *yuan fen.*"

"*Ge-men'er,* you like to talk about *yuan fen* a lot, don't you?"

"But it explains how everything works."

"Well, whatever it is," be it fate, cause and effect, a whole load of crap I can't even eat, "as it stands, I ain't got no *yuan fen* with girls, okay?"

Not unless you count my *yuan fen* with Madame, which at this point is awkward, to say the least, and potentially . . . who knows.

"Really?" Sun squints. "Maybe you just haven't done what it takes to kick-start it."

As in actually making an effort?

Okay, fine. Maybe it's not a good idea to just wait around for the right girl to come to me. If love takes a kick in the pants, so be it. Unfortunately, I've got no pants that I care to kick as of right now.

"Well, maybe you do," Sun says with a shrug, "but just don't know it yet. Like an old acquaintance, for example."

"Yeah, sure. Maybe."

"Well, whatever it is"—he rubs his silver hair a few times—"just don't let face get in the way."

"What's that got to do with anything?"

"Everything." He frowns. "Just ask yourself, how many times have you *not* tried something because failure might make you lose face?"

"Sure, I know that." For once upon a time, I was afraid to ask girls out for fear of being turned down too. Definitely not the case anymore.

"But then there comes a time when things don't work out on your first try," Sun says. "What do you do then?"

"Move on?" Life is too short as is. And there are 7.5 million females in this city alone, at least 30 percent of whom are between the ages of eighteen and thirty-five.

"But you don't get to eat hot tofu if you don't have the patience," Sun quotes China's quirky way of saying "Good things come to those who wait." "Sometimes you just have to keep trying."

"Even after the girl turns you down?"

"Especially when it comes to girls who turn you down."

That's the craziest thing I've ever heard!

"Well, I am not talking about girls who turn you down because they'd rather be *ernais,* but girls who turn you down for the right reasons. Like you were too sloppy, too lazy, too cocky, too whatever."

"But still, wouldn't that be kind of embarrassing?" I *am* a guy after all.

"See"—Sun gestures with his finger—"that's where it all goes back to *yuan fen.*"

"Again?" How many more parts are there to this thing?

"The point is," Sun continues, "when you are not honest with yourself, you don't make the right effort. You don't make the right effort, a *yuan fen* that could have been will never be. But in actuality, what's holding you back? If it is just face, is it really worth it?"

"Okay, fine. If he really must know there is this one girl."

"Yeah? What's she like?"

"Well, she's pretty."

Or to be more precise—pretty damn hot. And given how she can switch freely between Chinese and English, she is about the foxiest culture chameleon I know. Having spent the last three years studying traditional Chinese medicine right here in China, she probably knows a lot of things about this place that I don't. When we first met, things were going pretty well. The two of us even went for a long ride on my Yamaha once, and she even bought me Baskin-Robbins afterward.

Yeah, I am thinking about Ginger.

But then she gave me the deflection when I tried to kiss her at the end of our ride that day—twice! Things like that just don't happen to me.

"Have you guys ever talked about it?" Sun asks.

"You mean sex?"

"No, of course not. Do all Americans think this way?" He chuckles. "I meant about you liking her."

"Well . . . sort of."

"Sort of?"

Okay, no. Now that I jog my memory, I didn't exactly warm Ginger up for that kiss. Nor did I feel the need to. After a whole day of holding on to me for dear life, she had to know what was coming. And just look at her—big hair, big flair, and that naughty mark above her upper lip. As bling bling personified, she had to be free-spirited.

But then, what about from her perspective? After all, I was the bad boy of Sanlitun, and a girl like her would never want to be just another face in my harem. Without clear communication, how could she have known that beneath my wanderer's image, I actually liked her and was interested in more than just a one-night stand? Especially if I didn't even know that myself at the time?

"Then I suggest you send her a clear message while you still can." Sun seems to be speaking from experience. "*Yuan fen* doesn't wait forever."

"But what if it doesn't work out?" I hate to be realistic. For starters, there are a lot of guys after her all the time. Some of them own not one, not two, but five Range Rovers. And being an outsider, she just might pack up and leave town tomorrow. Even though my instincts tell me that she still likes me (or she would never even have said hello at Café 44 on the afternoon of my arrest), what assurance do I have that our *yuan fen,* if any, will actually endure? "And even if it does last for a while, what then? Pardon me for pointing out the obvious—" I pat Sun on the shoulder—"but your own marriage didn't exactly work out."

"True." He rubs his silver hair again with a sigh. "But you know, to keep a relationship going strong year after year is really like a job."

"That doesn't exactly motivate me, *ge-men'er*. I am more of a gig guy than a job guy."

"Or maybe you just haven't found a job that you are passionate about. When you truly enjoy what you do, even working twenty-four/seven won't feel like a job."

"Or it could turn into a real chore. How would you ever know the difference until it's too late?"

"You won't. But you also won't know anything until you try. How old are you now, anyway?"

"Twenty-eight. Turning twenty-nine."

"Born in the Year of the Tiger?"

"No. Year of the Rabbit."

"Well that means you are thirty already."

Fine, if you insist on counting my age on the lunar calendar, in which case a person is deemed one year old as soon as he is born and is thus always one year older in Chinese math.

"Then have you ever heard of 'A boy becomes a man at thirty'?"

84

A Chinese maxim says, If you haven't seen someone in more than three days, you'd better rub your eyes to get a good look. And now that I haven't seen him in a lot longer than that, Bill looks rather haggard. Even though it is rather dim in the unlit office, I can see that his complexion is sallow, his hair less spiky; and there appears to be a rather nasty sore on his upper right lip.

"How are you doing, kid?" He is sucking on his cigarette a lot harder than I remember him doing before.

"Not bad. Just waiting for, you know."

Frankly, I don't know how much longer I can last. In twelve nights and eleven days, I have probably had a total of fifty hours of sleep. Ever since I saw the nurse, I have been meditating up to five hours each day, especially when I can't sleep at night. I know she told me not to do it so much for nothing in excess is ever good, but what else is there to do? Here and now, I really wish I had the thick skin to jump on Bill's lap and beg like a puppy.

But then again, I wouldn't dare to. The last time I saw him, Bill was all smiles. But now, there seems to be a cloud hanging over him. In the flask on the table, I can make out at least four different types of herbs that are clearly not tea. Is he sick? That sore on his lip really doesn't look so good.

"Your rehab has been waived," he says in a scratchy voice.

Really? I'm gonna be free? He is not pulling my leg, is he?!

He nods.

"*Xie xie* [thank you]*! Xie xie! Xie xie! Xie xie! Xie xie! Xie . . .*"

"It wasn't easy this time." Bill exhales a fog of smoke with an uncomfortable frown. "There was a lot of pressure from above on this one. Year-end targets. The district is . . . coming up . . . short on the number of . . . rehab cases." He's coughing as he speaks, his shoulders convulsing painfully. "Drugs are on the . . . rise again." Bill gulps down half of his herbal tonic and follows with a sigh of agony. "The city really wants to make examples out of people like you."

"So . . . uh . . . when?" I would be sweating right about now if I hadn't heard the good news first.

Bill swallows yet another thick cloud of nicotine despite his apparent ailment. "I'll come and fetch you sometime after dinner."

"You mean today?"

"Yes." He manages a faint smile. "You are getting out today."

After all this time! All that sitting! All those *wo cao ta ma de mantous*!

Bill is rubbing his temple.

"Sorry." I sit back down.

I never thought I'd actually say this, but seeing Bill in his current state makes me feel like buying him a really nice dinner. Sure, fifty grand was a bit of money to pay by Chinese standards, but compared to freedom, what's cash? Given the number of people who had to be greased along the food chain, Bill might actually have pocketed very little for himself. And in relation to the amount of risk he had to take, which apparently amounted to quite a lot (if I take what he just said at face value), this whole thing could be more or less philanthropy for a cop who does not take home much to begin with.

Now that I think about it, it has been more than fifteen years since I was last saved by a nice guy. Back then, it was Joe, my first American friend. Without him, I could have been all alone at Indianola High for at least another week, which could easily have scarred me for life considering how much bullying a FOB thirteen-year-old had to endure. And now it's Bill, without whose intervention my life would still be hanging in a far-from-fair balance. All this time, I never got around to thanking Joe. In fact, I don't even know where he is anymore. Hopefully, it is not too late to make it up to him by showing Bill some extra gratitude.

"So what should I do in the meantime?" I ask.

"Well, why don't you write a short note to our mutual friend now and tell her that you are all right." Bill hands me a notepad. "She is expecting to hear from you."

"Right now?"

"Yes." He has exasperation written all over his face. "She is waiting outside as we speak. If you don't write this note, she'll make sure that I can't go home tonight."

"But what should I say?"

"I don't know, uh . . ." Bill blinks painfully as the smoke gets into his eyes. "Just tell that *shabi* to relax and you'll see her soon."

Whoa, he didn't just call her what he called her, did he? What happened? I thought Bill and Madame were practically family.

But then, knowing her the way I do now, I am pretty sure that Madame has been stressing Bill out ever since I got in here. Poor guy—I certainly hope she didn't try to throw herself at him, too. And poor Madame—how could anyone ever get used to her fruitiness? How does her fiancé do it?

And what am *I* going to do about her once I get out of there? How do you break up with someone that you were never even with?

"Here you go." I return the note to Bill, short and sweet, nothing specific.

"Good." He smiles, now clearly more relaxed than before. "Try to enjoy your last few hours here." Ha. Very funny. "I will see you later tonight."

85

"Congratulations!" Chairman pats me on the back. "From eight months to eleven days. That's got to be some kind of a record."

"So what are you going to do first after you get out?" Sun asks.

"Dunno." I'm still too busy smiling. "Haven't really thought about it yet."

"Then I'll tell you what," Sun continues. "You must go find a bathhouse and have a good sweat in the sauna."

"And don't forget to unload your cannon." Heilongjiang winks.

"Then buy some new clothes and burn the ones you have on now," Chunk follows.

"But most important," Chairman tops it off, "you must go to a temple first thing in the morning, burn some incense, and thank the Buddha for doing you a favor."

"I didn't know you were a Buddhist, *da ge*."

"I'm not." He shrugs. "But you've got to do it."

"All of it?"

"Absolutely."

"Why?"

"What do you mean 'why'?" the gang of four answers with amazing synchronicity. "To get rid of the bad luck, of course!"

Right, prison always makes one more spiritual than otherwise.

But then, was this whole prison experience just a matter of luck? Would such a conclusion be as incomplete as equating *yuan fen* to fate?

It brings me no pleasure to say this, but Madame's conspiracy theory actually stuck like crazy gum. To make sure that I wasn't making too much out of nothing, I even ran it by Chairman and Sun, and they both agreed with her.

So for days, I dwelled on evening the score. Lao Chu would have to pay for his treachery. His reputation must be ruined, his business run into the ground. The revenge would have to be perfect in every way, even more original, discreet, and effective than anything Madame and I had already discussed. It felt good to imagine his suffering at the hand of my wrath, especially when I couldn't sleep at night.

But now . . .

Maybe it is because of all the *yuan fen* talk as of late, but if I were really to reason it out, the seed of my imprisonment was planted the very first time I made a conscious decision to get high in public, which could in turn be traced to the very first time I smoked any big numb at all. As there is a cause and effect to everything I do, sooner or later, irresponsible behavior will catch up with me. Granted, Lao Chu could have had something to do with my eleven days of purgatory; but if so, *yuan fen* will eventually catch up with him, too.

And to be fair, the past eleven days really haven't been a total loss. At the very least, I know for sure now that I am not addicted to hash or, Mao forbid, morphine. Then figure in the new friends that I have made, the fresh (if odd) stories that I have heard, and the *qi* phenomenon that I am just starting to get a taste of, and this just might be the most productive eleven days I have spent in a long time. In fact, I would go so far as to say that I am a better person now than I was before I came in.

Now wait a second, this is not what they mean by the *Dao*, is it? To the Chinese, the *Dao* is the Way, which is in cap because it is the path to enlightenment. Some philosopher from more than two thousand years ago by the name of Lao-tzu said that the *Dao* varies for every individual and that it is never the path often traveled. Could this mean that enlightenment often lies in places where we least expect to look? Indeed, given how rare enlightenment has been in the history of mankind, the path there can hardly be the Autobahn. In case I get pulled over for something stupid and end up somewhere twisted, what else is there to do but to pay my dues and learn from the mistake? Hopefully one day, after enough of these potholes and falling rocks (and let's pray that they never ever get anywhere as bad as this), I would figure out everything that *yuan fen* stands for.

Or, alternatively, attain a state of sappiness even beyond that of the ancient Chinese philosophers.

86

"What have you been writing over there anyway?" Chairman sits down next to me.

"Oh, nothing really." Unless you consider my getting sentimental about my last *mantou* worthy of attention.

"Is this all in English?" He flips through the A4-sized notepad that I have scribbled on down to the second-to-last page. "Are you like a writer or something?"

"Me? No." The idea never even occurred to me. "This is just, you know, whatever."

"Then what do you do anyway? You never answered me when I asked you."

"Well, uh . . ." Sorry to disappoint him, but I really haven't figured that out yet.

In fact, now that I am getting out of Chinese prison, I might just get out of China altogether.

Of course, I am well aware of all the "reasons" for me to stay. I am bilingual, am relatively well educated, and have spent much of my youth—especially my twenties—in China. My friends are here. My network is here. And now that I have done Chinese time, I am about as close to a China insider as an outsider gets.

But the problem is, I have to be passionate about what I do. Yes, I can do well in China given my credentials; but who's to say that I can't do the same in America? As fluffy as the word may be, we still want some "fulfillment."

"Hey, what are you doing?" Chairman seems puzzled.

"Just getting some exercise. It might help me think about the future."

Besides, it's been long enough; I can't see my friends looking like this.

"Why don't you just take a nap or something?" Chairman sounds rather concerned.

"Why? What's the matter?"

"Because nobody said we can do that." He thumbs at the surveillance cameras.

"Did the rules say that we can't?"

"Well, no . . ."

"Then I am free to do my push-ups." I can't believe that it didn't occur to me sooner. Must have been too busy adjusting to these lovely new surroundings.

Okay, I know that I made some mistakes in the past when it comes to what "freedom" should entail. But now I am smarter. And unlike the freedom to get high, the freedom to stay fit is surely something that is good for everyone. At the end of the day, regardless of race or nationality, we are all human beings. No matter what kind of freedom jigsaw we are subject to, certain pieces must be common to all of them.

Of course, the chances are that no matter how developed this country becomes, Chinese freedom will never be the same as American freedom. But neither does it have to be any less; and the real question should be: "When will it be even more?" According to pragmatists, all will happen in good time. According to idealists, everything should happen now. Personally, I like to be a pragmatic idealist. While changes will undoubtedly happen out of nature, I am also a part of nature that can make changes happen. Here and now, I am not changing all of China just yet, but I am doing what I can—I *am* pushing up.

And to help me, the pain in my hip has vanished. Is it the patches that supposedly contained tiger penis, or could it be the *qi*? Ordinarily, my arms would be getting at least a little tingly after the first twenty; but now, my body feels as light as a feather.

"Come on, *da ge*, do a hundred!" Heilongjiang hollers.

"Yeah, come on!" Chunk seconds the proposition as usual.

Are these guys serious? I haven't done that many in one go since college, and there is certainly no cute girl around here to impress.

"Hey! What's going on in there?" A voice unfortunately too familiar decides to crash our party.

Fresh into his afternoon beat, Chiwarzenegger looks capable of pumping iron with his furrowed brow.

"Just getting some exercise, sir," Chairman replies with a hasty quiver in his voice, even forgetting the obligatory "Thank you, sir, you look wonderful today."

"Was this your idea?" His Muscularity keeps talking down to our puppet leader.

Chairman is already crying beneath his nervous grin.

If I knew any better, I'd stop right now to give Chiwarzenegger some face.

But how can I let down twenty-seven men who have cheered for me since the very first rep?

"It's me, sir." I tilt up to meet Chiwarzenegger's glare, "I just wanted to see how many I can do."

The giant hoodlum-in-uniform squints, as if searching for the whereabouts of his brain.

What's he going to do? Throw me in solitary?

I hate it when he bangs our gate with that big, black baton of his.

"There will be no trouble, sir." I muster all the respect I have for this dumbbell, "You have my word."

"Who the hell are you?" he sneers.

"Sir," I am going to stay polite even if this ungrateful piece of shit has already forgotten about all the English homework I have done for him; but today *is* my last day, and I *will* do my push-ups, even if it means that I have to say, "We are all just huge fans of your physique, sir. Even if we can't ever be as strong as you are, we'd still like to try, if you'd just let us."

I know, once upon a time, I would have slapped myself silly for talking like that. But here and now, inflexible pride just seems like an unnecessary impediment. As an old Chinese maxim goes, one who is truly strong must know when to take a bow, for our world is full of egos and putting pride aboue practicality for no good reason will only get you more time to sit around and do nothing. Thus, as much as I hate pumping Chiwarzenegger's already very juiced ego, I will take a bow here if doing so would allow me to keep pushing up.

"Very well then." The left corner of Chiwarzenegger's mouth almost hints at an upward tilt as he proceeds to turn and walk away. "Just keep the noise down. Don't blow it on your last day."

"...Six.........Five.......F-o-u-r..........T-h-r-e-e.............T-t-t-w-w-o ....O-N-N-N-E..."

HOLY PROLETARIAT MOTHER OF @#$!

"...O-N-E H-U-N-D-R-E-D!!!"

The only sound I can hear is that of my heart racing above the red-line.

No Ferrari can beat this.

From every direction, the sound of people cheering with their hushed "ooh" and "aah."

Victory has never been sweeter.

Or sorer.

And it smells like ... unwashed human feet?

Mao, lend me your strength, just enough to lift my face off the wooden deck beneath.

Out of the corner of my eye, Heilongjiang is giving me the most enthusiastic two-thumbs-up. "That was s-o-o-o-o *niubi*! I've never seen anyone do that many before."

"...No shit..." Would somebody PLEASE give me some water before I pass out?!

Honestly, I never really expected to squeeze out as many as I did, not even after the twenty-second breather I absolutely had to take between my first sixty reps and the painfully long march that followed.

It's amazing what a little cheer from your fellow men can do.

"Say, *da ge*," Heilongjiang pleads to Chairman, "can I try a couple too?"

"Now?" Our puppet leader glances up at the cameras reluctantly.

"Oh, come on, *da ge*." Chunk is adorably consistent in playing the cheerleader, except that this time he also adds, "Let's all do it."

And some of the People are already springing into action. One by one, they take up spots on the deck, and some even get into formation on the floor.

"But that'll make too much noise." Chairman shakes his head. "I don't want that guard coming around again. You guys don't even know how to do this right."

"But don't worry, *da ge*," Heilongjiang rebuts. "We have our own *da xia* right here. He can teach us everything."

Then, before Chairman can respond, he turns to me with a wink and says, "What do you say, *da xia*? Will you do the honors?"

Well, I have never been called a superhero before, but if that's what gets them going . . .

"Oh . . . all right." Chairman reluctantly signals Chunk to move over and make some room. "Maybe just a few."

A few? Are you kidding? Here and now, I wish I had a whistle!

Or better yet, a camera. Mao, what an ugly scene! Grimacing faces, trembling arms, oohs and aahs all over the place. Chairman is sticking his buttocks a mile into the air, while Chunk is barely lifting anything other than his head and shoulders off the deck.

"Come on, give me another rep!" I see pain on some of the People's faces, and Chunk looks like he is about to faint.

And then there is Heilongjiang. After only a minor adjustment, his form is nearly perfect. With every rep, his chest almost touches the deck and his extension is long and smooth. Not to be outdone, a few of the other juvis have already begun a new set after a short break; and even Chairman—after I forced his buttocks down level with the rest of his body—is now coming up on five clean reps.

Now I don't mean to be blowing my own horn here; but could Heilongjiang be right—that I really *am* a *da xia*?

Okay, so I don't ever wield a sword or leap from roof to roof, but who needs any more of that kungfu-tion outside of Hollywood? In real life, being a *da xia* has just one simple rule: to use one's own powers for the benefit of all. Between all the haves and have-nots in this world, can an outsider like me make a positive change in the lives of others simply by sharing his knowledge and experience, and sometimes even just an idea or perspective? Indeed, if I can be a catalyst for doing push-ups in a place like 801, can I do more once I get out?

Come to think of it, I just might've been working toward *da xia*-hood all along. Through Foodiez, I have brought a new idea to Beijing. Through Lawttitude, I have taken on a state-owned Goliath. As for *Happy Heroes,* that was a crash course caught on tape.

Is the lesson I've learned from all these to just pack up my bags and leave?

Fact of the matter is, there are countless things I can do in China to feel the fulfillment of being a *da xia*. And unlike with a lot of other noble causes in this world, I can actually live in relative comfort while doing it. As clichéd as the statistic may be by now, the market here is still 1.3 billion strong. If I just stay patient, keep an open mind, and pick the right opportunities from the many that will surely come along, I will eventually have my own piece of the rice cake, and perhaps even without becoming a part of the cliché in the process.

Of course, this means that I might never have a simple answer to "What do you do?" But then, given all the changes that are happening in our world, is it realistic to expect a person of my age to know exactly what he wants to do for life? Relative to my father's generation, who had barely an inch of soil to plant their seeds of dreams, which in many cases never bore the fruits they wanted no matter how much they prayed for rain, I now have the luxury of an entire green field to till and nurture, which, if given the right amount of commitment, could even one day become a forest.

"Now, listen up everyone." Chairman addresses the People as he curls his arms to feel the muscles he never knew he had. "From now on, there will be no more spitting on the floor. And I do mean that for *everyone*. Let's keep this place clean and tidy so that we can all use it to get some exercise. Got it?"

It looks like I may have planted a little something in here already. Better add a blip to my journal before I forget.

Speaking of which, what am I going to do with these pages once this is all over? Throw them away? Chuck them in the drawer?

It might seem a crazy notion, but maybe I ought to reconsider Chairman's question from earlier in the day:

Am I a writer?

88

You just can't trust the Chinese.

Last night, the night that Bill was supposed to set me free, nothing happened. Nothing. No word. No apology. Not even a gofer to deliver an explanation. Bill just never showed.

But I still tried to reason it out. Given his haggard state when I last saw him, maybe he was just too sick to last through the day. Or maybe when he said "later tonight," he really meant "much later to-night." So I waited, and meditated, and then meditated some more. At six thirty this morning, I woke up to find myself still sitting upright with my legs crossed—I had fallen asleep while meditating!

Then at noon, Bill finally showed up. And he looked perfectly fine, except that the sore on his lip had gotten bigger and darker.

"Sorry about last night." He kept covering up his mouth while talking. "I got tied up."

I still can't believe I responded: "That's okay."

I must be getting too good at this face-giving business.

"So when am I getting out?" I stayed calm and polite.

He replied, "I will see you after dinner."

"As in tonight?" Meaning tonight, tonight?

"Mei wen ti." He nodded definitively.

Then just as he was about to walk off, Chairman waved him down. "How does it look, *da ge*?" Chairman was as nervous as I had ever seen him.

"Not yet." Bill did not look happy to see him.

"Any chance I'll go down before year's end?" Chairman was presumably referring to the Farm.

"Not likely," Bill replied curtly. "It'll be at least a few more months."

"How many more exactly?"

"Honestly, I don't know."

"Then is there any chance I can wait until after the winter is over?"

"Look, I'll try, okay?" Bill put up his hand in annoyance and walked off in a hurry.

So I asked Chairman, "What was that about?"

His thin eyes squeezed shut beneath a helpless frown. "He is the one in charge of my file," he said.

"You mean he is your *tuo'er* too?" I thought it was rather interesting that we shared the same deep throat.

"No." Chairman shook his head dejectedly. "Or I wouldn't still be here."

"So what has he told you about your case?"

"It's been three months since he last said anything."

"Well what did he say before then?"

"The same thing every time."

"Which is . . ."

Chairman let out a long sigh, "He told me every time that it was *mei wen ti*."

As in "no problem"—the same thing that I last heard from Bill more than eight hours ago?!

In my three years in China I have come across a lot of "cultural differences," but the *mei wen ti* when there is clearly a lot of *wen ti* has got to be the most frustrating. For some odd reason, the Chinese just have a problem with saying "can't," "don't," or "won't." Instead of a simple "No," it's always "No problem." But what the hell for?! If you can't do it, just say you can't do it; don't string people along and abuse their hopes and expectations—not unless it was your intention to mislead and deceive in the first place!

And now it's almost time to scratch off Day 12 on the calendar. Where the hell is Bill? What happened to his promise? How many more *mei wen ti*s am I going to take before I stick it up his—

"*Da ge,* look." Heilongjiang nudges me in the arm.

On the other side of the gate stands Chiwarzenegger. He is fingering me to get up.

Is this it? Is he telling me to get out of here?

He is!

I never knew I could spring from the hip so fast.

Here we go—shoes, laundry . . . That's it? Have I really gone for this long with this little?

Maybe the whole world should spend a few days in prison—and there will be no more energy crisis.

Standing to my left, someone is waiting for something.

How do people actually say good-bye in these situations, bearing in mind that we are guys?

In my heart, I truly hope for Heilonjiang to stop stealing bicycles and get a real job, and for Chunk to emerge from his year down on the Farm a lean, mean, pushing-up machine.

But I didn't actually say that: one gets a squeeze on the shoulder, the other a pat on the paunch.

With his hands crossed behind his back, Chairman is standing alone by the gate, a hint of blue in his thin, slit eyes.

"*Da ge*," I want to find some powerful and moving words.

But Chiwarzenegger won't wait that long.

So here it goes.

Startled, Chairman tenses up his body like he has never been embraced by another man.

I think he might be the first virgin I have ever had.

"So long everyone; and good luck."

Maybe one day we'll see each other again.

But for now—

I'm getting the hell out of here!

Clang. Chiwarzenegger unhooks the lock from the outside latch.

The steel gate opens to a dull, rusted screech.

Even dragging the heels on my laceless lace-ups, the exodus took all but four hurried steps.

By the time I turn to look, the lock is back on the gate again.

And I am not behind those bars, nor am I ever going back. EVER!

WOOOOOO-HOOOOOO!!!

If I could only touch the sky; hell, I'd even hug this guy—

"Hey, what are you doing?" Chiwarzenegger flinches back.

Never mind, he is too dense to appreciate the music that is booming in my ears. Now if I only had a camera to record this moment. *Ah-oooooh, I feel good!* James Brown would have been proud: Chinese people can do the —

D'OH?!

"Cut it out with the chicken dance." Chiwarzenegger clearly enjoyed that loud smack across the back of my head. "You are not going anywhere just yet."

From behind the desk, Bill utters, "Things are going a little slow. There are some unexpected complications."

Complications? What kind of complications? Isn't that what the money is for? If it was going to be all easy breezy with no complications, why the whole damn fifty grand?

"But don't you worry," he continues. "It will be any day now."

"Any day?"

"Yes, any day."

Just not today.

89

It's been three hours and twelve minutes since lights-*out*, even though it should really be light-*on*. I have tried everything.

Stuffing toilet paper in my ears has been as effective against all the People's snoring thunder as the Great Wall was against the Mongol invasion. But there seems to be no other way.

Those two cold *mantou*s left over from dinner have sent me to the latrine twice in thirty minutes.

I've thought about another cold shower, which, in addition to being masochistic (considering how damn freezing tonight is) would probably have the effect of a triple latte instead.

Is there anything that I can use to block out that wretched, cold ceiling lamp? Anything at all?!

Yes, there actually is. And if I could be as brave in terms of hygiene as some of my fellow men are, I too would flip my dirty underwear inside out and use it as an eye patch.

90

All morning, I waited for him.

Every time there was any noise coming down the corridor, my heart would race and my palms turn sweaty.

But so far on this Day 13, still no sign of Bill.

Having slept even less in the past two nights, I can only meditate to help stay sane.

About an hour and a half ago, Sun left along with a few others. I let him keep the Polo sweatshirt given by Madame—it fit him well, and the temperature has been dropping every day for the past week. He said he was going to down a few shots of *bai jiu* as soon as he hit the street. I wish I could down a whole damn bottle.

Then fifteen minutes ago, Chairman came back with a dark cloud on his face. Pacing back and forth, he kept muttering the word *"hen,"* meaning "cold-blooded," to himself. Without a doubt, it had something to do with his future.

"So what did you do exactly?" I finally asked again.

Yes, it was rude. But I had to know.

"It was only a fight." The spite in his eyes could not have lied.

Yet he has been here for almost six months? With more on the Farm to go?

"Did you pull out a knife or something?" Surely someone must have been hurt.

"No. Do I look like someone who'd pull out a knife?"

True. "How about a beer bottle?"

"I never drink."

Well, "Then how about a stick?" "A bat?" "A crowbar?" "Any-thing?"

"*Ge-men'er!*" he snapped. "I was the only one who got hurt, and it was only a bloody nose!"

Like clockwork, the dinnertime ritual has begun. The water wagon just finished its pour; next will be the *mantou* cart, followed by the cabbage tub.

My stomach is growling. But I will NOT eat another *mantou*—for to do so would be to accept as fact that I am not getting out of here today, again.

But it's already 4:30 P.M., and I haven't yet seen anyone released after dinner.

"It's official." Chairman looks at the *mantou* in his hand. "Another day. Gone."

I am gonna kill Bill.

91

Inside Chief's dimly lit office, Bill is sitting across the table.

Unlike last night, I didn't bother to gather my stuff when Chi-warzenegger called me out of the cell again.

The chair feels icy cold against my spine. The temperature must be in the 30s (Fahrenheit) tonight.

Quietly, Bill swirls his flask of green tea, the color of the potion already yellow and pale after having been refilled many times.

If all he is going to do is just sit there, then I'd much rather go back to my cell and try to get some sleep.

"You should really have that looked at." I point to the sore that has already taken over Bill's entire upper right lip.

My tone didn't carry the same level of concern that it would have had yesterday.

"I was tied up with work again." Bill gives the same excuse he gave yesterday *and* the day before.

Except that today, he doesn't look concerned or apologetic, not even in the slightest.

"So, what now?" Given that it's already 11:45 p.m. on this Day 13, I'm guessing that an "early" release is now officially out of the question.

"Well, as you know, drug users have to do rehab." Bill takes a sip of his potion and rolls the taste in his mouth. "Getting that waived is extremely difficult."

Bastard! Here come more excuses!

"And since your hash had morphine in it"—he lights up a cigarette and contemplates the red hot tip—"a lot of people would ask a lot of questions if you got off so easily."

But haven't we gone over this already—all 50,000 *kuai* worth?

"So there are some people I still need to take out for dinners and drinks and, you know, the usual."

"So how much more?"

"Not much." Bill ashes his cigarette. I can't stop my jaws from clenching. "Only fifty thousand."

As in *another* fifty thousand? Does he think I have a money tree growing out of my ass?!

Oh I get it—this is all part of his diabolical scheme: Start with the

VIP treatment to buy my confidence, then the false news to hype me up about getting out early, followed by three days of waiting until I am mentally drained, then swoop in for the kill when I am willing to do just about anything. And that note he asked me to write for Madame—I should have punched him in the face for calling her a *shabi*. Now I know where that sore comes from: One with a venomous heart shall have his body ravaged by poison!

"That's a lot of abalone and shark's fin soup." I surprise even myself with my calmness. "And then?"

"Well . . ." His face turns jolly. "As soon as the money hits the account, you'll be on your way."

Yeah, right, do I look like a *shabi* too? If he comes back tomorrow with an even more egregious demand, do I just keep on paying out of my nose? When even thieves have a code of honor, how can this asshole call himself a cop? Make no mistake, this is not about pride anymore. This is about ethics.

Besides, now that I have done thirteen days already, what am I afraid of? If the law says that I should do rehab, then so be it—it won't be the first time I have done trials by fire. Moving to America wasn't all pleasant in the beginning either, but I survived, even excelled. If it is within my *Dao* to endure more hardship, then I am ready to be tested.

Is he?

"You know what?" I stare into the con man's eyes and wait a beat. "Don't bother."

"Pardon me?" Bill pulls back from another sip.

"You heard me." I cross one leg on top of the other. "If I have to do rehab, so be it. The deal is off."

"What do you mean it's off?"

"As in called off, canceled, rescinded."

I take a cigarette from his pack of red and gold and light it up with his fancy Dunhill lighter.

Well look at this, a Panda cigarette, the most expensive brand there is at more than 500 *kuai* a pack, whereas the Zhong Nan Hais that Lethal smokes cost only 8. First produced in 1956 for the exclusive pleasure of China's national leaders, Pandas allegedly have ginseng mixed in with the tobacco, making them Mao's favorite when he was still alive. Now, apparently, the brand is shared by dignitaries and dirty cops alike.

"But don't you want to get out of here?" Bill is still holding his tea in that awkward position.

"Two days ago, absolutely. But now . . ." I pause for a long, long drag on the cigarette. "I've changed my mind."

"What?"

"I kind of want it for the experience."

"Experience?" Bill follows his chuckle with a laugh. "What are you, a masochist?"

"You know what they say: no sacrifice, no glory; and definitely no story."

"Story? What story?"

"Don't know yet, will find out soon enough—anything can happen in rehab, right?"

"But then what?"

"Tell the people what I saw."

"Come again?"

"Sure. Television, newspaper, Internet—anywhere a story can be heard."

"Wait," Bill stops laughing. "No one said anything about you being a reporter."

"Eh, only when I see something worth reporting. By the way, did I tell you I used to be a lawyer too? Helps with writing about the law; you know, crime and punishment, cop and robber, and now, prisons and rehab centers and—"

"Wait, *what*?"

"Oh yeah, all that good stuff." I haven't blown a smoke ring this perfect in months. "By the way, I really ought to thank you for the pen and paper. Honestly, I didn't think it was going to be that easy."

"You mean you will write about this place too?" He takes a nervous gulp of his tea along with all the bitter herbs floating on top.

"Are you kidding?" I'm trying not to laugh as he spits out the roots and leaves stuck in his mouth. "Everything about China is hot these days, especially places like this. Foreigners would love to know more about Chinese prisons, but they hardly get in. Now, thanks to you guys, it's going to be great."

"Then what are you going to say?"

"Well, everything: how we sit, what we eat, where we sleep, sucking up to the *tou ban,* scrubbing toilet as the *mo ban,* the inmates, the jailers, the guy who got a metal helmet put on his head, folks I met when I was out of my cell, those who did me favors, those who were dicks, friends, enemies, *shabis,* you."

"Me? What about me?!"

"What do you mean?" Now it's my turn to laugh. "You are practically the main character."

"But haven't you had enough yet?" He scowls. "It's been two weeks already!"

"Oh, it's never enough. When it comes to things like this, it's all in the details. And if I have to do rehab, then I'll write about that, too. I have never been in a room full of Chinese heroin addicts; couldn't find them even if I tried. Thanks to you, this is going to be a really, really good sell."

"But you can't write about things like that. This is China!"

"And this is the twenty-first century. I write what I want, when I want."

"But aren't you afraid of rehab?" Bill's forehead is getting shiny.

"What's there to be afraid of?" I put out the cigarette that I have smoked only a third of. "I know guys who've gone to rehab. They all came back looking the same."

And now that I have begun my study of *qi*, rehab just might be the retreat I need to take it to the next level. Think about it: the food in rehab will probably be the same as here, with no snacks or junk foods or even any meat to contaminate my system, and there is bound to be no sex for distraction.

"All right. Fine." Bill leans over the desk, his lip sore seemingly ready to burst. "What do you want me to do now?"

"Simple." I light up another Panda just to piss him off. "Give my money back."

"What?" He flinches.

"Don't play the fool with me, mister. Give me my money back, and I'll go to rehab. Otherwise, get me the hell out of here and I am not paying you another cent, got it?"

"This is blackmail!" He slams down the flask.

"Cao ni da ye!" I swear I'll ram that flask up his grandfather's ass if he keeps on playing games. "If you don't want your damn face plastered all over television, then I suggest you do as I say, understand?!"

That felt better than sex.

Bill is fumbling for his cigarettes.

Poor bastard, why do this to yourself? I know, given all of China's growth of late, your paycheck is probably the only thing that hasn't increased by tenfold in the last decade. But that doesn't make it right for you to gouge people. Compared to those more-connected cops who own whorehouses and nightclubs, you are just a small-timer who doesn't know who he's messing with.

"But wait a minute." Bill takes two hard drags of his cigarette. "You don't even know my name yet."

"So? Just a small detail that no one is going to care about." "Bill" alone will do.

"But who is actually going to read any of your stuff if you are kept locked up?"

Beg your pardon? They can't do that—it's not as if I killed anyone or even robbed a convenience store. They can't just lock me up forever for one pesky joint!

Can they?

"Let me make something clear to you, kid." Bill snickers. "If I can give you pen and paper, I can take them away. Then once you are down in rehab, we'll make sure that you never, ever write again!"

Bill slams down his tea flask for the second time.

Like a freight train on steroids, Chiwarzenegger bursts into the room, practically taking the door off its hinges.

WAIT, this is not working out the way it was supposed to!

Chiwarzenegger's coarse talons claw into the sides of my neck.

"You know, kid," Bill is shaking his head. "I actually wanted to help you. In fact, I was willing to bargain on the fifty thousand, just like we do with everything here in China. Frankly, I was willing to go as low as twenty thou. But you had to pull out that American attitude and demand everything your way. *Cao*, have you forgotten where you are?!"

"Let me go!" I swear I'll make Chiwarzenegger pay for this.

All I need is one punch. Even if I never see daylight ever again, I shall see Bill in his nightmare every night!

Goddamn it, why can't I break free?!

"Lock him in the hole and heat up my tools," Bill orders his henchman with a sinister grin. "I will take care of this one myself."

The hell he is! You can lock up my arms but you can't lock up this: Fourteen days, UP YOURS!!!

Like a bullet, my last weapon rockets toward Bill's frightened brows. If I had any *qi*, this one took it all. Yes, I might do life for maiming a pig with the biggest, baddest loogie in all of Chinese history; but here and now, I am—

"*Da xia!*" A faint voice cuts in just before Mad Mao hits its target.

And something is interfering with the trajectory!

STOP SHAKING ME!!!

Ouch, who just punched me in the chest?!

That faint voice is growing stronger.

Where the hell is that stupid white light coming from?

I'm too young to die of a heart attack!

Through my finger cracks, I can almost make out a face:

Square jaws . . .

Chapped lips . . .

Some random peach-fuzz and a head of short, greasy hair . . .

Heilongjiang?

What the—

"Psss, over here." A man whispers from a short distance away.

Bill? I rub my eyes.

And again.

"Hurry up and gather your stuff." He speaks urgently while fiddling with a key.

The clanging on the lock sounds real.

Up above, the same ceiling lamp looks as ghostly as ever.

To my left, Chairman's body is curled up in deep sleep.

To my right. Chunk is snoring away with his mouth wide open.

I am . . . still in 801?

And everything that just happened was only a bad dream?

My chest still aches.

"Come on, *da ge*." Heilongjiang is pulling me up by the hand. "You are going to sleep somewhere else tonight."

92

For some mysterious reason, the white ceiling lamp seems to have gotten a whole lot softer.

And that latrine stench. Where has it gone?

But for Heilongjiang and the two other juvies standing watch, everyone seems sound asleep.

Outside the window, a murky darkness.

"What are you looking at?" Bill's hushed voice sounds anxious. "Put your clothes on and let's go!"

Strange. With freedom looming at the gate, it's almost as if I want to stay a little longer.

Truth be told, I never thought that I would grow attached to this place one bit. But now as I stand between the edge of the deck that has been my home for two weeks and the heads of two juvies snoring away on the cement floor, I must admit that I have. Indeed, I'm starting to miss folks like Chairman and Sun already. They have become way more than mere acquaintances in the little time that I have known them, and have seen and heard me in ways that not even my closest friends have. And while I don't necessarily care for the title of "big brother," I will certainly miss the sound of closeness whenever Heilonjiang called me *"da ge."* As someone who grew up without any siblings, this was the first place where I felt a sense of brotherhood under adversity. Then add on all the other bits that I first considered to be torture, including the cold showers, the sleepless nights, and yes, even the *mantous,* and how could I ever forget this place?

"Here, *ge-man'er*, make good use of this." I hand Heilongjiang the meal card that I have used only once.

Who knows, maybe by the next time I see him, he will already have his own syndicate of some sort.

Judging from the way he is curled up in his blanket with his back toward us, I can't tell if Chairman is awake or not.

What could I say to him now that would actually make him happy?

Thank you, old man. Maybe one day, *yuan fen* will have us meet again.

Once again the gate swings open to a dull, rusted screech.

With my shoes in hand, I tiptoe around the heads of those sleeping on the cement floor.

As I hunch down to fit through the squat gateway, something tingles in the pit of my stomach.

Relief?

Elation?

Anxiety?

One discovers something new every day.

In the corridor, a symphony of silence.

Without movement, my final victory dance.

As Bill returns the lock to its usual place, I wave good-bye to Heilongjiang.

As usual, he is grinning like the eighteen- (or seventeen-) year-old he claims to be.

On the wall of the corridor, the clock reads:

00:05, 10-28.

93

The long staircase was much easier to walk down than up. I counted forty-eight steps in all. Lucky number.

"How is your lip, by the way?" It's strange to hear my voice in the wide open space.

"*Ai,* almost healed." Bill shakes his head in helplessness. "It gets like this every year when winter hits. One day, I'll move away from all this dryness. Too much fire in the *qi,* not good for my health."

Right, I think I got some of that too; except that my fire came in the form of paranoia, which happens easily when one loses confidence in the nature of man.

"I am sorry to have made you wait for so long," he continues. "It's these new regulations. Got to follow them to the last stroke for now. Even I had to be discreet this time. I hope you understand."

Well, after a few more breaths of this free air, I doubt anything in the past will matter much anymore.

Cutting through a patch of shaded darkness with the metal detectors behind us, Bill stuffs a package into my hand.

"What's this?" I shake the manila envelope.

"Your belongings," he says. "Check it and make sure it's all there . . . except for your leather jacket. I don't know where that went."

I guess that's my cue to consider riding a scooter from now on instead.

"Then what's this?" I discover a stack of pink Mao-bills inside the envelope.

"Five thousand *kuai*." He dry-coughs once. "Go ahead, count it if you want to."

"What for?" I am pretty sure that it was just a dream I had, in which I demanded ten times this amount back.

"That's for breaking the promise." Bill dry-coughs again. "I told you that you were getting out three days ago; but, you know . . . This is all that's left after paying off the others."

"But what about yourself?" No one should have to do this for free. I know I wouldn't.

"A man has to live by his word." He shrugs.

"Are you sure?" The sting in my bitten lip confirms that this is not another dream.

"As long as you remember this lesson." He grins. "I'd rather make a *ge-men'er* out of this anyway."

"Yeah? . . . Then can I ask you something?"

"Sure."

"What's the story with the *tou ban* in my cell?"

I hate to be nosy, but Chairman is a friend too.

"Oh, that guy." Bill sighs. "All I can say is that he and his partner got mixed up in some shady business that reached rather high places. Now his partner has fingered him as the scapegoat and is using some strong *guan xi* to keep him in jail. The whole matter is rather messy."

"But is he going to be okay?"

"Well, our system is not perfect." He lights up a cigarette, the same Zhong Nan Hai that Lethal smokes. "But we are trying to make it better. If you don't see what I see, you don't know how difficult it is. Even a pigeon has gizzards and intestines that loop around forever, whereas our system is mammoth."

"But he *is* going to be okay, right?"

"Let me put it this way." Bill exhales deeply. "Here in China, where the rule of law comes short, we try to make up for it with *ren qing*. Ever heard of it?"

Sure. Translated literally, *ren qing* means "human kindness." But in line with China's tradition of saving face whenever possible, it is often a euphemism for giving and receiving favors. If someone does a favor for you, you owe him a *ren qing;* if you do a favor for someone else, he owes you a *ren qing*.

"Isn't that pretty much the same as *guan xi*?" After all, the owing of favors often forms the basis for connections.

"But more than just that," Bill says. "*Ren qing* is for when the rules yield unduly harsh results. Our society is too complex to be governed by rigid rules alone. Once in a while, a little *ren qing* is necessary."

Well then, I guess he is actually using the phrase for its literal meaning. How refreshing.

"But still, what about all the dirty *guan xi* that arises out of *ren qing*?"

After all, humans can be manipulated, deceived, and even coerced to do things against their will or conscience. Sometimes even a seemingly good thing might result in situations where one will be forced to compromise not only pride but also ethics. And in real life, not every nightmare ends in waking up.

"You are right," Bill says, with a nod. "By its very nature, *ren qing* creates ambiguity in our system. But nothing is absolute. Even in America, a judge can exercise discretion to achieve fairness when the written law would otherwise yield an unjust result. Here in China, we also need to find a compromise between rules and *ren qing* rather than choosing one over the other."

"But when is that going to happen?"

"Well, aren't you the lawyer?"

Touché. "So I take it my friend *will* be okay?"

"Again," he says, chuckling at my persistence, "one can never make any guarantees in these matters."

"But give me like, you know, a percentage." Like, say, 40 percent?

"Well"—he exhales with a smile—"I managed to get you out, didn't I?"

Nuff said.

"Well, thank you for everything." I really wish I could say something more meaningful to mark the occasion.

"Mei wen ti." Bill gives my hand a firm squeeze with three dips. "Can I just say something before you go? A suggestion, if you will?"

"Sure, anything."

"Well, don't take it the wrong way, but you still have a lot to learn about China."

"Yeah, no kidding."

"Then may I suggest you read more about China's culture and history?"

"Oh, absolutely, I am already planning to read more about the *qi* and the *Dao* and a whole bunch of other cool stuff I just picked up."

"But make sure you also read the classics, like Confucius for example."

"Yeah?" I hate to disagree with his advice, but Confucius is just a bit dense. "I mean, how relevant are they, really? A lot has changed since when Confucius was alive."

"Well, not every word of the Bible is relevant to the Western world anymore either, but you still say 'Oh my God' all the time, don't you?"

"Hey, I didn't know you were a Christian."

"No, I am a Communist." He waves good-bye as the giant metal gate opens with a dull rumbling. "But the Bible was a mandatory read when I studied at Party College."

94

In the distance, a yellow-and-green taxi awaits under the lone streetlight.

"*Ge-men'er!*" A tall, thin man in cowboy boots opens his arms.

He has cut his hair. The beard is looking fierce. A big, scruffy smile on a razor-sharp face. *Wo cao ta ma de,* Lethal Weapon.

From inside the car, a girl screams. It's Rockette. Her petite body is bouncing with excitement all over the backseat.

I'm the luckiest man in the world to have friends like these.

"How are you doing? Are you hungry? Thirsty? Need some clothes?" Madame steps out from the passenger side.

I know it's wrong to say this, but I am, for lack of a better word, scared. She looks too concerned, like a mother for a child, a wife for a husband, a *sha* . . . And what's that paper folded neatly in her chest pocket? My note?

"Great to see you." I give her a hug.

I can feel the sin in it. But I've got to. She has done so much for me. It's a tight hug, strong, firm, and rigid. Like men hugging.

"What's with the color of this cab? And what is this, a Hyundai? What happened to the Volkswagens and Peugeots?"

I am used to Beijing cabs being red instead of whatever this two-tone scheme is. And it's a good diversion.

"New city ordinance." Madame is quick on the explanation as usual. "Soon, most of the cabs in this city will be two-toned Hyundais. Almost sixty thousand of them. Aren't they much nicer?"

Indeed. Roomier, cleaner, plus that new-car smell instead of the familiar Anchovy 'n' Swiss.

"And it's made right here in China, bumper to bumper," Madame adds.

And not Japanese; surprise, surprise.

"Hey, where did this on-ramp come from?" I definitely don't re-member ever going back into the city this way.

And when did that building come up? Or the three other giant towers of neon right next to it? Wasn't it some giant, rusting amal-gamation of Communist relics the last time I paid any attention?

"Two weeks can be a long time," Rockette says. "Wait until you see all the other things that have changed around here."

"So," Lethal asks, "how you feelin'?"

"Relieved, I guess. And a bit . . . strange." Barely two weeks away. "It's as if I am FOB again."

"Is that good or bad?"

"Well . . ." At least the "F" in FOB stands for "fresh."

"So what do you want to do now?"

Well, let's see . . .

Maybe I'll get a bite to eat first. Ghost Street should just be hitting its second wave of the night right about now. Get a bucket of crawfish and two dozen lamb skewers, with three times the cumin and peppers to help free the prisoners in my mouth.

Or maybe I should first go for a really hot shower to wash away all the bad luck, a change of clothes to get back my trademark look, then a very, very Long Island ice tea at Transit to see if my kidneys still work.

Or how about a massage? Yes, from head to toe. Even a 20-*kuai* job at one of those back-*hutong* hair salons will do. Heck, I might even go through all the missed calls and unread messages and let the world know who is back in town.

Or perhaps I should call my old man first and let him know where I have been all along.

But like Rockette said, two weeks can be a long time. Maybe there is something new in town that I haven't even heard of— something fantastic, something revolutionary, something to help forget that the past two weeks ever even happened.

Or, perhaps I'll just savor this moment a little longer.

FAST-FORWARD . . .

"Can I help you with something, sir?" The head of a young lady appears from behind the screen of a silver iMac.

Just like that, it's October again.

"If you don't mind my asking"—I honestly cannot believe what I am seeing with my own eyes—"is this still Café 44?"

For it sure doesn't look like the old hideout where I spent almost every 4:20. The tables are gone; chairs are gone; even those wall shelves where Lao Chu kept his Japanese-style double-bubble coffeemakers that sold for a bargain 300 *kuai* each, gone. What was once the bar area is now a working desk and a flowerpot. The floor has been upgraded from bare cement to wood-textured tiles. There are even retractable blinds for the windows.

"This is an office now. For the shopping mall in the *hutong* next door." The young lady stands up to answer politely.

And what a pleasant sight she is: wavy black hair, big brown eyes, a pair of long legs in black-and-gray Louis Vuitton heels. . . .

"Sir?" Her two hands lock fingers gently before the small of her belly, right in the center of her black-and-white Mandarin dress.

"Oh, I'm sorry." I guess I must have blanked out for a split-second déjà vu. "You reminded me of someone I knew. She liked to wear Mandarin dresses as well."

Just a different pattern. Thank Mao.

"How nice." The young lady actually seems flattered by my stare. "Was she a friend of yours?"

"Yeah, well . . . Yeah."

Actually, it was rather sad to hear "friend" and "was" in the same sentence.

The truth is, it's been a while since I last saw Madame. For two months after 801, she took it upon herself—and only herself—to be my "girlfriend." Without ever consulting me on the matter, she bought things for me, cooked dinners for me, stood outside my door till three o'clock in the morning, and basically took the concept of "crazy Chinese chick" to unprecedented heights. To be fair, I had no good reason for letting it drag on for as long as it did; but being human, I just felt like I owed her too much to refuse. By the time I finally managed to walk away, her fiancé had as well. The whole experience almost turned me off women for another ice age; and, needless to say, Madame and I are not in contact anymore. But considering all that she did for me, the effect of which has been nothing short of life-changing, the least I can say to strangers would be:

"She and I used to meet for coffee here."

"That's what I thought." The young lady keeps smiling politely. "When was the last time you were here, sir?"

"Oh, that would be a while ago."

As much as I wanted to come back here on so many previous occasions, some memories always held me back.

"Well, we have taken over this place for a few months already," she explains, seemingly pleased by the way I am studying her working space.

"So whatever happened to the previous owner? His name was Lao Chu."

"Not too sure." She shrugs. "He probably found a way to make more money elsewhere. Did you come here a lot before?"

"Yeah, you could say that."

In fact, it seems like just yesterday when Lethal and I had our last debate here about something. I can still recall all his gestures and phrases and the way we laughed out loud without a care. I never had a friend who was as good as pushing my buttons as he was; and I will always look forward to the day when the two of us can meet up again.

Not too long ago, Lethal Weapon decided to take "a break" from China. As he never said why, I naturally thought it was difficulty at work that hastened his departure. After all, even Superman would have to realize his limitations after being Kryptonited by censorship enough times. Indeed, at the moment we last bid *zai jian,* I myself got a little disillusioned as well.

But lately, I've been feeling a little different. Maybe my buddy didn't fold because it got difficult; maybe he had a better plan all along. Maybe, instead of trying to make everything happen before its time, he stayed in the game long enough to impress and motivate the insiders working around him so that even after he took his bow, his ideas had a shot—and in fact a better shot—at one day changing China. Indeed, the last time I tuned to his old network, it truly surprised me with its much-improved and suspiciously Lethal-inspired social commentaries.

Sometimes, I honestly think Lethal works for the CIA, even though he is really too smart for them.

But no matter where his next mission takes him, I hope he will look back on our trek through Inner Mongolia and laugh. For two weeks we roamed the wide-open plains on horseback, pitching tents and eating lamb. It was even more grueling than Madame had predicted, and the Ambiguously Gay Duo looked more like Dumb and Dumber in those blazing Mongolian saddles. Frankly, we never came close to finding Xanadu, but we did find out a lot more about ourselves, friendship, and just how massive and diverse this country truly is.

"So what can I do for you today, sir?" the young lady continues. "Are you looking for a commercial space? We are currently looking for new tenants in our mall."

"Your mall? Isn't it full already?" Or so it seemed when I had a Big Bite at the Kiosk only ten minutes ago.

"I meant for our new development, sir," she explains. "It will be ready soon."

Man, these guys just keep on building and building. "Will it be in Sanlitun as well?"

"Of course, sir. This is where all the action is. Would you like to see our brochure?"

"Oh no, that's all right." Not after I've been bombarded with dozens of brochures, flyers, and even spam text messages about all the real estate projects mushrooming around this city since eight o'clock in the morning, every morning. Besides, what would I do with the information in the brochure anyway? After all, "I'm not really in business for myself." At least not one where I use a fancy storefront to peddle sweatshop-grade goods bearing space-age packaging.

Of course, in actuality, Foodiez is still delivering, and doing more of it than ever before. To my very pleasant surprise, the operation ran just fine during my stint in 801. In the absence of their ill-tempered boss, my staff relied on their own good sense and actually did a fine job. So I decided to delegate more responsibilities to the most capable of the bunch and put them in charge of their respective departments. Then, faster than anyone had anticipated, revenue went up, customer complaints went down, and together with their performance incentives, my boys are now making more than twice the amount they took home in a good month before 801, not to mention having been upgraded to safer and faster vehicles and proper, seasonal uniforms. As a result, I have not done—nor felt the need for—any yelling or screaming in months.

"So what *do* you do, sir?" the young lady asks.

"Well"—I still get a kick out of saying this—"I used to be a lawyer."

"Used to?"

Well, okay, once a lawyer, *always* a lawyer. And it's not because lawyering is a trade that I can always fall back on, but because a great lawyer who does it for the right reasons is just what this place needs.

But to become that great lawyer, I must first find the time and focus to do it right. Though there are now more legal headhunters in China than one can shake a chopstick at, and the list of law firm openings keeps getting longer and longer, the right fit given my personality is still one in a million. But I'm not sweating it. If and when the right opportunity finds me, I'll be happy to put on my lawyer hat once again. Of course, there is always the possibility of having first to defend my bar license before some ethics committee for my little trouble in big China; but then it may just turn out to be the "big case" that Lawttitude was meant to try.

"So what do you do *now,* sir?" The girl seems less enthusiastic than before.

Well, at least for the moment, "You can say that I am a writer . . . *cha bu duo.*"

"Really?" Her pursed lips loosen up a little. "What do you write about?"

"Oh, you know, this and that. The usual Sanlitun stuff."

"You mean for a magazine?"

"No, more like a book, *cha bu duo.*"

"Really? That sounds like loads of fun."

"Yeah, well, as fun as it is difficult."

Or lately, just difficult.

The thing is, as willing and eager as I am to tell my stories, what's the point of telling them? It sure as hell can't be for shit and giggles, not after drafts upon drafts, thinking after rethinking, over and over again.

From a purely commercial standpoint, I of course thought about writing something that would one day be touted as *"the"* book on modern China. But seriously, how can I, or anyone, pull off such an impossible task? This place is so big, with so many people and so much history and culture, that anyone who claims to be an expert on China as a whole has to be a quack, and any book that purports to be the authority on China should go straight to the Dumpster.

So to be perfectly honest, I've been a little stuck, which is why I came back here today, hoping to find something, anything at all.

"Then"—the young lady tucks some loose hair behind her right ear with a small flick of her wrist—"do you have any idea when your book is going to be on the shelf?"

"When?" Did she not just hear my inner monologue?

"Yes. Do you have a publisher yet?"

"Well, uh, soon?" Hopefully?

"But you have been published before, I take it?" Her eyes seem to be looking for something. "Writers can do really well these days, you know."

Oh wow, is she hitting on my wallet already? It hasn't been even two minutes yet. These girls are practically working on Wall Street time!

But unfortunately, sweetheart, as much as I can appreciate your silky hair, porcelain skin, and Hollywood smile, the days when beauty alone could make a sale to me are history.

For, believe it or not, the bad boy of Sanlitun is now a one-woman man. No bullshit.

It all started with a groundbreaking text message that I sent to Ginger on the very night I was to turn thirty (according to the Western calendar, that is). The two of us had been hanging out as casual friends again for a few months before then, and the three or four conversations that we managed to have one-on-one turned out to be more than I had ever expected. Beneath all the bling-bling, there was something very special about her; and I became more intrigued than ever.

So with only ten minutes to go before the clock struck midnight, I decided that I wanted Ginger to celebrate my thirtieth birthday with me. Given that it was on a weekend, I honestly did not expect any reply, as she would surely be dancing the night away at Vic's. But for whatever reason, she had stayed home that night. And maybe because I started the message with her real name instead of just "babe," she replied, "Come on over."

Two days later, we decided to give "it"—as in a relationship—a try. The decision was actually not so brave given the circumstances, as she had already decided to move back to America in about two months for her family business. In other words, we already had an *out* before we decided to go *in*.

Little did we know that the *out* was never going to happen. Perhaps because we only set out to have two months of being open and genuine with each other instead of making a much longer commitment, we gave everything that we had without holding back. After letting go of the single-and-fabulous image that concealed our true selves for many years, we discovered a fountain of affection, respect, and understanding in each other. Without trying very hard (or much at all), we have somehow achieved a level of synchronicity that I never thought possible: at a frequency far beyond coincidence, we would think and say the same things at the same time; lately, we have even shared similar dreams.

So not long ago, I did the impossible: I asked for her hand in *marriage*. Neither of us ever expected to come full circle this way; but that's exactly how *yuan fen* likes to operate. Just as an example of how whimsical our finding each other truly was, we had actually been neighbors on two different occasions during our singlehood in a town twice the size of New York City, without either of us ever knowing until years later; and our birthdays turned out to be only one day apart. Of course, we still have our arguments (like two Capricorns ramming heads); and my list of a relationship's pros and cons has only grown longer since 801. But overall, it has certainly been more "better" than "worse."

"Well, if you are really into reading"—I take my hand out of my Levi's pocket so the girl can see my ring—"I can let you know when it's published."

As long as she doesn't hit me for a free copy plus autograph.

"Then can I interest you in one of our office spaces?" She looks slightly disappointed but is still relentless in her salemanship. "Writers need a place to work too, right? And these are very reasonably priced, only fifty *kuai* per square meter per day."

"Per square *meter*? Per *day*?" Let me do the conversions here . . . That'll break the bank at more than US $1,800—no, make that US $2,100—a month for a measly one hundred square *feet* of space (and Mao knows how much more if the exchange rate keeps going south). "Ehhh, that's a bit too pricey, don't you think? Especially considering how much one *kuai* is worth these days."

"But consider the area, sir. This is Sanlitun, after all."

Right, Sanlitun, a village for peasants who couldn't afford to live inside the old city walls barely a hundred years ago; a strip of cornfields up until thirty years ago; and now, a bastion of malls and office buildings where the nouveaux riches go.

And while all this was happening, the rest of Beijing changed right along with it, now boasting more buildings, more billboards, more wealth, more people—including FOB outsiders by the hundreds of thousands. Along the way, some changes left me sadly nostalgic, including the complete demolition of Transit as part of the city's continuing and sometimes illogical reconstruction, while others have been promising, such as the promulgation of a nationwide traffic law that is almost halfway to being actually enforced, including random Breathalyzer checks for all the fast and furious coming out of Vic's, Mix, and all the other nightclubs that are now doing better than ever.

According to some statistics, the population of Beijing is now more than seventeen million, and up to many more across the greater metropolitan area when floating migrant workers are included. According to some cabdrivers, who are widely acknowledged to be the barometer of public opinion in this town and the largest captive audience for government radio, China will one day regain its past glory as the hegemon of our civilized world, at which time it can do whatever it wants, just like all the other hegemons that have come before it.

I, for one, don't particularly find such a prospect very exciting. As necessary and inevitable as development may be, let's not only focus on the monetary and, Mao forbid, military parts.

But what can I do? How can one man make a difference in the way this country is changing so that everyone, regardless of nationality, can look forward to a brighter tomorrow?

Back in 801, I discovered for the first time that I can be a *da xia*. But as much as I enjoy the idea of being a superhero, just one of me isn't enough to change even Sanlitun. Instead, there must be a critical mass of like-minded individuals who are strong (and arguably masochistic) enough to brave the Wild Wild East, with the firm belief that certain short-term sacrifices are a small price to pay for the long-term benefit of all. And I know that these people exist, for if I can be such an agent of change from time to time, so can even a Republican.

But how do I get in touch with these *da xias*? Cold-calling? Mass e-mail? Facebook?

How about just a book?

Well, if I do that, it would likely mean the beginning of yet another very long and painful process of rewriting, reediting, recompiling, reformating. . . . How many more nights do I want to work till five in the morning? It might even have to get a bit personal.

But then, how else would I write a book worthy of superheroes?

Of course, the same book might also fall into the hands of those who are not quite *da xia*s and have no aspirations of making a difference; but that's okay. For those deadweights, at least the story starts in Sanlitun, which, as the young lady has said, is "where all the action is."

"Well, I'll tell you what." I suppose this girl should get a little face for that last bit of inspiration. "I *will* take one of your brochures."

After all, never say never. Even though Café "Death Death" is now officially dead, who knows what might soon bring me back to Sanlitun again?

And would you look at this thick packet of fancy! Crisp, laminated pages; cool, technicolored inserts; interestingly (if not oddly) designed spaces with an area of 1,888 square feet as converted (or a multiple thereof); everything to help convince me of the unparalleled success that this new mall—and, of course, China—is destined to achieve.

Mao as my witness, my book will never look like this brochure!

Now don't get me wrong. For some people, working in places as posh as this new mall and breathing air as pristine as Lysol is absolutely key to finding happiness; and there is probably nothing wrong with that. But I'd rather hold the key to a more exciting world—one where anything can change with the blink of an eye, and anyone with a sense of responsibility can help make that change meaningful. With patience, humility, and an open mind, we can even help guide the way an entire one-fifth of the world's population sees, hears, thinks, and acts, all with a view to improving their society, and thus our world at large, faster than economics alone would allow.

Of course, riding a Chinese train into the future could get pretty rough sometimes. But as much as some aspects of living in China still get to me, including the fact that there are still Spit 'n' Squatters (albeit in noticeably smaller numbers) and that some FOB outsiders still make complete fools out of themselves once drunk (and they are not all just Americans anymore), their cumulative downside is more than offset by the adrenaline of seeing the good changes happen right before my eyes. Case in point: now that all the construction is finally winding down a bit (at least on the east side of town) and trees are being planted on sidewalks even far from the embassy areas and tourist traps, blue sky has become an almost common occurrence. In fact, when I looked out of the window after my meditation last night, I actually saw stars in the Beijing sky. And I wasn't even smoking a Zigarette.

"So, sir," the young lady says, handing me her business card without my asking for it, "would you like to see one of our spaces?"

"Beg your pardon?"

"I can show it to you now if you like."

"As in now now?"

"Yes. It's just down the street."

"But I thought it wasn't finished yet."

"But we do have demo spaces ready for viewing."

"Oh no, that's all right. Just the brochure is enough."

"But it'll take only a second."

"No, really."

"We are having a special right now. I can give you a great discount."

Like 88 percent of the original price? "No, that's not necessary."

"I can go as low as forty-five *kuai* per square meter per day."

"But I haven't even seen the place yet."

"If you really like it I might be able to get it even lower."

"Please. No. I'm serious."

"You'll regret it if you don't."

Cao, I'm starting to regret something already!

Okay, I guess some things are slower to change than others—every time I say something nice about this place, it still likes to pay me back with a bite in the ass.

But with Mao as my witness, I'm okay, honest. As much as this young lady is starting to remind me of my One A Days, I'm not going back. I'm a little older now and hopefully a little wiser. And even though this is China, where everything is more likely than not to be different from anywhere else in the world, and hardly anything works in the way that you might be used to, the alarm on my trusted Nokia still reminds me that it is now precisely 4:20 P.M. on a beautiful, breezy afternoon in the red capital and that the rest is, well, as we like to say in this part of the world:

THE FUTURE

GLOSSARY

bai jiu: "White liquor," a strong-smelling Chinese spirit derived from grains.

bao an: Security guard.

cao: The F word.

cha bu duo: Colloquial expression for "give or take."

da ge: "Big brother," a term of respect for the dominant male.

da ma: "Big numb," the Chinese name for marijuana.

da xia: China's concept of a superhero, traditionally in the form of kung fu masters who fight injustice like Robin Hood.

Dao: The way to enlightenment, the foundation for the religion of Daoism (or Taoism).

dou di zhu: "Fight the land baron," one of the most popular Chinese card games as of late.

ernai: "Second wife"—refers to a woman who gets paid for being a mistress.

er bai wu: The number 250, colloquial for "idiot."

fa piao: Official tax receipts issued by the Chinese Treasury.

ge-men'er: Chinese equivalent of "dude," the default way to address a male counterpart casually.

guan xi: Connections.

hai gui: Overseas returnee—a person who was born and raised in China, went abroad to study or work, and then returned to China.

hutong: One of Beijing's centuries-old narrow alleyways.

jie fu: Brother-in-law.

kuai: Colloquial for RMB, the local currency, like "buck" for "dollars."

lao wai: Literally, "old outsider"; colloquial term for "foreigner."

lao ye zi: Colloquial for "old man," or father.

lin shi bao fo jiao: "Holding on to the Buddha's foot in last-minute prayer," meaning to scamper for solutions when it is already too late.

mantou: China's equivalent of white bread, but more like a bun.

mei nu: "Pretty girl," a frivolous greeting for a female.

mei wen ti: "No problem."

mo ban: "Last on deck," the title of the least senior person in a Chinese prison cell.

ni da ye: "Your grandpa!" Used more like "Bullshit!"

ni hao/nin hao: Most common greeting, meaning "How are you?" The second variation is the more polite version, reserved for people worthy of respect.

niubi: "Cow pussy," used to mean "cool" or "awesome."

pai ma pi: "To slap a horse's ass," meaning to brownnose.

qi: The mystical force that is believed to be key to a person's physical and mental health. Also known as *ki* in Japanese.

ren: Person or people. Someone from Beijing would be a Beijing-*ren*.

ren qing: "Human kindness," colloquial for humanity in general.

shabi: "Stupid cunt." The nastiest word in Mandarin Chinese.

shuai ge: "Handsome chap," a frivolous greeting for a male.

si hai wei jia: "To live among the four seas."

tang yuan: A Chinese dessert consisting of sticky rice wrapped around sweet fillings; usually served with the water in which it was boiled.

tou ban: "First on deck," the title of the most senior person in a Chinese prison cell.

tuo'er: Someone who is entrusted to carry out a favor, often with a clandestine twist.

wo cao ta ma de: Lethal Weapon's favorite curse, literally meaning "F*#! his mother's privates!"

wu jing: China's military police.

wu liao: Bored, boring, monotonous, etc.

xie xie: Thank you.

yuan fen: A uniquely Chinese concept that is often cited as the default reason for why everything works out the way it does, especially when all other reasons fail.

zai jian: "See you again," colloquial for "Good-bye."

zao fan you li: Mao Zedong's famous phrase; "to rebel with reason."

Zhong Nan Hai: Beijing's favorite cigarettes, named after the ultrasecretive compound behind the Forbidden City where China's top bureaucrats live and work.

Zong: A term of respect used when addressing a person who occupies a management or leadership role within his or her company. Typically used by attaching it after the person's surname.